Ech
in the
Halls

An *Unofficial* History
of the University of Alberta

ASSOCIATION OF PROFESSORS EMERITI OF THE UNIVERSITY OF ALBERTA

DUVAL HOUSE
PUBLISHING
LES ÉDITIONS DUVAL

The University of Alberta Press

Published jointly by

DUVAL HOUSE PUBLISHING
18120 - 102 Avenue
Edmonton, Alberta T5S 1S7
Telephone: (780) 488-1390
Fax: (780) 482-7213
e-mail: pdr@compusmart.ab.ca
website: www.duvalhouse.com

UNIVERSITY OF ALBERTA PRESS
Ring House 2
Edmonton, Alberta T6G 2E2
Telephone: (780) 455-2200

Canadä Duval House Publishing and the University of Alberta Press gratefully acknowledge the financial support of the Government of Canada through the Book Publishing Industry Development Program (BPIDP) for our publishing activities.

Printed in Canada.

Canadian Cataloguing in Publication Data

Main entry under title:
   Echoes in the halls

ISBN 1-55220-074-4

1. University of Alberta--History--Anecdotes. I. Spencer, Mary,
1923- II. Dier, Kay, 1922- III. McIntosh, Gordon.
LE3.A619E33 1999   378.7123'3   C99-911163-9

Cover photos:
Front: Dr. Mark Arnfield adjusting the Argon-driven dye laser with the sixteen
         fibreoptic cables for interstitially applied PDT in Dunning R3327 rat prostate
         cancers (photo courtesy of Malcolm McPhee)
Back: The trunk esker at Exeter Lake with its black and red beach concentrate of
         diamond indicator minerals (photo courtesy of Robert Follinsbee)

Contents

Foreword

A S WE APPROACH THE Millennium, we pause to look at the University of Alberta—its roots, the forces that shaped its development and will certainly influence its future. Many people were involved—the public, governments, university governing bodies, and staff at every level. And so, perhaps appropriately, this book is one of apersonal recollections.

The Association of Professors Emeriti saw both the usefulness and interest in recording these times, and initiated this collection. These are accounts of events by people who experienced, and sometimes guided them. They are inside chronicles about the University, about how it works, the people who made it what it is today and how they did it.

Who better to tell these stories than the people who lived them? Authors had complete freedom to choose their own subjects or events. A fascinating picture of the University, its wide interests, diversity and accomplishments, emerges. Equally interesting and entertaining are the people—their ideas and contributions, personalities and ideals.

The response to our invitation to participate was excellent, but too large to include completely in this book. All contributions as originally submitted are available through the University of Alberta Archives. (See the complete list of submissions at the end of the book.)

We did our best to solicit articles from all retired professors and senior university personnel. Unfortunately, we could not reach everyone. We regret this most sincerely.

Herewith—as a gift from the Old Millennium to the New—we invite you to enjoy *Echoes in the Halls*.

Acknowledgements

WE HAVE MANY PEOPLE TO THANK for their assistance in bringing this millennium project of the Association of Professors Emeriti to a successful conclusion. First and foremost, we say a special thanks to the nearly 100 retired members of the academic and administrative staff, Board of Governors and Senate who responded to our invitation to write about the University. In reading their papers, we became happily aware that their years at the U of A were a time of great satisfaction and considerable accomplishment.

Our publishers, Jean Poulin of Duval House Publishing and Glenn Rollans of the University of Alberta Press, played a major part in helping us reach the finish line. We set out in heedless innocence on a great adventure to prepare an informal history of the University, and in due course we discovered that we needed the discipline and know-how that only experts in the publishing business could provide. Jean and Glenn were our disciplinarians—gentle always, but firm when necessary, and generous with their time.

Scott Rollans, as editor of the manuscript, was the good-humoured and tough-minded artist who drew from the bounty of papers—the number both delighted and dismayed us—and created an interesting and beautiful book that we have called *Echoes in the Halls*.

For the title of the book, we acknowledge the creative enterprise of Hank Spencer. He provided us with a mittful of suggestions, but *Echoes* was so obviously the right one that little discussion was necessary in making the choice.

It was our happy lot to have been immersed in the creative side of this project, but many people asserted their own creativity and did the hard work on the business and production side.

This project may have been lost in a quagmire of financial uncertainty were it not for the timely intervention of our fundraising committee, Don Bellow and Brian McDonald, the financial stewardship of John Young and the leadership shown by Roger Smith in providing bridge funding for production costs. Jim Malone took on the responsibility of marketing *Echoes*. The executive of the Association of Professors Emeriti offered moral support and practical assistance throughout the course of the project. Many members of the Association, too many to name individually, assisted us in contacting retired members of the academic and administrative staff to inform them of the project and to enlist their participation as writers.

Our secretaries, Nancy Smiley and Julia Mamolo, played key roles in managing the flow of information that sometimes threatened to inundate us. Lynda Vivier provided yeoman service in transcribing one of our balky interview tapes.

Various University offices and individuals helped us with specific tasks: Public Affairs, Alumni Affairs, University Archives, and the office of the Senate. In addition, the Edmonton Public School Board Archives helped us to locate an elusive photograph.

Our heartfelt thanks to all of you. This was a labour of love for us, and we think it likely was for you as well.

Mary Spencer, Chair
Kay Dier
Gordon McIntosh
Organizing Committee and Volume Editors

Editor's Remarks

WHEN MARY SPENCER first presented me with my personal copy of all of the submitted articles, about 1000 pages stuffed into a binder with a six-inch spine (okay, it was only four inches, but it looked bigger), I wondered how we could possibly turn this deluge into one coherent (and portable) book.

As I began reading, I found myself in the company of dozens of lively and engaging minds, each with an important story to tell. The collection as a whole represents a valuable addition to the University of Alberta Archives. It paints a collective portrait of University life that cannot be found in more conventional, less personal accounts. Everyone who invested the time (and the considerable effort) to contribute deserves our thanks and our congratulations.

When you read the excerpts printed throughout the book, you will get a sense of the wealth of material that lies beyond these two covers. I hope you will be inspired to delve into the archival materials and (this is my greatest hope) to sit down and record some stories of your own.

In compiling this book, every effort has been made to secure copyright. If we have failed in any instance, please contact the publishers and we will do our best to remedy the situation.

I thank Mary, Gordon and Kay for the countless hours they devoted to this project (since they wrote the acknowledgements, they couldn't very well thank themselves). I also salute the contributors for their gracious tolerance while I fiddled with their text, and for their gentle tact in correcting me when I went too far. It's painful when you construct a single elegant, expansive paragraph (the way you were trained) and some upstart carves it into three clear, concise paragraphs (the way I was trained). Here lies the real generation gap!

The leaves are now turning, and in less than two months I will be sipping refreshments at the book's launch. As is the case with most large projects, it's hard to believe that this one is nearly over. It has been quite a summer!

Scott Rollans

Student Days

Life on both sides of the lectern

C. FRED BENTLEY

'Call Me Tubby' and Other Free-Wheeling Ramblings

AS A STUDENT

IN 1936, MY FRESHMAN YEAR, many of the students came from remote rural places and didn't know a single soul at the University. The year's first major social event was the "Wauneta Dance," where the ladies in Pembina Hall would each select a gentleman to be her escort. Of course, every red-blooded freshman desperately hoped to be honoured with an invitation.

Unfortunately, there was only one female student in Agriculture—and she was a sophomore! So we 20 freshmen Aggies had to scramble to find some girl who might choose us.

Then—good luck?—there was one woman student in the Animal Science laboratory, a weekly three-hour session with livestock at the University Farm. Not surprisingly, my classmates and I showered her with attention. Although she was always pleasant with us, she remained quiet and very standoffish no matter how we persisted.

Then, one evening, at a University function I was attending, the respected Chemistry Professor, Dr. Reuben Sandin, was introduced to the audience, along with his wife. My jaw dropped. There stood the *girl* in the Animal Husbandry course! No wonder she had been a bit aloof to all of us attentive young males.

Fortunately, the experience wasn't a total loss. I managed to win about $1.25 in wagers with my classmates, who steadfastly refused to believe that the pretty young lady in the Animal Husbandry lab was a professor's wife.

Many years later, Mary Sandin was a foremost weaver in Canada and a good friend of my wife. It was great fun telling her of the problem she had been to the boys in the A. H. course!

The Agricultural Students Club had a tradition of welcoming freshmen with a tour of the campus to show them where their various classes and laboratories would be held. One year, at the annual banquet of the club, one of the student speakers brought the house down with his rendition of a "tour" for next year's freshmen:

> *And as you approach the 'West Lab,' don't be alarmed if the students burst out on a dead run. There is no fire—they are just leaving Professor Henry's class and trying to get to their next class on time! And if you are on the second floor of the Arts Building and hear a voice with a strong Scottish burr saying '...and other things being equal,' well, that is Professor Stewart (later President Andrew Stewart) talking economics. We conclude our tour in the North Lab. If you are going along the hall and hear 'ping, ping, ping,' don't worry; nothing is about to explode. It is just Dr. Wyatt trying to light his pipe.*

As undergraduate students, we all got to know Dr. Ignatieff, a new Professor in the Soils Department. He conducted research directly below the most used lecture room in the North Lab. That ancient building had generous holes around the plumbing and heating pipes that came up from Dr. Ignatieff's lab.

Dr. Ignatieff loved to sing at his work, and his joyful sounds often overpowered the lecture in the classroom above. When that happened, the lecturing Professor would go over to the corner and hammer on the pipes to get the thunderous singing turned off!

Dr. Sheldon was a legendary Professor of mathematics. As first-year students, we Aggies, with about 150 other students, took his introductory course in statistics. On return to the campus after the Christmas break, three of us were walking along in the Arts Building when we met Dr. Sheldon. He stopped and greeted us. He then expressed his disappointment in our poor grades in his course—and mentioned the exact marks that each of us had received!

He was a very entertaining lecturer. Each year, somewhere in his statistics course, he would discuss what or where infinity was. He would stride around the front of the room looking everywhere for infinity. In 1947, with a huge class (many, many were veterans) in Convocation Hall, Dr. Sheldon began to look for infinity as usual. Suddenly, one of the veterans jumped to his feet with the stance of a rifleman and shouted, "Bang, bang, bang! Got him for you, sir." Thus ended the search for infinity.

In 1935, I took French 1 during the summer session. My Professor, the renowned Dr. Sonet, was one of the last Professors at the U of A who insisted upon wearing an academic gown for his lectures.

As a Frenchman, Dr. Sonet was very worried about political developments in Europe and the effects on his homeland. He strode back and forth in the classroom, ranting about his concerns, gesturing and jerking to emphasize his views. A true Latin, he often got so worked up that he actually tore his gown.

Two or three decades later, the U of A granted him an Honourary Doctor of Letters degree and asked him to give the Convocation address. Of course, the Registrar's Office provided him with the usual firm guidelines for the address, including a precise six-minute time limit. However, Dr. Sonet was not to be so constrained. He brushed past the microphone, strode to the very edge of the orchestra pit and gave a scintillating lecture of nearly twenty minutes!

AS A FACULTY MEMBER

It was exciting to return to the U of A as a faculty member in 1946 and take my place among my former Professors. Soon after my arrival, I was walking across campus when I met Dr. Harold Thornton, the Professor of Dairying, who happened to be very short and very rotund. I said, "Hello, Dr. Thornton."

He looked me in the eye and said, "Fred, we are colleagues now. Please call me Tubby, or call me Hal as you prefer."

What a pleasant welcome to the faculty!

In 1948, the Chair of the Soils Department was Dr. J. D. Newton, one of five siblings who all had Ph.D.s in agricultural disciplines. His brother, Dr. Robert Newton, was President of the U of A. Poised and confident, he was quite different from J. D.

J. D. was very shy, restrained, self-controlled, oath free and always exceedingly proper. One day, he and I were out on a field trip. He drove, while I kept busy observing the passing soil landscape.

We were travelling along a narrow, rather high-graded "market road" (as they were called in those days). Suddenly, we were in the ditch—fortunately right side up—with no damage to the car and neither of us injured. J. D., showing unusual perturbation for him, exclaimed mildly, "Oh, dear."

A few years later, the U of A hosted the Agricultural Institute of Canada's annual conference. At the formal presentation of committee reports, the Chair invited questions or comments regarding the Education Committee's presentation. Dr. William (Bill) Newton, the third male member of the Newton family, jumped to his feet at the back of a jammed Convocation Hall and shouted, "That is a damn awful report, a disgrace to this meeting." He then advanced down the aisle bellowing out why he thought the report was so bad, ending up at the front of the hall directly addressing the audience. One of our Soils graduate students, who was sitting beside me, leaned over and whispered, "Who is that?" When I responded, "J. D.'s brother," the student looked at me with disbelief and said, "You can't pull my leg like that."

The inquisitors and their victim (Jim Carson's thesis oral examination). L to R: John Bowland, J. D. Newton, Mary Spencer, Fred Bentley and Jim Carson

In the middle 1950s, the University administration was highly informal. The President appointed me, along with two or three other faculty members, to a new body—The Promotions Committee. The other members were all Deans and Senior Officers of the University. Soon after that I also became a member of the Staff Association's Salary Committee.

The meeting of the year between our three-member Staff Association Committee and the University President—the administration—was held one evening in his home! In those days, nobody saw this as a conflict of interest.

By my standards, there were a few "bad apples in the barrel" on the University staff. Once, a group of four or five of us from various disciplines got into a long discussion on "teaching." Finally, one person, who had said little up until that point, stated his view. "I don't worry about teaching," he declared. "The honours and graduate students can get the knowledge they need from textbooks and the library; since the other students are of no account, I don't worry about them." Fortunately, that person left for a different job soon after. That employer's gain (?) was certainly no loss for the U of A!

Overall, however, I have always felt at home among my colleagues. In the late 1970s, a new stenographer/secretary came to our section of the Department of Soil Science. For the preceding couple of years, she had held a similar position in an adjoining building.

One day, about two months after her arrival, I asked her how things were going and whether she was comfortable in our department. There followed an outpouring of pent-up emotions. She had never imagined there could be such a difference in work atmospheres in the same institution, and in such close proximity.

"Over there, everyone was constantly trying to thwart the others, and as secretary, I was caught in the middle. It was terribly unpleasant. Here, people work together, are friendly and helpful. I am so very happy now."

That heartwarming compliment was fully justified. Our Department of Soil Science was a remarkably pleasant and cooperative place to work. For instance, for more than a decade, I was out of province several times a year for periods of about three to ten days each time. Through the superlative help of my colleagues, and some judicious planning on my part, not a single lecture or laboratory session was ever cancelled in any of my courses.

I am exceedingly fortunate to have attended and worked at the University of Alberta. As a student, I was so excited and enthusiastic about university life that I dreamed of ways I might one day help my University in return. I am still driven by such feelings. I am not retired; although it is nearly two decades since my paycheques ended, I am still trying to repay the University of Alberta for the wonderful life it has enabled me to have.

In 1946, I was accepted into the predentistry course. After spending nearly five years in the Air Force, it had been a long time since I graduated from high school, but I was determined to obtain a higher education. I was taking advantage of a program which paid a living allowance and tuition fees for veterans attending educational institutions.

The University had to cope with a large influx of veterans. They built temporary buildings and rented off-campus classrooms in the district to handle the load until new buildings and additions could be constructed.

Because the University only had three student dormitories, the Students' Union organized a canvass of homes on the south side to find people willing to rent accommodations. The city purchased suites in Dawson Creek, formerly used by workers and their families during the construction of the Alaska Highway, moved them to 70th Avenue and offered them to married students with children. We were able to afford a comfortable one-bedroom suite in the "Dawson Creek" complex.

Immediately after the war, many items, especially appliances, were in short supply. It was not until two years after we moved in that my wife was able to quit using the scrub board and enjoy the luxury of a wringer washing machine.

Although it was a busy time for me, we did find time to socialize in the evenings or listen to the radio after putting the children to bed. We made many good friendships during this time, which we still cherish.

Richard McClelland

Charlie Lockwood

The Chancellor Drops In

I N JULY 1963, a couple of weeks after I joined the Department of Extension, I was in my office, with almost no one else around. Suddenly, a short, jolly, well-dressed man came through my door and said, "You must be new here. My name is Walter Johns. Where is everybody?"

"I'm Charlie Lockwood, just started with the University, err... ." I was not sure what to say. In my uninitiated state, I was not aware that University offices were normally pretty quiet during the summer. "Professor Campbell just left on a short holiday (I had no idea how long he would be gone), and I understand that Mr. Eyford (the Assistant Director) will be back on Monday."

The President gave me a big smile. "I hope you enjoy your work here. I am glad you have come to the University."

During the 1970s, we ran Arctic Summer School. This was a residential school centred in Inuvik and designed for managers working on northern projects.

Late one night, I was sitting in our makeshift office in Grollier Hall, the Northwest Territories Government student residence where we stayed, talking to Val Smyth. Suddenly, in walks Ron Dalby, the University Chancellor. He was in Inuvik with Edmonton Alderman Buck Olsen on a Chamber of Commerce tour of the north. He had heard his University was in town and came over to see what was going on.

I handed him a copy of our course timetable and then casually mentioned that at that very moment (it was about 11 p.m.), we had a group on an overnight camp-out in the Mackenzie Delta, about fifty miles down river from Inuvik. It was late June, so the sun was up all the time. Ron said, "Can we go down there right now?"

I was taken aback, but said, "Sure, as long as Val can find us a plane and, more importantly, a pilot."

"Then let's try," said Ron, and Val started working the phone.

The reluctant pilot agreed to meet us at the lake, so we were off to the camp. I was somewhat concerned about the condition of our students because I had heard talk of an evening "party" at the camp. I also knew that a quantity of beer had gone with the group, and to the best of my knowledge, the Chancellor was a temperate man.

As we started circling the camp to make a landing approach, my worst fears were confirmed when I saw two of our people swimming across the Mackenzie. However, once we landed things seemed okay. It was about one in the morning by then, and the booze had long since run out. A small clutch of students started haranguing the pilot to fly them back to Inuvik for more supplies, but the rest cottoned on to Ron and Buck. They proceeded to introduce our guests to the wonders of the Mackenzie Delta ecology, taking them to look at the fish net that had been rigged in the river. After a short visit, we sent an impressed Chancellor on his way.

We had lots of great people during my years with Extension. They made it possible for our department to lead the way in developing university continuing education in Canada.

An apocryphal tale from the St. Stephen's oral tradition ...

In earlier years, theology students were housed at St. Stephen's College along with students from other faculties. These budding young ministers-to-be were sent into the countryside on the weekends to practise their craft on the rural congregations.

One weekend, a candidate returned with a case of eggs, a reward from a local farmer. Setting his prize on the sideboard in the old dining hall, he announced to all present that these eggs were for his exclusive use. Given the limited resources available to theological students in those days, one might sympathize with his apparent lack of Christian generosity.

Apparently, though, not all present were so understanding. In response to this declaration, someone standing nearby picked up an egg and sent it flying across the dining room. Before the Dean (who might have been the beloved Charles Johnson) could intervene, the air was filled with eggs. When the escapade was over, not an egg remained. The saga, as it has been passed down, doesn't mention who cleaned up the mess, nor what penalty was imposed on those perpetrating such behaviour in the hallowed halls of a theological college.

The most widespread St. Steve's stories, however, are *not* apocryphal; they centre on the old tubular fire escapes that once graced each end of the building. Frosh residents, in various states of undress, would be carried to a fire escape and dumped into it, along with copious amounts of cold water, for a fast ride to the ground. At other times, those who fell out of favour with the ruling elite suffered this same indignity to remind them of what a privilege it was to live at St. Steve's. In winter, the cascading water paved the fire escapes with ice, adding to the ecstasy of the trip.

When old Stevites gather, they resurrect these memories again and again. While I was Principal of the College, whenever I travelled in Alberta and across Canada, graduates would come up to me, introduce themselves and then recount their own tales about the infamous fire escapes. Each time, I could see the pleasure the teller felt in reliving the St. Steve's experience.

Garth Mundle

JOAN MUNRO

University of Alberta, 1953
A Taste for Learning

I T'S 1998, IT'S FALL and I'm a student again. I guess I'm one of those people who just can't stay away. I've already been back three times since I first came to Edmonton as an undergraduate in 1953. Maybe I do this because Edmonton in the fall reminds me of my first university years, when classes began in late September and we regularly skipped any that conflicted with the World Series.

When I was a little girl, I used to like to listen to my parents talk about the olden days, about buggy rides and one-room school houses and all-day revival meetings. When I was twenty-one, married and in second year arts, I thought I would never have comparable stories to tell my children and grandchildren. Nothing seemed very different from my own childhood. But looking back with nostalgia at my university years, I can see that times have changed a bit.

Both Jack and I had been in the very first arts and science class offered at what was then called the Calgary Branch of the University of Alberta (that in itself is a bit of history). We came to Edmonton to finish our arts degrees, and I've lived here ever since. There were a few married couples on campus, but most of them had one partner working—usually the wife who, as we used to say, was "putting her husband through." I remember only two other couples who were both students.

That first year at U of A, we lived in two rooms on 98th Avenue just east of 99th Street. We did have an old car, a Willys, but it mostly didn't go, so we either walked to school along Saskatchewan Drive very fast (we were usually late) or took a trolley, which came up 99 Street and along Whyte Avenue, ending its journey by the Garneau tennis courts. The walk from there was nearly as far as on Saskatchewan Drive. You could catch a transfer if you were lucky, but you usually weren't.

Next year, we moved into a different suite, to use the term very loosely, in a house on 81 Avenue near 112 Street. It was actually the attic, one large room with a stove and a bed that slid out of sight under one of the lower portions of the ceiling. No fridge. I still remember the singular taste of butter that had been left on the window sill to keep cool. Sun does interesting things to food, even in mid-winter. Some sort of regulation prevented the installation of plumbing above the second floor, so we hauled water up the stairs from the bathtub below and ladled it from the bucket with a long-handled dipper. Still, it was relatively pleasant and much closer to the University than our first apartment.

I often watch today's students parading down 112 Street every morning. We did that, too, our ranks swelling block by block as we drew nearer to campus.

Classes were held in the old Arts Building, except those for medical, dental and education students. These met in what are now called the Dentistry/Pharmacy Building and Corbett Hall respectively (we had our teeth fixed by dental students). The Students' Union Building was what is now University Hall. There, snooker was the game of choice, played on the lower floor.

As a music major, I had several classes in an army hut behind the Arts Building. The Music Department used the east end, and I believe CKUA had the west end. Professors Richard Eaton and Art Crighton taught music, with prominent musicians Edgar Williams and Ernest Dalwood (later Professor) coming in to instruct in strings and woodwinds, as we were expected to know something (not much!) about every instrument. They held their classes in the rooms behind and above Convocation Hall. Some years later, as the music program expanded, I instructed flute students in the same rooms. I remember well the choir rehearsals, the music history courses and the harmony and counterpoint.

My music courses were interesting and valuable, but they took time from my other favourite subjects—English and philosophy. Professor Salter, a recognized authority on Shakespeare, still taught in a black academic gown; Professor Baldwin was young and dynamic; but Professor Mardiros in philosophy probably influenced me most. I also remember my art history and geography courses, taught by Professors Taylor and Wonders respectively. The Dean of Arts, Professor Johns from Classics, saw every student at some time or other, much as each department's undergraduate advisor now attempts to do.

Like today's students, we took out student loans and worked summers. During the term, we laboured part time for Bruce Peel in the Rutherford Library, erasing the old Dewey Decimal System numbers on the file cards and typing in the new Library of Congress numbers.

In those days, the Rutherford (now called Rutherford South) opened to the outside. Once, on the spur of the moment, a large group of us picked up a Volkswagen Beetle parked outside the Arts Building, carried it up the library stairs, set it down just outside the doors and then scattered. To be honest, I think I just watched.

We studied for exams at the long tables (still there) on the second floor of Rutherford, or lounged/slept in the big, red leather easy chairs. At one point, I earned extra money by hosting a noon-hour classical music program, where the audience sat in those chairs and just listened or daydreamed.

We wrote our exams in the Drill Hall. I still remember the canvas curtain that separated the waiting area from the writing area (filled with rows of desks, much as the Butterdome is now). Whenever anyone opened the outside door, that canvas flapped noisily.

The cafeteria was in another former military building. We didn't frequent the Tuck Shop, a favourite hangout for generations of students, but we usually had dinner once a week in the cafeteria. The cooking was better (and faster) than mine, and they had wonderful whole wheat buns.

The army buildings were an eyesore, admittedly, but the other buildings had a certain red brick pseudo-grandeur about them. However, even then, plans were being made for expansion. Nothing, we were assured, was to be built north of the space in front of the Arts Building nor between the Quad and Saskatchewan Drive. But first came the Tory Building, and then a series of buildings north of the Quad.

As the old military buildings came down, the whole eclectic conglomeration that we have today went up, gradually robbing the campus of much of its dignity. Fortunately, the Quad was left undisturbed, as was the open space in front of the Arts Building. For years, the latter was little more than a chopped-up field, constantly being torn up to repair pipes or wiring. Years later, however, Professor Hugh Knowles and his colleagues landscaped the empty space with mature trees and pleasant paths so that now it is the most beautiful spot on campus.

I must include a word about Corbett Hall, known in 1953 as the Education Building, and before that as the Normal School. I attended grades one and two there and cannot imagine a more exciting beginning to my education. This was the one school where student teachers practised their skills, and for that reason, we had specially chosen teachers in our regular classrooms. They subscribed to John Dewey's Progressive Education theories, later much maligned (and wrongly, I think).

The building itself was superior to any school I have been in since. The classrooms had movable desks at a time when most were bolted to the floor. There was an observation area where whole classes of student teachers could watch a lesson being taught without interrupting. The hallways and washrooms had marble floors (just take a look the next time you're there), and the toilets flushed automatically!

Imagine my disappointment when I moved to Calgary and attended an old-fashioned school with fixed desks, manually flushing toilets and a teacher at the front of each room holding a pointer.

Well, in 1955 we convocated, not in Convocation Hall (the University had long since expanded too much for that), nor in the Jubilee Auditorium (which did not yet exist), but in the Stock Pavilion at the Exhibition Grounds. The building smelled of recently evacuated horses and cattle. Sparrows flew about above our heads as we actually knelt before Chancellor Fred McNally to be ordained with our degrees.

I couldn't say those were the best years of my life, but September's falling leaves never fail to bring back poignant memories. The University gave me a taste for learning that will never leave me.

VERNE NYBERG

A Not-So-Nostalgic Look at University Life

ALTHOUGH I SPENT THIRTY YEARS as a Professor at the U of A, my strongest memories come from my student days in the early 1940s. Readers should bear in mind that most of the experiences related here are those of a scared undergraduate, fresh from the farm, whose social contact had been limited largely to downtown Amisk. Further, the memories have been exhumed from beneath half a century of subsequent experiences and have been adjusted to present the author in the most favourable light possible. With that caution, let us look back to another era.

University life during wartime was quite different from any time before or since. The residences were closed (except for St. Joe's and St. Steve's), so out-of-town students had to find accommodation in the surrounding neighbourhood. Some, inevitably, landed in outright dumps.

I was much luckier. I stayed in St. Stephen's College for the first year, which was ideal, and then used my knowledge of the area to choose good housing for my second year. Unfortunately, my only criterion was that it had to be close to the University. I made arrangements by telephone during the summer, and sent my truck to the address. When I arrived at about 8:00 a.m., I was met by a surly female who told me I could not stay there because I had failed to provide a deposit. I was not unduly disappointed because the house was a textbook example of a slum.

I ended up finding quarters nearly a mile from the campus. Two weeks later I was pleased to notice a "Room for Rent" sign on the house where I had been rejected. The sign remained there for the rest of the year.

During the war, Alberta was on daylight saving time all year long. When you left your dwelling at 7:30 a.m. in January, it was so dark that you knew that you would never, ever see daylight again. To make matters worse, there were huge snowfalls early in the winter of 1942 to 1943. I remember waiting for a streetcar at 109 Street and seeing an American army vehicle stuck in the middle of Jasper Avenue. This was a "six-by-six," a monster propelled by ten wheels. But it had encountered weather that was even more monstrous. Incidentally, the streetcar never came, so it must have also gotten stuck.

University students generally kept a low profile during the war. Some of the locals wondered why this large group of young people wasn't overseas like their own sons, brothers, uncles, cousins and so on.

As physically able males, however, we were required to take military training for a minimum of two university years. This consisted of putting in two hours twice a week. In my first year, only army training was available. The army had maintained a presence on the campus prior to the war, the Canadian Officers' Training Corps (COTC). When the war commenced, the Auxiliary Battalion (AUXBAT) was added.

The COTC consisted of the officers, most of whom were senior students. Their main job, which they performed with gusto, was to show how mean and tough they could be to the freshmen and sophomores in the AUXBAT.

At the end of the university year the scene shifted, for two grueling weeks, to Sarcee Camp just west of Calgary. An advance party of AUXBAT types set up about a million tents, and then the rest of us arrived. I will forever remember it as the worst two weeks of my entire life.

In 1942, early May in the Calgary area was even colder than usual. Our tents had no heat, but this was no problem because we had been issued four wool blankets instead of two. After all, we pampered souls were not yet ready for the rigorous life of the army. That line wore thin when we noticed that the commando unit, training in another part of the camp, was put up in wooden, heated barracks.

We were also each issued a large cloth bag to serve as a mattress and introduced to a pile of straw with which to stuff it. We now had what was called a "pally ass." Years later, I learned that the proper term is paillasse, which is French for pally ass.

That night I dutifully removed my clothes, dressed in my flannel pyjamas, crawled into my four blankets on top of my pally ass and promptly froze to the marrow of my bones. In the morning, I donned my fatigues right over the pyjamas. That night I left everything on (well, not my boots), put my regular uniform over everything and froze again, as badly as ever.

It seems that wool blankets absorb moisture from the air and lose their ability to keep a person warm. Oh, yes! I should mention that when a person is that cold, the kidneys work double time. Every night I was forced to abandon my blankets for a hasty trip to the latrine. I was in no danger of losing my way, thanks to the steady stream of other shivering apparitions making the same trip.

U of A students in the COTC, circa 1943

All of this suffering had no discernible purpose. The muddled activities we performed were completely foreign to what Canadian soldiers actually endured. We practised with rifles left over from WWI in trenches left over from the same unpleasant period. After two weeks at Sarcee, I decided that I would consider joining the army when Hitler got to Leduc. Mind you, I was very careful about voicing this opinion. I may have been a lowly freshman, but I was not completely stupid.

The next year, when the air force and navy introduced their own versions of military training, AUXBAT suffered a mass exodus. People did not mind facing two more years of training instead of only one for those who stayed with the army. I switched to the air force and found that they had a better idea of how to train and motivate people. And their barracks were always comfortable.

This journey into the past would not be complete without some reference to Joe Shoctor. A fellow freshman, he seemed immune to the pangs of shyness generated by moving to the city from the farm. Joe was a bit of a clown and had a gift for sensing how far he could go without incurring the wrath of the authorities.

Joe was subjected to the AUXBAT like the rest of us, but he managed to have a little fun. One day we were all being instructed in the intricacies of the "slope arms" command—the army's way of saying, "Pick up your rifle and put it on your left shoulder." Our officer demonstrated what was expected, which consisted of three distinct moves. When he was finished, Joe spoke up with, "It was too slow, SIR!"

The rest of the platoon waited aghast for the thunderbolt to strike. Instead the officer took the bait and snarled, "If you're so smart, YOU show us how it's done." Joe took his rifle and at the command, made the required three moves quickly, crisply and absolutely flawlessly. All of us, including the officer, gaped in surprise.

At the time, we did not know that Joe had spent several days practising the maneuver at every opportunity until he had it down pat.

Joe stars in another memory that is printed boldly in my mind. The U of A used to stage a Gilbert and Sullivan operetta every year, and in 1942 it was *The Pirates of Penzance*. We took each show to Calgary for two performances, one in the afternoon and one in the evening.

The makeup facilities were about a block from the theatre, which meant that the cast had to walk down the street in full makeup. The males in the chorus all played either pirates or policemen. As we were walking along, Joe, a pirate, borrowed a helmet and billy club from one of the policemen and began directing traffic in the middle of one of Calgary's busiest intersections. Most of the motorists did not notice anything untoward about a traffic cop wearing the helmet of a London bobby. Two real policemen stood by and laughed throughout the performance. Had anybody but Joe tried that scene, there surely would have been hell to pay.

Graduation brought with it a feeling of accomplishment and self-importance. In wartime, this was enhanced by the fact that every science graduate had to register with the Wartime Bureau of Technical Personnel.

I received my B.Sc. in mathematics and physics after three years; however, I was scheduled for a fourth year in order to qualify as a high school teacher. I therefore sought a summer job, eventually working for a prospecting company based in Yellowknife.

After two or three months on the job, I got an official letter from the Wartime Bureau of Technical Personnel. It said that I was a science graduate working in a non-essential industry and would have to mend my ways forthwith. I was directed to report to work at the Abasand oil sands project and (to completely deflate my ego) begin duties as a bus boy in the mess hall.

I talked the matter over with my boss, giving him an outline of the nasty reply I intended to send, reminding the Bureau that I was scheduled to return to university in a few weeks. My boss, well versed in the ways of the bureaucratic world, warned me that this would be a big mistake. At his suggestion, I waited ten days, then sent a letter saying that I would be pleased to do as they said, but that I needed more detailed instructions as to where to go. As my boss predicted, I never heard any more from the Wartime Bureau of Technical (and dishwashing) Personnel.

While life at the University was different during wartime, one thing has remained constant and will probably remain so forever. Then, as now, older people (anyone over thirty) firmly believed that learning standards had seriously declined since they were undergraduates.

In my freshman English class, after the return of our first term paper, our Professor told the entire amphitheatre full of students that we had absolutely no writing skills whatsoever. He claimed that there was only one student in the whole class who knew anything about writing.

As it turned out, this student, a very fine young man, was so bright that he had ulcers by the time he was twenty-five, and was an English Professor (not at the U of A) by the time he was thirty.

That was in English, but what about mathematics, where many self-appointed experts just know that standards have gone down? For these people, I submit this little anecdote.

In my third year at the University, I helped mark examinations in the beginning calculus course for engineers. The November examination was marked out of a total of 30. In the whole group of 100 or so, one student managed to achieve a mark as high as 24. This was another one of those people with brains to burn.

Once the marks had been scaled, the passing grade was determined to be a raw score of four. Only about half the class achieved this lofty standard. Of course, most of these low achievers graduated in due course and can now look back on successful careers as engineers.

I do have some memories related to teaching at the University. One that comes immediately to mind dates back to the 1970s when (according to some students) nothing "relevant" was being taught at the University, and when society in general was mired in yesterday's outdated procedures. In this period, it became University policy that students in each class would evaluate the Professor and the course.

Near the end of one of my courses, I passed out the required forms to the students. I knew that I had done a reasonably good job, although, as always, there were things I would like to have done better. After responding to a group of short questions related to instructional matters, students were asked to comment on any aspect they deemed important. Although most of the comments were favourable, one student wrote, "This course has all the attraction of a pitcher of warm spit." The submission was anonymous, but the handwriting was very distinctive, so I knew without doubt who wrote it.

Early in life, I learned to always look at the bright side of things. I thought to myself, "It could have been worse. He did, after all, say SPIT." So, what the heck! He passed the course.

I have no real memories of University life after the mid-70s. Everything is a blur of classes, meetings, dissertations, golf tournaments, research projects, grading papers, bright students, not-so-bright students and the like. But with age has come the realization that I would not change anything, including the AUXBAT stuff, and, further, that University people, especially students, are the finest on earth.

While opening the mail recently, I was delighted to find two long-forgotten cartoons that I had drawn (along with many others) during my 1951 OR stint at the University of Alberta Hospital. Eleanor Stares (née Rogers), a Regina Hospital grad who was a wonderful Theatre Nurse at the U of A while I was training, found the drawings in one of her memory books and thought that I should have them.

Because there was another Shirley in my B.Sc. class, I had chosen to go under the alias of Shay, which is what I called myself as a small child, unable to get the gist of my real name. That is how I signed this cartoon, in the puddle on the floor of this Autoclave Room where we students washed, tested and autoclaved hundreds of rubber gloves every day. This scene would likely be totally foreign to any nurse who trained after the late 1950s.

As I had never kept any of my cartoons (I simply posted them on the Autoclave Room bulletin board and left them until they disappeared), I greatly appreciate Eleanor's thoughtfulness in giving me the two she had saved.

Shirley Stinson

Arrivals

First impressions

ABDUL N. KAMAL

Braving the Frontier
Remembrance of My Arrival in Edmonton

IN 1961, A YEAR BEFORE completing my Ph.D. in Theoretical Physics at the University of Liverpool, I started to ponder my future. There were three Canadians in the department at that time, two young postdoctoral fellows plus Harry Schiff, a Physics Professor on sabbatical from the University of Alberta.

One day, over coffee, I asked the two young postdocs if there were any good universities in Canada where I could apply for a postdoctoral fellowship (which is a sort of physicist's purgatory). One of them said to me, "How about the University of Alberta? Talk to Harry." The other offered a little extra incentive. "They don't do much physics there, but they have lots of money!"

I found this remark only mildly amusing, so you can imagine my puzzlement at the sight of these two fellows doubled over with raucous laughter. I knew nothing about the oil riches of Alberta at the time. In fact, I did not know where Alberta was on the map of Canada.

Two years later, in 1963, I remembered their advice. I wrote Harry a handwritten aerogram asking if there might be a job for me at the University of Alberta. He wrote back immediately, offering me a postdoctoral fellowship. For the first time, I looked up Edmonton in an atlas, expecting to find it somewhere in the frozen tundra.

Several Physics Professors at the U of A had links to the University of Liverpool. Among them was Avadh Bhatia (after whom the Physics Building at the University of Alberta is named). In 1963, he spent a sabbatical in Liverpool, along with his wife, June.

Over tea one lovely autumn afternoon, Avadh gave me some advice that would make my first day in Edmonton memorable: "Don't do what the Canadians do. You will see them go out in minus thirty-degree weather in shirt sleeves. At that temperature, exposed flesh freezes in a matter of a few seconds! Wrap yourself up well, even at the risk of looking a tad overdressed."

Meanwhile, a Canadian graduate student had been filling my head with far-fetched tales of Canada. "Out west," he assured me, "when people kiss, sparks really do fly!" And, "You can get quite a charge off the doorknobs." I laughed. Something literally as dead as a doorknob would suddenly come to life and zap me with a bolt of lightning! Yeah, very likely.

By the time my (then) wife and I left England, we had formed an image of an Edmonton where grizzlies roamed the streets alongside gun-toting cowboys wearing Stetsons at a jaunty angle, chewing on blades of grass, swaggering bow-legged in their pointy boots with spurs and spitting like lizards in heat.

In fact, when I informed my father (in what is now Bangladesh) that I was going to Canada, he sent me some advice, as any caring father would. "Watch out for bears and wolves when you go to the outhouse. And don't answer the call of nature after dark, even if it means doing some extra laundry the next day."

We arrived in Edmonton at 3:00 a.m. on the last day of October 1963, by a Trans-Canada Airlines' Viscount on a milk run from Montreal. The airport building only helped to reinforce our image of Edmonton as a frontier town. As we walked through the ramshackle hangar, I was summoned to the Trans-Canada counter on the PA system. There I was handed a message from Harry. The missive was brief: "Welcome to Edmonton. Take a limo to Athabasca Hall."

Now, coming from England, where the longest car was all of eight feet, taking a limousine seemed the height of wasteful extravagance. Instead, we took a bus to the Park Hotel on the south side and a taxi from there to the campus.

That morning we woke up late. We drew the curtains warily, fearing to see the ground covered in snow. Instead, to our surprise, we were greeted by a stunningly clear day. Limpid sunshine bathed the trees as I had never seen. It looked like a crisp, cold day.

As I entered the bathroom, I was literally shocked when the seemingly inert doorknob delivered its promised bolt of charge to my unsuspecting hand.

It was too late for breakfast and too early for lunch in Athabasca Hall, so we decided to go downtown for brunch. Paying heed to Avadh's advice, I wasn't about to take any chances. I wrapped my head and upper torso in my Liverpool University Science Faculty scarf, a veritable blanket in bold blue and white stripes designed for survival in emergencies such as being marooned on the Hebrides. Thus mummified, I put on my thick tweed jacket and a pair of grey flannel pants (the kind that only the English seem to know how to make, which last you a lifetime). Having fortified myself thus, I donned a thick dark blue winter coat as a final defensive measure against the flesh-freezing weather. A pair of leather gloves completed my accoutrements. Only my eyes were exposed to the harsh outside world.

As I took my first few tentative steps outside, I attracted bemused looks from the locals, who were indeed walking about in their shirt sleeves — just as Avadh had told me! Good job that I was forewarned, I thought to myself.

We walked to the bus stop to go downtown, and, lo and behold, there were more of the crazy Canucks in their shirt sleeves! "Cold nuff fo' ya?" one of them said to me. As I felt the sweat beginning to course down my body in runnels, I have to admit that I was beginning to doubt the wisdom of Avadh's advice.

By the time the bus reached Jasper Avenue, I could feel my soaked shirt clinging uncomfortably to my body. I was swimming in my own sweat and on the verge of drowning. Just as we found a restaurant (well, actually more of an eatery, as there were no memorable restaurants on Jasper Avenue), we saw a neon sign flash the time and the temperature: 11:30 a.m. and 63°F!

You can imagine my embarrassment as I laboriously unswathed myself, layer by woolen layer, much to the amusement of the motley crowd assembled in the restaurant for their morning coffee.

I came to Edmonton for a two-year stint and stayed a lifetime. How things have changed! These days, a handwritten letter would hardly be deemed a serious application for a job.

And what of the people who influenced my incipient career? Harry still lives in Edmonton with his wife, Sarah. Avadh, unfortunately, is no longer among us, but his wife, June, a well-known novelist better known as Helen Forrester, still lives here. And the two young postdocs in Liverpool, whose jocular advice brought me to Edmonton, are Professors at two of Canada's prominent universities.

And yes, we now do lots of physics here at the U of A, but no longer have much money!

My earliest recollection of medical teaching at the University of Alberta dates back to 1914. A three-year School of Medicine had been organized in 1913, under the Faculty of Arts and Science. For the next ten years it, continued as a three-year course, after which students were accepted for their final two years at McGill and the University of Toronto.

In 1914, the Low Level Bridge was the only link between north and south Edmonton. To reach the University from the north side, you either walked across the river ice in winter or took a trolley car over the bridge. It dropped you off at the intersection of 82 Avenue and 109 Street, and from there you walked along a trail in dense bush to Assiniboia and Athabasca Halls, the only University buildings at the time.

Mr. Cecil Race, the very kindly Registrar, examined my credentials, indicating that I had passed the English Matriculation Examination in Belfast, and allowed me to register. The following year, I registered in the School of Medicine. By 1915, the Arts Building had been constructed, and most of my first-year medical courses were carried out in it. Our subjects included physics, inorganic and organic chemistry, botany, zoology, French and German.

Those pioneer teachers were a dedicated group who carried their heavy load with few assistants. Graduate students did not exist. Our teachers included R. W. Boyle in physics (who later distinguished himself in the field of ultrasonics in submarine detection), A. F. L. Lehman, a gifted teacher in chemistry, and J. B. Collip, a youthful and enthusiastic zoology teacher who, of course, later became famous as a co-discoverer of insulin.

John Scott

PAUL R. GORHAM

The Throne Room

I FIRST CAME TO the University of Alberta in January 1969, to be interviewed as a potential replacement for a retiring professor. While on campus, I gave a seminar on toxic blue-green algae, the focus of my research at the time.

After my talk, Professor William A. Fuller invited me for dinner at his Parkallen home. Edmonton was in the grip of a prolonged, extreme cold spell. The car heater wasn't working well on the ride over, and my clothing was not warm enough. When Professor Fuller introduced me to his wife, I was so cold that my teeth were chattering!

My visit included an interview with Donald M. Ross, Dean of Science. He described for me, in some detail, the plans for the large biological sciences complex that was under construction and scheduled for completion in the summer of 1970. He had been instrumental in getting this approved, designed and built. I also remember how impressed I was by the dining room at the Faculty Club—especially by the view across the river valley of the city lights on a cold winter's night. I was very pleased, then, when I was eventually offered the position.

I joined the faculty in August 1969, and was warmly received by Professor Wilson N. Stewart, Chair of the Department of Botany. I was assigned an office in a two-storey, cream-colored house (later dismantled) on the east side of 112 Street, at the corner of 91 Avenue, not far from the Tuck Shop.

Prior to its acquisition by the University, this house had been the Palace of the Roman Catholic Archbishop of Edmonton. The ground floor, to one side of the hall and stairwell, was made up of two large rooms. One had a raised dais where audiences with the archbishop had taken place. The adjoining room had served as the reception and waiting room. The upstairs rooms were now used as offices and laboratories by several botany graduate students.

On the main floor, another new staff member, Dr. James M. Mayo, occupied the waiting room, while I was installed in "the Throne Room." Its ceremonial ambience soon disappeared. The dais was immediately buried under stacks of large moving cartons containing my books, periodicals and files from the National Research Council, and I requested filing cabinets and bookshelves from Lloyd Carswell, the departmental executive assistant, to bring some order to the place.

Jim Mayo and I got to know the Cameron Library, the Students' Union Building and other buildings on campus together and soon we were close friends.

During my thirteen years at Faculté Saint-Jean, I witnessed events ranging from the sublime to the absurd, and everything in between.

I'll never forget my first day at the Faculté. As I entered the door, my heart beating fast with excitement, what did I see? A young woman washing her hair in the sink! When she saw me out of the corner of her eye, she quietly wrapped a towel, Hollywood-style, around her dripping hair and asked if she could help me. She was the secretary. Still in her Carmen Miranda "hat," she showed me to my office: a totally empty room, except for a phone on the floor.

Talk about first impressions! Keeping my cool—which over the years I became very good at—I decided to view the situation as simple culture shock. The shock continued when I went hunting for someplace to live other than my hotel room. Well, guess what? I was not able to rent or even to buy an apartment or a house. Why? Because I was a single woman!

In the course of my search for a dwelling, I chatted with many people and heard many stories. One person told me about a middle-aged woman who swore that she smelled roses every Saturday as she passed a statue of the Virgin Mary erected on the Faculté grounds. Her story had been passed from one person to another, taking on such proportions that an official inquiry was conducted. The findings: in the house next door to the statue, they did the laundry every Saturday using a rose-scented detergent!

I had inherited the "Collège Saint-Jean" from the Oblate Fathers and was given the task of guiding it into the non-confessional "Faculté" it is today. Fulfilling that mandate, with the invaluable support of countless others, is the brightest spot in my forty-three-year career.

Gamila Morcos

GERALD MCCAUGHEY

How I Met
"THE PRESIDENT"

I HAD BEEN TEACHING at Victoria's (now sadly defunct) Canadian Services College, Royal Roads for a decade, since graduating from McGill in 1951. We enjoyed an elaborate Graduation Day Parade every spring, when our latest band of immaculate, intelligent Officer Cadets moved on to higher challenges. Although we instructors were, by and large, civilians, we always dressed up in caps and gowns, pinned on our World War II medals and carried out our part in the parade ceremonies.

In 1962, my family and I were watching the splendid affair yet again. My oldest son turned to me and asked rather plaintively, "Dad, when are **you** going to graduate?" I, indeed, had begun to wonder if the time hadn't arrived for me to move on from what was essentially a junior college.

Shortly thereafter, I met George Baldwin while we were both teaching summer school at what was then Victoria College. George did a splendid job of selling me on the outstanding quality of the University of Alberta and suggested that I apply for a position there. I decided that yes, my son was right. It was time for me to "graduate"!

That being the early sixties, academic jobs were available at the drop of a hat. My only problem was deciding which of the many offers I would accept. George, however, had done his work so well that I didn't take long to choose. With appropriate back and forth letters to Henry Kreisel, Head of the English Department, and ultimately Dean Smith, Faculty of Arts, I was committed to the U of A.

I spent some time in Edmonton finding a nice, new, suitable house to purchase. After borrowing funds for a down payment, I returned home to the bad news (typical for a Canadian Government employee) that my accumulated sick leave money (which would have covered the loan) had been cancelled for all and sundry. These days, I suppose we would have taken a class action against the "feds," but back then it was simply "tough luck, chum" from the government.

Fortunately, the University of Alberta was not so penurious, providing up to $750 in moving costs for new faculty. This was just about the exact amount needed to move goods and chattels and a family of six from Victoria to Edmonton. So I called in the movers and they loaded up. After packing our tent and family into our 1950 Buick Riviera coupe, we set out on our new venture. We camped along the way in such beautiful spots as Bridal Falls, Mount Revelstoke and Jasper Park.

When we arrived in Edmonton at about 11 a.m. on Labour Day Monday, we found the big MacCosham van waiting at the door of our new home. "Well," said the driver, "we are ready to unload and glad you are here. As soon as you pay me, we can begin."

"Sure," I replied. "I have my chequebook right here. Exactly how much do I owe you?"

"I need a certified cheque or cash," he insisted, arms folded across his chest. Behind him stood the moving van, loaded with my every earthly possession.

How on earth, on Labour Day Holiday Monday, was I supposed to solve this problem (credit cards had yet to be invented)? No one in Victoria had as much as mentioned payment to me (even if the driver found this hard to believe). The fault probably lay with the fact that we moved out of the Royal Roads married quarters, and all the movers were used to dealing with military personnel and being paid directly by National Defense. Now, suddenly, I was faced with the very sticky business of "pay or else."

What could I do? I phoned MacCosham's in Victoria, but only some junior manager was on duty for the holiday, and he couldn't have cared less about my problem. Finally, we managed to reach a senior man from the Edmonton branch at his summer cottage. He happened to have some vague knowledge of University matters, his brother, uncle or whatever being a Professor at Queens.

"Well," said this one to me, "isn't the University going to reimburse you?"

"Yes, of course they are. I am not about to give you a bad cheque!"

"Well then, all we need right now is a confirmation of that fact from the University, and I will authorize the release of your shipment."

"And how, precisely, do you expect me to get that on Labour Day Monday?"

"No problem," said Mr. Mac's Man. "Just phone the President and have him call me to confirm that you are joining the staff. That will suffice."

"What do you mean, call the President? How do you think I can do that? He probably doesn't even know who I am. Perhaps I could call Henry Kreisel or even maybe Dean Smith, but the President...?"

"Listen," said my helpful moving executive, "either I get it direct from Dr. Johns or you **don't** get unloaded!"

By now, this long-winded telephonic dance had been going on for about two hours, much to the amusement of the moving crew. Although they seemed genuinely sympathetic to my dilemma, the driver kept repeating, "It's as much as my job's worth. I simply cannot unpack a load without being paid unless our Big Boss here says it's okay!"

My kids were getting more than a little restive, and I realized that I didn't have any options. I had to phone the President and just hope he felt kindly about cutting this particular Gordian knot.

With much trepidation, I placed the call. He sounded as if he didn't really know who I was and found it very hard to believe that nobody had bothered to tell me about this essential fact of moving. Even so, he did all the right things. He phoned the moving company executive, guaranteed my account and instantly returned my world to normal. Suddenly, all those very positive things George Baldwin had told me about the U of A proved true.

Of course, I later got to know Walter Johns personally and came to realize what a fine person he was both personally and professionally. In my opinion, he was the greatest President the University of Alberta has ever had.

U of A President Walter Johns hard at work counting pennies

MARY SPENCER

Learning to Love Muddington

IN 1953, I ARRIVED IN EDMONTON to look for a job. It turned out that my taxi driver had just done the same. After checking his map of the city, he decided that the shortest route to the University campus was over the Groat Bridge. We found our way to the appointed place on the riverbank without difficulty, but lo and behold, either the bridge had sunk, or it had not yet been built. The latter proved to be true.

I eventually did manage to cross the North Saskatchewan River and became a U of A faculty member.

After spending five-and-a-half years in the San Francisco Bay area, coming to Edmonton was like entering a different world. Early in the oil boom days, the overwhelming impression was of mud (*Muddington,* a visiting friend from Sweden called it!). As the residential and industrial areas rapidly expanded, construction of paved roads and sidewalks could not keep pace, and there was little in the way of sod or landscaping to cope with the gumbo.

In those times, Edmonton's ballet performances were held in the Sales Stock Pavilion, for lack of a better venue. The makeshift platforms "whomped" with every graceful landing, and long, lonesome train whistles created melancholy discords within the music.

I remember being in Eaton's basement one Saturday, during our first November back in Canada, and being almost overwhelmed with nostalgia for the fresh daffodils that would have been blooming in our California garden. Grey November, with its bare deciduous trees and no snow cover, was (and is) surely Edmonton's bleakest month.

Nevertheless, even though our California employers had offered to keep our jobs open for a year, my husband and I decided to stay in Canada. For all of the most important things in life, we made the right move.

Since housing was extremely scarce in those boom days, the University provided incoming faculty with short-term accommodations in Pembina Hall, the ladies' residence. Every morning, I had to scout the hallway to

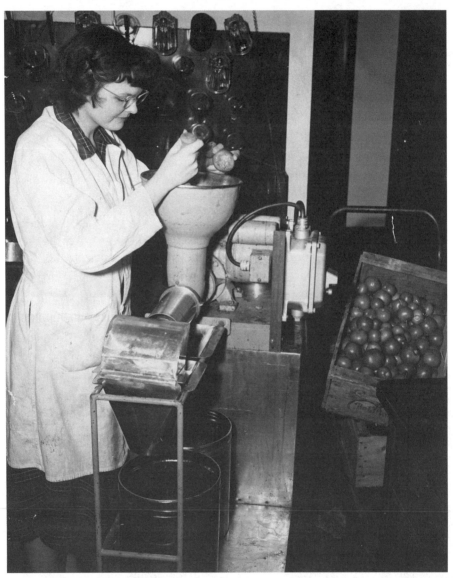

Mary Spencer in the lab

make sure it was safe for my husband to emerge. Even then, he would back into the hallway from our suite.

In the big Athabasca Hall dining room, we all stood as grace was said (in Latin) before every meal. Proper dress and manners were the order of the day. Faculty members, a number of whom lived permanently in the residences, ate at a separate table. Dr. D. G. Revell, retired Head of Anatomy, always had interesting stories to lighten the heavy discussions around the table. ("Daddy" Revell, M.D., came to the University in 1907 and was a prime force in the establishment of the University Hospital on campus and its fusion with the newly established Medical School.)

There was a definite pecking order at the table, with the Junior Professors being kept in their place while the more senior ones expounded at great length (the topics were no different than they are today, except in detail). This came as quite a shock after the casual and often irreverent atmosphere at the University of California.

The elusive Groat Bridge figures large in another story of my early times in Edmonton. My husband and I had moved to the north side, across the river from the University. The bridge, designed by U of A faculty engineers, was nearing completion. The wooden forms and steel reinforcing rods had been installed for the final concrete arch, which would be poured that evening.

The forms were held in place by long wooden braces to the river bottom. At around midnight, a flash flood descended on the bridge in full force. It loosened the supports and swept them away down the river. The forms, with the reinforcing rods inside them, began to slowly sag under the weight of the concrete. By morning, an upside down, fully reinforced, hardened concrete arch was solidly in place.

To say the least, this presented a very difficult demolition problem for the engineers! A certain Engineering faculty member, George Ford, had steam coming out of his ears. Although the failure was legally judged to be "an act of God," the Groat Bridge remains famous in engineering circles as "The Bridge with the Fallen Arches."

I first came to the U of A on a one-year appointment in the Department of Biochemistry, replacing Alf Harper who was taking time off for further studies in nutrition. Fortunately for me, he accepted another position, and I was appointed in his place.

I inherited a small class in plant biochemistry and also assisted our Department Head, Dr. H. Bruce Collier, in the large general biochemistry course taken by non-medical students (science, pharmacy, agriculture, home economics, etc.). I soon found that agriculture students were always ready to settle right down into hard work, thanks to their childhood farm responsibilities.

Biochemistry occupied part of the top floor in the old Medical Building. Beginning biochemistry classes were held in the large lecture theatres, which still exist in almost their original state. One outstanding feature in the department was the "tin room," where all the benches and floors were covered in tin sheet, which could be easily washed down. The sheeting was installed when Dr. J. B. Collip, early Professor of Biochemistry and co-discoverer of insulin, made the first isolation of parathyroid hormone.

When I came to the University, the department looked just as it must have when the Medical Building was constructed. Lab floors were brown battleship linoleum, common to most large structures built earlier in the century. (In 1929-30, the University of Alberta Hospital had replaced theirs with brown terazzo tile in order to save the $600 per year in floor wax!) The woodwork and lab benches were stained dark brown and the benches had repaintable black tops. The laboratories were pervaded by a faint, unmistakable odor of rats, mice and "checkers" (their food) emanating from "the rat room."

In those days, chemistry was the major part of biochemistry. One standard method of laboratory teaching was the measurement and identification of unknown substances obtained from living organisms. I was shocked one day, on approaching the student laboratory, to see a nun kneeling in front of the lab bench. "What?" was my immediate thought. "A student calling on divine powers to help her identifying her unknown?" As I drew closer, I realized, to my great relief, that she was merely kneeling down to read the meniscus curve on her burette!

My first office was a small cubicle off a research lab where I was given a bench to do my research. I shared the lab with Dr. Collier, his technologist (Sheila McRae) and Peter Solvonuk (one of his graduate students).

We were in the midst of a lively but friendly competition to see whether Genetics or Biochemistry would graduate the first Ph.D. at the U of A. Clayton Persons won the race for Genetics, but Peter was a close second and went on to a fine career in clinical biochemistry.

We had a very good rapport in that laboratory, and in the whole department. Like most scientists, we had our share of practical jokes. When I moved to Alberta, I brought along a "picnic lunch," tiny samples packed in dry ice, laboriously collected for two years from materials that I would never be able to obtain in Edmonton.

One day, while working with my precious samples, I placed one of them, a yellow liquid, on a hot plate and ducked into my cubicle to get something. When I returned a few seconds later, the liquid had turned a brilliant royal blue. My reaction had best be left undescribed.

You guessed it. My lab mates had obtained an identical pyrex flask, filled it with just the right amount of blue liquid and then waited patiently for the perfect opportunity to switch them.

Bruce Collier was an ideal Head, but he did have one failing—he could tell some awfully corny jokes. I came across an old letter the other day in which he mentioned that he was thinking of returning his new typewriter because it made just as many mistakes as the old one!

Dr. Jules Tuba was next to him in seniority in the department. One cannot describe Jules Tuba without also mentioning his office companion, a handsome and well-tempered orange chow named Ching. Ching was a great favourite on campus and a pleasant character in his own right.

In addition to having an unusual name, Dr. Tuba was blessed with a rather large nose and often joked about it. He used to tell about the time he and his charming wife, Vera, had tea at a friend's house. Their friend's preschool daughter pointed directly at Jules' face and loudly pronounced, "You have a very large nose!" Without missing a beat, he replied, "Yes, and you have a very small one!" The little girl promptly touched her nose and ran to the mirror, wide-eyed.

Jules had been in biochemistry during the war, when governments put a great emphasis on nutrition for both the armed forces and the general public, many of whom were employed in war industries. I have a souvenir from this era: an Alberta Agriculture pamphlet extolling the high Vitamin C content of wild rose hips, and giving a jelly recipe for them.

Jules used to tell us a story about the patriotic citizen who brought for analysis a small bottle of the most disgusting looking and vile smelling dark brown liquid. He boasted that he had found a new and plentiful source of Vitamin D, but was not about to say what it was. The poor man was crestfallen when tests on the sample failed to find even a trace of Vitamin D. Only then did he describe the work that had gone into preparing the sample. He had melted and concentrated a snowbank, convinced that it had absorbed enough sunshine to produce huge amounts of Vitamin D.

Jules, a great raconteur, had a special rapport with the Med students. He used to swap stories with them during their Saturday morning biochemistry labs. Since Friday was party night on campus, these labs were a challenge to all concerned.

Percy Beaumont, a warm-hearted and generous lab technician from England, also exchanged stories (of dubious nature) with the students. Bob Clelland, who took care of the lab animals, had a similar taste in humour. The two of them used to try to outdo each other telling off-colour jokes—definitely not during afternoon tea time when the whole department always met together. Percy and Bob had worked in the department through the Depression in the 1930s and were two of the most conscientious reprobates I have known.

A high point of our Social Season was the Annual Biochemistry Curling Party, in which every able-bodied person curled, regardless of experience or ability. Alan Stewart, our clinical biochemist (and an honest-to-goodness curler), showed remarkable forbearance to the rest of us.

The most memorable curler of all was Eugenie Triantaphyllopoulos, a postdoctoral fellow from, as you may guess, Greece. She and her husband, an M.D., had never even heard of curling before arriving in Edmonton. It was a sight to see, I tell you, when Eugenie bounced those rocks down the ice. If one happened to do something it should, she would raise both arms above her head, clasp her hands in triumph and utter great huzzahs!

Everything was always upfront and out in the open with Eugenie, whose abilities (noncurling ones!) were highly respected. We all enjoyed her company, except possibly the fellow who worked across the bench from her. In the heat of an argument, she was known to shake her fist at him and utter her worst possible insult, "You—Turk!"

Friendships also reached across departmental and faculty boundaries. Everybody attended Studio Theatre performances, held in an old "temporary" wartime hut. We were royally entertained by such shows as *Love of Four Generals*, *Death of a Salesman*, and *Look Back in Anger*, with the likes of Walter Kaasa, Jack McCreath and John Rivet, not to mention talented student actors, directors and stage managers.

We had other social gatherings in the rooms of the Wauneta Society, (a sorority for all girls on campus), on the second floor of what is now University Hall. Our Faculty Lounge was presided over by Mrs. Young, a statuesque and most dignified blond lady of a "certain age," possessed of an extremely well-developed sense of propriety. The tea and cakes were good!

At our Christmas parties, Walter Harris and Buzz Hunter carved turkey for each of us, standing at the end of long buffet tables spread with all the trimmings. After the feast, Richard Eaton would lead us in carols and games. In one game, he would play the accompaniment for a piece and we would have to guess what it was. General jollity ensued with these and other homemade entertainments and skits.

Alcohol was forbidden on campus, and I cannot recall it appearing at these Christmas parties. I did have my suspicions, however, about the New Year's Eve formal dances at Athabasca Hall.

Then, as now, faculty members were deeply involved in many community good works. One of the most tireless was Merv Huston in Pharmacy, later Dean of the faculty. He sold boxes of apples in the fall for the Kiwanis Club, and espoused at least one good cause for every season. My clearest image of him is of the time when he and a number of other University Hospital Auxiliary husbands stood in a chorus line at the annual Auxiliary fundraising show and danced the can-can in red flannel long johns.

Many science departments, including Chemistry, were housed along with Biochemistry in the Medical Building in the '50s and '60s. As Dr. Gunning notes in his article, our early research facilities were not only inadequate but downright antiquated!

Nevertheless, when he arrived in 1949, Dr. Collier began to transform our Biochemistry Department through his own high standards in teaching and research, as well as skilled administration. He realized that an organization's strength lies in its people. Through two appointments— Dr. Larry Smillie (replacing Dr. Stewart in 1955) and Dr. Cyril Kay in 1958—he built a solid basis in protein biochemistry that eventually won the department great national and international respect.

Department members regarded Bruce with admiration and affection. He never sought personal power. He had a talent for evoking cooperation and honest effort from his staff, both professional and non-professional. He was also a leader in creating the Faculty Association of the University of Alberta, and in 1954 served as its President. In 1961, the Association asked him to Chair a committee on University Government, to recommend revisions of the University Act. The new University Act gave control of

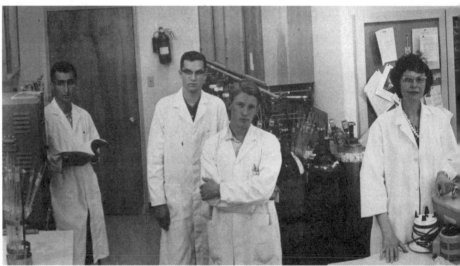

"Ethylene Alley," Mary Spencer and students: Michael Meheriuk, Kim McCalla, John Vose, Art Olson, Jamie McTeague, John Thompson, Hugh White, Don Graham and Bob Stinson (photo by Tom Tribe, technologist)

academic matters to an elected General Faculty Council.

Nineteen sixty was a pivotal year in my life. (I could also think of a few other words to describe it.) Dr. Collier resigned as Department Head and went to London, England, on a year's sabbatical leave. Dr. Walter Mackenzie asked me to be Acting Head. During that year, our old Biochemistry quarters were extensively remodeled for the first time ever.

To complicate matters even further, my daughter was born as soon as classes were over in the spring. As an expectant mother, I discovered a new advantage to lecturing in a white lab coat. (I also wore them to avoid chalk dust decorations on dark winter clothes.) Dr. Ray Salt, whose Anatomy Lab was just across the hall from my office, was totally chagrined that he had not noticed my condition, though he must have been quite alone in that respect!

Yes, there was no shortage of good times and interesting characters, and these helped make up for the lack of money. We had to make do largely with small grants from the Medical Research Council and the National Research Council because the provincial government believed that its role was limited to providing us with our physical space.

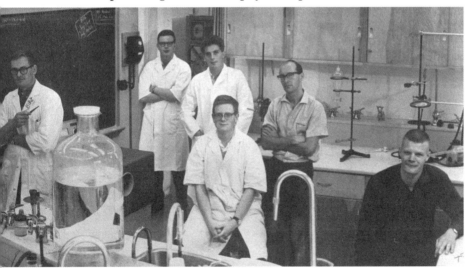

With little money for new equipment, we often had to improvise. For my metabolic studies, I had to be able to analyze for minute amounts of chemicals. With ethylene, for instance, as little as 0.1 parts per million can affect certain biological processes. To measure such minute amounts of ethylene, you need a gas chromatograph, a device that was not even commercially available at the time. And so, with my husband's help, I fashioned one out of empty jam cans and other bits and pieces. It looked terrible, but it served well for several years.

Many of my best memories of this period involve the students I taught, both undergraduate and graduate, and the technologists who worked in partnership with us. I'm happy to say that the U of A still continues to enjoy this genuine, and remarkable, community of effort.

Campus Life

---

*Making a home at the
University of Alberta*

HUGH KNOWLES

Life and Times on Rabbit Row

W E ARRIVED IN EDMONTON on a cold snowy morning in late December 1947, after a three-day trip by train from southern Ontario. I can still remember travelling slowly across the High Level Bridge in the department car as we followed a horse-drawn sleigh transporting the day's milk on its way to those Garneauites awaiting door-to-door delivery.

We'd been met at the station by a blue-nosed easterner, whose claim to this distinction arose not from the weather but from his place of origin, the rural valleys of Yarmouth County in Nova Scotia. This was our first meeting with Dr. Bob Hilton, the Head of the Division of Horticulture, Department of Plant Science, a man who was to become a mentor, friend and colleague for the next forty years. Bob was far more than a horticulturist; he was a person with a vast knowledge and a sense of humour greatly appreciated by both colleagues and students.

Earlier that year, the University had provided twelve townhouses, in three buildings, for the housing of new academic staff. The buildings stood at the corner of 87 Avenue and 112 Street, just south of St. Stephen's College, a space subsequently occupied by the Education and Household Economics Buildings.

If you were lucky enough to get one of these units, you were allowed to occupy it for four years. After that, your family was alleged to be wealthy enough to afford to go out on its own.

It was a great place to live. Our neigbours were all young and about the same age. Because most of us had children, the complex soon became known as "Rabbit Row."

We were a cosmopolitan bunch; in addition to the families of the Hiltons and Knowles, there were those belonging to a singer called Eaton, a tone-deaf soils specialist named Bentley, a geologist called Follinsbee, a play producer named Robert Orchard, a couple of chemists with the names Brown and Harris, a couple of Campbells (each with the first initial D), another Scot named Tweedie, a philosopher named Mardiros and an artist by the name of Jack Taylor.

The complex even had a father figure, Harry Sparby. Harry and his wife, Cynthia, had no children, but he was the Provost of the University and, therefore, deemed well qualified to serve our small community in this capacity.

During our time in Rabbit Row, many of the original group gave in to the urge to put down roots elsewhere. There was no shortage of suitable replacements, however. Families of Bakers, Goodales and Godfreys, Johnsons and Whiddens, Baldwins, Davys and Elders all applied for, and received, citizenship.

I don't think anyone, including the abundant offspring, would say that they did not enjoy their stay at Rabbit Row. We were a good social group, in spite of the fact that some of the men played bridge and the women had no time for it.

Group picnics were a regular event, with all the fun these entailed. As you might expect in a group of this kind, some of the children were well advanced for their age. I was the father of an attractive four-year-old daughter, and on at least one occasion, I recall being asked to consider a request, in advance, of course, for her hand.

During this era, U of A Professors enjoyed two regular events in particular. The first was the monthly meeting of the Science Association, held in the amphitheatre of the old Medical Building (now the Dentistry-Pharmacy Centre). We all participated, and I recall with pleasure many excellent presentations.

The second event was more social. One Saturday evening each month, the Men's Faculty Club assembled in the common room of Athabasca Hall. I don't recall being offered anything stronger than coffee at these gatherings, and certainly there were no women invited, but the meetings were well attended. Eventually, the association was the prime moving force in the acquisition of a faculty common room in the new Students' Union Building, now University Hall.

Presentations at the Men's Faculty Club were generally serious and philosophical. One regular attendee was the beloved Chancellor, Dr. George McNally, a very fine old gentleman who never forgot your name.

Two well-known and well-liked people, Maimie Simpson and Reg Lister, presided over the student residences, Pembina, Athabasca and Assiniboia. In addition to her academic contribution to the Faculty of Arts, Maimie was the person to whom you would direct your daughter when the more ladylike aspects of university life were to be addressed. The life and times of Miss Simpson, as she was known to all, is a revered part of the University's history.

New staff members from out of province were directed to Reg Lister, Superintendent of Residences, for temporary accommodation. Reg had a large staff, ran a good ship and provided comfort for many beneath his roof. He also always found space for the staff's New Year's celebration. Apparently he would make some sort of deal with student residents who were going home for the holidays and acquire a block of three or four rooms for our use. Alcohol was officially forbidden in the three residences, but Reg managed to make an annual exception without alerting the President, the President's wife or the Board of Governors.

Of the many faces I recall from the late 1940s, three botanists of the day stand out in particular: Dr. Moss, Dr. Cormack and Dr. Whyte.

Moss was Head of the department. He was a taxonomist of renown and, among other things, the author of *The Flora of Alberta*, still the standard text on the subject. During the summers, he led the Botany Club on monthly field trips and did a fine job of introducing its members to the flora of the region.

Bob Cormack, a plant anatomist, was much beloved and respected by staff and students. A fellow of the Royal Society, he was considered a world authority on the functioning of plant root hairs. Those outside the University remember him for his excellent book, *Wild Flowers of Alberta*, but to those of us who knew him, the most vivid memory will be of Bob's delightful habit of humming a little tune as he nonchalantly strode the halls.

Jim Whyte I got to know as a plant physiologist. His particular interests in cultivated plants and stream fishing led naturally to an association with horticulturists, particularly with this one. Now, forty years later, I can still recall Jim's unbridled enthusiasm for a botanic garden. Part of the explanation stems from the fact that the tall Scot had spent part of his life studying at Edinburgh, site of the Royal Botanic Garden.

Jim was able to help realize his dream. An old army man from WWII, he had connections with Colonel H. A. "Sandy" Dyde, now a prominent Canadian lawyer. Jim and others were able to persuade Colonel Dyde to donate eighty acres of land for the establishment of the University of Alberta Botanic Garden, now known as the University of Alberta Devonian Botanic Garden.

Yes, that slow trip across the High Level Bridge back in 1947 turned out to be the beginning, rather than the end, of a wonderful journey.

I'm sure a lot of people have wondered over the years why the Faculty of Arts has its General Office on the sixth floor.

During the era of student unrest in the 1960s, our own revolutionary, Jon Bordo, was trying to stir up some action, without much success. One Sunday, the Dean called me in a state of alarm and asked me to come over to the old Arts Building and help him deal with what could become a tense situation. Students were gathering on the main floor, and it looked as if they might demand to see their files. If that happened, there was no way that we could find enough space in the vault to lock them away.

As it turned out, only a few students came to the office asking for their files. We dutifully produced them, and when they found that there was nothing in them that they did not already know, the revolution petered out.

When Dean Smith planned the Arts office for the new Humanities Centre, he put it on the sixth floor where it could be made inaccessible by elevator or stairway.

Bob Middleditch

FRANK BUECKERT

Memories of an Opening Nighter

A LTHOUGH FIFTEEN YEARS have passed since I retired from the Department of Drama, my wife and I remain regular "opening nighters" for Studio Theatre at the Timms Centre. We sit in a marvelous, state-of-the-art facility and are entertained by the talented students of one of North America's most renowned acting programs. On nights like this, I can't help being filled with pride as I reflect on my early days at the University, and on the changes I have witnessed over the years.

When I first arrived in the fall of 1955, the Drama Division and Studio Theatre were housed in Quonset Huts left behind from the Commonwealth Air-Crew Training Program. Two huts, side by side, connected by a walk-way, formed our basic unit. Studio Theatre was in one, with offices, lobby and dressing rooms crammed into the other. Across a sidewalk, another Quonset Hut served as the set-building workshop. The rest of the Drama Division, including props and costume workshops, offices and classrooms, was scattered among other, less-distinctive, wartime buildings along the bank and elsewhere around campus. It was a makeshift operation, but it worked—thanks to the innovative and energetic staff, students and around-town willing helpers.

Professor Robert Orchard founded Studio Theatre in 1949, in a 149-seat auditorium. Opening night was a major local event, with audience members (mostly University staff) dressed in their finest. After the performance, over coffee and goodies, everyone was clearly excited about the birth of a new Edmonton theatre institution.

Orchard insisted on making Studio Theatre the best, near-professional experience possible. An actor of note himself, he would usually act in plays he directed and occasionally appear in others as well. Gordon Peacock, the second staff member, would direct one play each year, while the other two (in a season of four plays) would be directed by others from around town, who had either professional or high school directing experience.

Initially, the actors were largely drawn from the community and included some with professional training and European theatre experience (including Walter Kaasa, Max Planinc and Ivor Roberts). As the Drama Division began to come into its own, acting students were used more and more often.

Some of our most memorable theatrical evenings actually took place outside in the courtyard beside Corbett Hall. At "Torches Theatre," gas torches at either side of the stage lent a warm glow to the proceedings. Another venture, called "Barter Theatre," allowed patrons to pay what they pleased.

When Cameron Library was enlarged in 1967, the wartime buildings had to be demolished. Happily, Herbert Coutts, the Dean of Education, had himself spent some time on the Studio stage. He generously invited the Drama Department (formed in 1965) and Studio Theatre to find space in his Education Faculty Building (now Corbett Hall). Any lingering nostalgia over the Quonset Huts quickly vanished, as Studio Theatre settled into the lovely old Education Auditorium, and the department found equally excellent space for offices and classrooms.

In 1974, with the completion of the Fine Arts Building, Drama at last had its own state-of-the-art teaching classrooms, with specialized rooms for Movement, Dance, Speech, Acting, Directing and Design. Studio Theatre remained in Corbett Hall for fifteen more years until the space had to be given up for Rehab Medicine needs (they were the "owners" now, as the Education Faculty had moved to new quarters). In 1989, Studio Theatre found a temporary home at the Myer Horowitz Theatre in the Students' Union Building, but the long, narrow stage proved a problem. Finally, with the completion of the Timms Centre in 1995, Studio Theatre had, for the first time, a facility custom-made for its needs.

Over the years, the composition of casts and crews changed, as the Acting, Design and Directing programs all began to prove themselves.

When the B.F.A. Acting Program was launched in 1965, students began to fill more and more of the roles. Eventually, entire Studio seasons were selected based on the specific composition and training needs of the graduating class.

I have had the great pleasure of seeing so many of our graduates do well; directors going on to head local theatres and actors appearing on local and national stages, as well as TV and the movies. Recently, U of A graduate Kenneth Welsh earned a Lifetime Achievement Award as one of Canada's most respected actors. I still recall the thrill of witnessing his first appearance at Stratford.

The success of our professional programs gave me the opportunity to work with top teaching talent from Europe and the U.S.A. Our reputation did carry a bit of a price, as some of our best people were lured away (including Gordon Peacock, who left for Austin, Texas). Others made the U of A their permanent home. Tom Peacocke moved briefly back to his M.F.A. alma mater, Carnegie Tech, but soon returned to Edmonton. A consummate performer and director, he remained the cornerstone of our B.F.A. Acting Program until his recent retirement. James DeFelice has likewise had many tempting offers, but (thankfully) has spurned them all. A stalwart in our theatre history and directing programs, he still finds time to direct and act at local theatres, especially the Fringe.

Upon my retirement, a scholarship was established in my name to be awarded annually to the most promising M.F.A. Playwriting or Directing student.

With so many wonderful memories, of people, events and achievements over the years, it's no wonder that the University of Alberta Drama Department holds such a large place in my heart. And it's no wonder that I still come back for opening night.

ART BURGESS

An Old Time Skating Party

RECREATIONAL ICE SKATING has lost some of its lustre since people first started skating on public outdoor ice. At the turn of the century, skating involved entire communities, adults as well as children. People skated purely for fun and for self-expression, practising and perfecting individual and group skills, and then performing them in public. With its emphasis on proper etiquette, gracious manners and civilized interaction between the genders, going skating was more than an on-ice workout. It was like going to a ball.

In those days, formal skating parties were held several times each winter. In Ottawa, the Governor General's Skating Party ranked as the principal outdoor event of the entire winter. Similarly, Alberta's Lieutenant Governor invited the social elite to his own annual skating party.

Elegant ladies and gentlemen, in furs, muffs and hats, danced around the ice while a military band played waltzes, polkas and marches. The people socialized, played on the ice, danced and performed for each other. There were no body checks, no penalties—just the exhilaration of gliding effortlessly to pleasant music in good company.

Nearly a century later, in 1982, I was given the unenviable job of coordinating the University's Recreational Skating Program. At the time, the noon-time skate (with an average attendance of twelve) looked like a drop-in shinny hockey practice. Recreational skaters largely stayed away, intimidated by the random on-ice action.

First, we brought in recorded music, which was quite a shock for the hard-nosed hockey buffs. Then we began to gently take control of the activities. Sticks and pucks were banished, along with excessive speed and dangerous hot-dogging. We brought in a staff of volunteer skating helpers, ready to assist anyone who asked—even the hot-doggers.

Within three years, attendance tripled. Recreational skating had become more safe, more civilized—and more rewarding because people had time and opportunity to practise their skills. On a typical Wednesday noon hour, sixty-five skaters would take to the ice. People could skate in couples, responding to the music changes with different steps and activities. At centre ice, aspiring freestylers had room to jump and spin.

Outdoor skating party in 1989 in Victoria Park. L to R: Equerry (not named), Hon. Helen Hunley, Dr. Art Burgess, young skater (unknown)

In 1985, Campus Recreation decided to host An Old Time Skating Party, scheduling the event on the first Sunday after reading week. It was a great success. Over 200 skaters came out for a memorable afternoon, including special activities, free refreshments, demonstrations by local figure skaters and—coup of coups—live music by the University of Alberta Concert Band, directed by Professor Ernie Dahlwood. Everyone present agreed—a new U of A tradition had been born.

By 1988, word of the annual party had reached the Lieutenant Governor's office. The Hon. Helen Hunley, herself a skating enthusiast, asked to become the event's patron, and we eagerly agreed. She arrived with an old pair of CCM Flyers, right from the 1950s, escorted by her equerry, a stalwart RCMP-looking man in blue serge. He skated ahead of her at a safe distance and steered through the crowd. The guy could skate. Ms. Hunley followed and skated with various partners who were first scanned by the equerry.

All went well for a while. I, as the impresario, got to skate with the Vice-Regal Lady. At first, she was a bit breathless and unsteady, and she kept straightening her knees to correct her balance (dangerous indeed). I slowed the pace and tried to get her to keep her knees bent. After a round or two of the rink, I returned her to her seat. I mentioned her unsteadiness to her equerry, and he had her rest awhile.

However, a few minutes later the caller announced a reverse-direction skate. Before anyone could act, Ms. Hunley was up skating by herself. Too bad! After a few strokes, she tottered and sat down abruptly, with one of those soul-shaking ice landings. Trooper to the end, she got right up and skated twice more around the rink (to the consternation of everyone) before leaving the ice for good.

If Ms. Hunley was in discomfort at the post-party reception, she hid it well. She insisted on personally greeting all the Campus Recreation staff, Professor Dahlwood and the band, along with a number of the skaters. Later, her secretary discreetly advised us that she had been "significantly bruised."

We sent flowers, along with a note of condolence, and assumed that it was game over for the Lieutenant Governor. Not so. In late April, we were advised that Ms. Hunley was delighted by the event, but disappointed that it was held indoors thus limiting the number of people who could participate. She suggested that we move the event outdoors and open it to the general public.

We held the 1989 Old Time Skating Party February 12 at the Victoria Park Skating Oval. It was extensively promoted, both by Campus Recreation and by Edmonton Parks and Recreation, but, as luck would have it, the weather took a nose-dive. By 2:00 p.m. the temperature had struggled its way up to −16°C, but with a brisk wind. Only about 120 brave souls took the ice, and music had to be supplied by a large sound system since it was far too cold for the concert band's brass instruments.

Even so, it was a memorable afternoon. Ms. Hunley made an impressive entrance in a cutter drawn by members of the Edmonton Speed Skating Club. After one trip around the rink's perimeter, she stepped from the cutter to be received by Dean Gerry Glassford and the party began with them skating together.

Outdoor skating party in 1989 in Victoria Park. Lt. Governor's entrance in a skater-cutter. Skaters from the Edmonton Speed Skating Club and Gateway Figure Skating Club. Hon. Helen Hunley and equerry in cutter.

The various events held the skaters' interest despite the cold. A rugged people, these Edmontonians. Skaters from the nearby Royal Glenora Club dazzled the crowd, even with one or two small glitches caused by the super-hard ice. The Edmonton Speed Skating Club led an "All's in" 3000 m race involving everyone, male and female, of all ages. The party ended with the traditional Grand March. Everyone began in a large circle and then skated single file in an ever-tightening spiral until there was no more room to skate. Watching from her chair in the centre of the circle, the Lieutenant Governor was surprised and delighted as the spiral gradually wound its way around her, finally enveloping her in a cheering throng of skaters.

At the end, everyone was invited to the Fourth Floor Lounge in the Van Vliet Centre for the Lieutenant Governor's reception. The hot chocolate was particularly attractive to the student helpers, many of whom had come skating in their jeans and jackets—long underwear being the depth of "uncool." The oldest skater present, seventy-four-year-old Joe Taylor, was thrilled to be introduced to Her Honour, and regaled her with vivid stories of parties in the 1930s.

The following year, Ms. Hunley stepped down from her position and moved to her home in Rocky Mountain House. There was less interest in the Skating Party from the Lieutenant Governor's office, so Campus Recreation moved the event back to the Clare Drake arena. I'm pleased to say that fifteen years later, the annual Old Time Skating Party continues to thrive.

GEORGE BALDWIN

It's Been Good to Know You

EDMONTON HAS BEEN A GREAT place to live and work, but I would have been surprised to encounter anyone back in the fall of 1951 who would have picked it, given a choice.

People had been born there, of course—at least that was the popular belief, though you could not prove it by the makeup of the University I was joining. Nearly everyone on faculty at the U of A was from someplace else.

Since then, of course, some have come back after trying it elsewhere, and even more have chosen to stay put because of what the city and its people have to offer.

But in the early '50s, for someone from Vancouver via the University of Toronto, Edmonton was scarcely a household word. In fact, I had to look it up.

Even then, my wife, Bobbie, and I had little to go on—a faint whiff of oil and gas somewhere north of the Calgary Stampede, a hint of far-out Social Credit doctrine and more or less interesting claims about the vastness of the city's green space and its low pollen count. What it did have, however, indisputably, was a surprisingly large river valley, the serpentine entrails of the place, apparently; and most important of all, proximity to the Coast and 1700 miles between it and the Toronto we could no longer stand.

Toronto the Good bore little resemblance then to the splendid metropolis it has since become. It was one of North America's major centres of English literary studies, and the people I was to study under were superstars—Northrop Frye and Marshall McLuhan, for instance. But the city had the spirit and ways of a small town, an unprogressive one at that. My senior Professor there took delight in saying, "Toronto can boast a thousand churches—and often does."

We never looked back when we left it—and all the rest of the effete East we had never come to know. I had jumped at Alberta's $3700 per annum for joining its seven-man Department of English (now consisting of some sixty Professors, both men and women, of course, fifty or more sessional lecturers and a multitude of graduate teaching assistants).

The invitation came on the recommendation of Professor F. M. Salter, who had interviewed prospective candidates in Toronto and elsewhere some months before. He, it should be said, was a star in his own right; one among many already there at the University. Edmonton and Alberta, indeed anything west of Etobicoke, may have been untamed wilderness in the minds of Torontonians, but the University itself had a sound reputation—virtually guaranteed by its illustrious founder, Henry Marshall Tory, and given momentum by a nucleus of fine scholars who understood from the beginning the meaning of academic excellence.

Salter's key question during the interview was how I would teach a Keats poem about the colours in a stained-glass window to kids who had never seen one. We thought him a bit odd, I must admit, though I now

The Baldwins (and Hillman) arrive in Edmonton.

suspect he was trying to discover whether I was a smart-aleck grad-school type who was likely to sneer a lot.

He had nothing to fear from me. In Toronto, I sometimes felt that I barely understood what my more sophisticated classmates were talking about. As a graduate assistant, I never felt superior to my students, many of whom were older vets. In fact, I would sometimes shake so much in class that on one occasion, I never did get back on my nose the glasses I had taken off at the beginning of the hour. What is more, during my first year on staff, I twice had to find an excuse to cancel lectures because I could no longer keep up with the assignments I had given my students.

With coveted job in hand and fire-sale Hillman (probably the single-worst car ever made to cope with Edmonton's winters: we took the battery in at night), it was Westward Ho! for my wife and me and newborn son. We headed for a place with oil, a river valley, weird politics and an absence, apparently, of stained-glass windows—a country at the outer edge of most known things, except for a university environment.

As a student, I had already come to love the University during my seven years in it and would, as Professor, happily stay with it for at least another thirty-three. There I pursued, from then until now, the most civilized and rewarding of activities in the lively company of bright and stimulating people, at least half of whom were perfectly normal. The other half included an absent-minded Professor who, at a stop sign, got out of his car to assist a woman who had dropped her shopping bag and then hopped on a bus and went home.

That lay ahead, of course. For the moment it was exciting enough to set out for Edmonton, by a route simply picked off the map and never used since—through Glacier National Park and then straight north forever until the Calgary Trail reached Edmonton and 87 Avenue, where a sharp left turn towards the University seemed indicated.

You should try that particular route through Strathcona sometime: there isn't one. But two hours later, by now thoroughly conversant with back-street Edmonton, its sagging snow fences, clotheslines, telephone poles and garbage tins, we made it to the University-owned semi-detached house that was to be our home for a couple of years—two storeys complete with finished basement, fireplace and ten-foot by twenty-foot garden plot right where the Education Building now stands, built at a cost (I am told) of $13 000 a unit.

At $56 per month, utilities included, this was prized accommodation, available only to staff with at least one child and preferably another on the way. The units were part of what, inevitably, was called "Rabbit Row," and just as inevitably, our ladies were known for their overblouses.

Close and abiding friendships were readily made. That was characteristic of Edmonton, more than most places, probably for the reason that we had to rely on each other more than in larger centres.

The major hotels had their dining rooms, of course, though we were rarely in them, but there were few good places to eat. The Ham Shack on the city's eastern rim was popular (now hard to recall why), and the cafeteria of the Macdonald Hotel catered to those of us who could afford not much more than a Mac and Movie, as we called it. Otherwise, eating out was uncommon, except for picnics, of course, when we were all trying to survive our young families and the cabin fever they brought on. We worked at occupying them as best we could—at Whitemud, with its sleigh run down the hill from what is now Grandview; or Borden Park, where there was what must have been the saddest zoo in captivity; or the University Farm—a sure winner when the kids could stare at the experimental sheep with taps and windows in their sides.

Not that there was a shortage of things for adults to do: even then we had more theatre than any other place our size; and at the back of Hurtig's Bookstore there were poetry readings open to the public (well, a tiny piece of it); and a "five-cent football team in a million-dollar league" that answered our prayers by beating the East in '54.

The campus was alive with things to do: Studio Theatre, where Bob Orchard directed Henry Kreisel in *Chekov* while Bob's infant son became famous for consuming (according to Henry's account) a whole tube of contraceptive jelly; a Philosophical Society (so named) that attracted a good crowd to its wide-ranging program of talks by such faculty luminaries as William Rowan, who designed the Whooping Crane Stamp, and economist Hu Harries, who was even then trumpeting the virtues of real property; a Mixed Chorus conducted profanely by a Dick Eaton, who was himself something of an institution; and (hard to believe now) a Men's Faculty Club that met once a month on Saturday night to hear learned papers.

It was even possible to say in those days that the most fun place in Edmonton to be on New Year's Eve was the faculty dance in Athabasca Hall. Liquor was officially banned from the campus, but custodian Reg Lister would rent us rooms in the residence to drink our way into the new year (and, one night, a windchill of 90 below).

People from all over town angled for tickets to the ball—even Mayor Hawrelak—before one of his inaugurations was disrupted by three or four protesters from the University. On the whole, though, in those days we were less involved with the outside community than now, or at any rate less sensitive to what the city or provincial government thought of us.

Some sort of strain inevitably exists between town and gown. But back then, especially as enrollments began to go up, we were preoccupied with ourselves and utterly certain of the things we believed in. Academic arrogance had not yet been tempered either by a developed sense of social responsibility or the sobering effects of waning popularity.

We were young and energetic and growing mightily, like the city itself, and happily gave ourselves over to managing hordes of students, recruiting staff from all over the world, lobbying for additional buildings, developing new courses, new programs, new degrees. We were the Sputnik kids, riding high on the crest of the worldwide popularity that academe enjoyed.

Perhaps we had always been valued in Alberta. The University certainly did not have anything to fear from Ernest Manning's government. We were, from time to time, accused of being a godless place (most often, as I recall, by Alfie Hooke), but Manning himself never interfered. Though not university-educated, he seemed to understand perfectly what a university was, its role in society, the particular contribution it makes. We respected him greatly on campus.

I particularly recall one instance of his intellectual stature. As befits a university, we sheltered a few mavericks and intellectual hellraisers. We did not have as many genuine characters as in earlier times (the North

American process of academic selection tended to weed them out), and certainly not the wild-eyed radicals of popular belief, but we had our share of angry young men who satisfied their egos by shouting at the Establishment whenever anyone would listen. A couple of them took on Manning (for some reason, I cannot remember) and challenged him to public debate on their own turf, on campus.

To his great credit, Manning accepted the challenge. In a packed Convocation Hall, he proceeded to dismember them with his sharp wit and cogency. That could not happen in many places.

So, Bible-belted though we may have been, I do not think we ever felt constrained except perhaps by Social Credit's ultra-conservative fiscal practices (as distinct from its theories). While UBC was building energetically on what turned out to be cheap borrowed money, the Alberta government paid for what it built as it went along, incidentally erecting through Public Works some of the dreariest buildings imaginable. The semantic relationship between "aesthetic" and "anaesthetic" was clearly demonstrated on more than one occasion.

Lambasting campus architecture was a favourite pastime of our more established social critics, ever alert to the failings of others. In fact, just after settling in, I was visited by a hard-sell political scientist flourishing a petition for me to sign condemning the University authorities for keeping Red China sympathizer James Endicott off the campus. It was, of course, Grant Davy in the early days of his career as resident debunker.

Three weeks into my first job, I refused to sign, on the grounds that it might tend to incriminate me—and thereby earned, I think, his undying contempt, though he did compliment me on having the strength of my cowardice.

We could not, of course, be unaffected by what was going on in the city, and I suppose we were caught up in civic politics, for instance, as much as anyone—the idiocy or otherwise of the traffic circles; fluoridation (ex-President Newton actively fought against it); encroachment by the Royal Glenora Club on our park land; the fall from grace of William Hawrelak, a mayor in whom we had all taken great pride.

And there was also, of course, an outside world that impinged on us in

1951: Churchill was elected Prime Minister again; Libya came into being; General MacArthur was fired by Truman; the Rosenbergs were found guilty; McCarthy called General Marshall a communist agent; *Catcher in the Rye* and *The Caine Mutiny* were published; commercial colour television began, and so did *I Love Lucy*; *The African Queen* was on at the movies; *Billy Budd* had its premiere at Covent Garden; Mickey Mantle joined the Yankees; and the Maple Leafs were winning the Stanley Cup.

But through these past thirty-odd years, it is the University that has, predictably, been at the centre of my particular universe, ever since that first autumn. With the graduation of the last large group of 400 veterans, our enrollment in 1951 stood at 3200, served by 230 full-time staff (now including me), on a budget of $3.2 million. Peter Lougheed was student President; our first Ph.D. student was on his way through; Murray McDonald, Jack Taylor and H. G. Glyde were among our leading painters; hats and gloves were still worn at teas given by the Faculty Women's Club; evening refreshment—to the confusion of newcomers—was called "lunch"; the University ran CKUA, or at any rate had responsibility for a number of its programs, including a horror called "Champs or Chumps" that pitted staff against students; and popular among us was a drink called "Belgravia Punch" (equal parts ginger ale, apple juice, sherry and rye).

Much of my time seemed to be spent avoiding the office of my then Dean, Walter Johns, by going the long way 'round so as to escape his invariable enquiry into the state of my unfinished Ph.D. dissertation—well-intentioned but unnerving to a guilty conscience.

Construction had just begun on the new Engineering Building and the huge Biological Sciences complex, but West Garneau had yet to be expropriated and buried under Fine Arts and the Humanities Centre; Tubby Gerhart's Tuck Shop still served the corner-store needs of our community; and President Andrew Stewart was solemnly pronouncing that the optimum size for the University was 6300 students.

The Ring Houses, occupied by our senior administrators, yet stood in quiet dignity on the edge of the campus, beyond which the hillside fell away to a gravel pit and golf course without Groat Road approaches to scar its face.

So very close were we to the valley, in fact, that it was possible one Christmas for a newly arrived lecturer and his wife in search of a Christmas tree to go out into the country (they thought), be overtaken by failing light, but locate at practically the last moment before dark a beautiful spruce of just the right proportions. They proceeded to cut it down only to discover, to their horror, that it carried a brass plaque identifying the occasion when the Chancellor of the University had planted it just west of the President's residence. The tree still lies there for all I know.

In this setting, classes began and with them—for this rookie—a teaching orgy that would end twenty years later in the University administration. I gloried in the classroom, dreamt each summer about getting back to it, even though I would emerge from each new encounter bathed in sweat from the sheer exertion of holding onto a class while trying to shape it with ideas and intellectual experiences from English literature.

Some rounds I won; others I lost, including one in particular that I count among my treasures: a freshman essay on Shakespeare's play *Othello* that ought to be enshrined somewhere as an endangered species.

> *Julius Shakespeare's novel* Orthello, *written in the Victorian era, tells the story of how this Moor marries Desdemonia, a high-class super supple white girl and how this villian Iago breaks it up.*
>
> *At the beginning logo starts throwing doubt on how long the elopement can last.*
>
> *When this wedge has been inserted in Orthello's mind and the fish has been hooked, Iago feeds fuel to the fire by bringing up Desdemonia's cheating: she had lied to Orthello, deceived her father, and slept with Cassius. But worst of all she had given away his hanky.*
>
> *Orthello swallowed everything logo told him—hook line and sinker (up to a point). Superstition, which was a common belief in the Victorian Period, had a bearing upon the situation.*

So did Cassius:

Like all other men he had one prominent weakness—he could not drink.

– Orthello fired Cassius as his flag-bearer

– Laid Desdemonia on a bed and smothered her

– Smote a circumcised dog

– And stabbed himself with heavy heart.

In this way Shakespeare succeeds in giving us a great interest in humanity as such.

I really would not have missed that for all the writing competence in the world; nor for that matter, any of the things that made it difficult to leave when I retired fifteen years ago.

It's been good to know you. I would have added "So long" except for a fuss over its usage at the University of Oregon some years ago when, so the story goes, a new President chided his staff for employing "So long" instead of "Good bye," which means "God Be With You." His colleagues, always agreeable, could thereafter be heard saying, whenever appropriate, "So long, for Chrissakes."

Perhaps it should be left at that.

In 1963, I accepted a position in Extension because I knew that the University of Alberta had established Canada's first educational film library in 1917 and that the Department had a long history of support. Extension also appealed to me because the University in Wisconsin, my home state, also had a long history of extension activity.

I later discovered that Henry Marshall Tory had been familiar with the "Wisconsin Idea," promoted by an early president of the university who stated, "The boundaries of the campus are the boundaries of the state." Dr. Tory based his Extension Department on this philosophy, knowing that he needed the support of the citizens of Alberta, many of whom would never have the opportunity to attend university.

The summer of 1964 was extremely hot. Duncan Campbell dismissed the staff one day because of the heat and complained directly to the President's office about the problem. I ended up alone on the ground floor that afternoon, and the door had been locked because all the offices were closed. I heard someone knock and opened the door to find Walter Johns, the President of the University, standing there with a bowl of ice cubes. He was planning to deliver them to Duncan Campbell, in joking response to his complaint.

James Shaw

Art Burgess, George Baldwin, Henry Kreisel and Myer Horowitz starting the day right.

Innovation

Blazing new trails

KAY DIER

The Northern Nurse Practitioner Program

IN THE SUMMER OF 1973, I came home on leave from Africa, where I was a Senior Nurse Educator with the World Health Organization (WHO). I got a call from Ruth McClure, the Dean of Nursing, asking if I would consider heading up a new program designed to improve the knowledge and skills of nurses working in the Canadian North. I had previously served in the Territories and loved it, so her offer instantly interested me. On top of that, life back in Malawi was becoming very tense, as the "Life President" spread his tentacles into every facet of people's lives, locals and foreigners alike.

Ruth set up a cordial meeting with Dr. Walter Mackenzie, Dean of Medicine. Together they outlined the Northern Nurse Practitioner Program, a joint project intended to strengthen health services in isolated communities. Northern Nursing Stations, staffed by one, two or three nurses, provided public health services as well as emergency care. Medical backup was hundreds of miles away and the communication links were unreliable at best. High-risk maternity cases and the seriously sick or injured were evacuated by air. However, weather conditions, breakup and freeze-up often delayed these flights.

Medical Services, a department of National Health and Welfare, aware of the heavy responsibilities that their nurses were expected to assume, had provided funding to seven Canadian universities to offer a Nurse Practitioner certificate course. The University of Alberta program started in 1972.

I met with Dr. Sue Miller, the new Director (Medicine), Phyllis Craig, former Nursing Director, and Cliff Nelson, the physician who had set up the program.

Cliff had recently returned from Africa and was familiar with the WHO initiative to introduce Primary Health Care (PHC) worldwide. The PHC model places more emphasis on offering basic services out of easily accessible community health centres. Nurses assume an expanded role in health promotion, prevention and the treatment of minor ailments. Physicians are brought in for more serious cases, and patients are transported to acute care centres when necessary.

PHC is effective and affordable but requires a commitment by the governments involved. Unfortunately, political realities too often interfere, making WHO's goal of "Health for All by the Year 2000" an impossible dream.

However, at that time we were still full of hope. When Cliff enthusiastically promoted the Northern Nurse program as an opportunity to introduce PHC to Canada, I accepted the position of Co-Director (Nursing). I returned to Malawi and submitted my resignation to WHO. I had no regrets; during my absence, my African counterpart had been declared persona non grata and her husband, the Chief Medical Officer of the country, was thrown in jail.

Nurse Ruth Sutherland (left) and Visiting Doctor Joanne Pyper in front of Cambridge Bay Nursing Station, October 1962

I arrived back in Edmonton on the first of September, and the next day dragged my jet-lagged bones over to the Clinical Sciences Building. I was immediately engulfed in reverse culture shock. Having been overseas for more than six years, I was overwhelmed by the abundance of everything— books, audiovisual equipment, paper and people (the latter, curiously, all being white). To add to this, I was completely cowed by the technology—electric typewriters, fast-moving photocopiers and telephones with banks of buttons that I had forgotten how to use. But in no time I once again came to accept all this affluence as my Canadian birthright.

The curriculum was in place. The students attended blocks of lectures, followed by rotations at the Charles Camsell Hospital in emergency, pediatrics, obstetrics and health assessment. They also practised with the then very new computer simulation program developed by Dr. Dick Rossall.

The nurses brought surveys of their northern communities to serve as the basis for discussions on public health issues. These sessions had to be squeezed into a very busy schedule. The students spent a week studying addictions treatment at Henwood Alcohol Rehabilitation Centre, and later at Poundmaker Lodge, the Native treatment centre. Other shorter visits were arranged to facilities such as the provincial lab, the Diabetic and STD clinics and even an afternoon with the RCMP to learn about substance abuse problems in the North.

Believe it or not, in those days some of the nurses were not familiar with marijuana. The police obligingly grew a small plant so the students could identify the spiky leaves, and then burned a few to familiarize them with the pungent odor. No one got high!

We also added a session on legal responsibility. Because northern nurses often dealt with crisis situations, they were at risk of litigation and were frequently called upon as expert witnesses in court. Sexual assault cases were particularly difficult. After treating a victim and offering emotional support, a nurse would later be expected to act as an objective witness.

Incest was even more upsetting since there was no help for young victims trapped in their isolated villages. I'll never forget approaching a prominent physician and asking him to lead a discussion. He dismissed my request saying, "Incest is not a problem." That was in 1974 when such issues were still being swept under the rug.

The course placed enormous demands upon the students. A complicated system of pre- and post-testing only added to their anxiety. The written tests weren't too bad, but the students also had to demonstrate their abilities in action. This involved someone (usually me) playing the role of the patient. The consultation was videotaped and the pre- and post-tapes compared—hopefully showing a vast improvement after taking the course!

I was particularly adept at portraying gastric problems. One day an AV technician became so caught up in my performance that he popped his head in during the session, completely blowing the diagnosis. "I think you have an ulcer, Kay," he said earnestly. "I had a friend who got that from taking too many aspirins."

Despite the success of the Northern Nurse Practitioner Program, it faced constant obstacles. If I thought that leaving Africa would mean an end to my political problems, I was sadly mistaken. Sue and I were fortunate in that we had unfailing support from our two Deans. However, Ottawa had a very narrow vision for the program, which they referred to as "clinical training for nurses."

Every year we had to submit a brand new funding proposal, and every year our high-flying plans for improvements were shot down. We had no time to advance the program academically; as it was, we could barely cover

The Changing of the Guard, September 1973. (L to R): Eileen Hourigan, Cliff Nelson, Sue Miller, Phyllis Craig, Walter Mackenzie, Kay Dier, Matt Matas. (Missing: Ruth McClure)

the extensive curriculum during the time allowed.

Meanwhile, at the local level, we were often pressured by Medical Service officials to add their pet priorities to the already over-crowded curriculum. They also maintained the prerogative to select the students from among their staff, meaning that the University had no control over the qualifications of entering students. On top of everything else, the students themselves did not fit the traditional expectations of either nursing or medicine, so we frequently faced criticism from both sides.

To add another dimension to this grand collaborative experiment, a vast and extensive evaluation study had been initiated with Health Services Administration. They later received funding to complete the project, but in the meantime, we helped to support the evaluation with our own time and money.

The evaluation grew and grew until it practically took over the program, like the tail wagging the dog. We started by writing program objectives, and this soon expanded to include all the seven programs across Canada. Under the guidance of Clark Hazlett, we had meetings at various universities and diligently came up with objectives for every imaginable ailment and situation. These were then all submitted to the University of Alberta, where Sue and I reviewed each and every one of them for accuracy.

In typical academic fashion, we complained bitterly that we got very little credit in the book that was finally published. But I did have the satisfaction of seeing it used as a reference when I was later consulting in Thailand and Australia.

In the summers, Sue and I visited various Nursing Stations to see how the students were integrating what they had learned and to glean suggestions for course improvements.

Despite the trials and tribulations, I have warm recollections of the program. We were strongly supported by the University, deeply appreciated by northerners and—above all—we had a lot of fun. Sue and I were invited to speak at several conferences, and we received good media coverage.

The students themselves were interesting, high-spirited and independent. Because they were used to running their own show, they were definitely not shrinking violets. Although there were only eight in a class, I got constant complaints about our noisy discussions, which frequently spilled out into the hallways. The nurses thought nothing of challenging a medical specialist in class if they thought his or her advice was not practical. The doctors enjoyed these lively exchanges and always told the students to call them directly any time they needed help.

Each course concluded with a wind-up party planned by the students. The only thing these parties had in common over the years was their originality. One class presented the staff with vividly coloured T-shirts. Our names appeared on the back and on the front, in large letters, RCNP— Real Crazy Nurse Practitioners! We had to agree to wear them all day, which netted Sue and I some quizzical looks in academic circles. That night the whole group, bedecked in our colourful RCNP shirts, startled the patrons at a rather upscale restaurant when we floated in and settled around a large round table, like a living rainbow.

We also had a number of part-time people who lent their expertise to the program, and together we formed a cohesive group. Among these were Joyce Baird, midwifery tutor; Matt Matas, retired Regional Director of Medical Service, who taught physical assessment; Eileen Hourigan, the first licensed Pediatric Nurse Practitioner in Canada; David Secord from the Animal Lab, who taught suturing; Harriett Ferrari, Northern Zone Nursing Officer; Cliff Nelson, General Practitioner; Phyllis Craig, Health Sciences Administration Master's student working on the evaluation project; and Jean Moisey, who became the Assistant Nursing Director (we really got two for the price of one here as her husband, Claire, a pediatric resident, gave a lot of free help and advice to the program). Dr. Mackenzie never missed our welcome tea for incoming students, and when he retired, the group presented him with an Inuit carving.

I left the program in 1976 to accept a WHO assignment with a Public Health Nurse Practitioner project in Thailand. Upon my return to the University of Alberta, I continued to have contact with the Northern Nurse program. As Associate Dean, I was a member of the Executive Committee, and subsequently served on several ad-hoc committees.

When the Northern Nurse Practitioner Program closed in 1984 (the last of the seven original programs to do so), it had graduated 182 nurses. If this promising initiative had been allowed to develop into an ongoing comprehensive academic program, a well-prepared cadre of nurse practitioners would now be available, not only for the North, but for the struggling health system as a whole. Perhaps we were simply ahead of our time. Since 1998, a number of academic institutions have once again established Nurse Practitioner programs.

I joined the Faculty of Nursing in October 1974. The challenges, the mood, the morale of working in a university environment were great. The support system was more than I had ever experienced. There was a community of willing resource academics to approach for advice and consideration, an outstanding library, a visual aid department and a wonderfully collegial relationship among the faculty.

One of several "firsts" in Nursing during my time with the faculty was our development of programs for continuing education among registered nurses. The professional nursing association was now requiring their members to meet stated credits for re-registration. The faculty led the way, developing conferences, seminars and workshops on a wide variety of topics. Because many nurses worked in rural settings, the faculty also organized distance study packages, audiotape programs, modules of learning and visiting teams.

Looking back through the past thirty years, so much has happened. The hospital schools of nursing have been phased out, and the University and Baccalaureate nursing programs have expanded in numbers and course offerings. Community College programs for diploma preparation have been thriving, with possible transfer arrangements to the University. Graduate education at both the master's and doctoral level is in place.

I feel great pride and gratitude for having been involved with the changes, the progress and leadership shown by the University of Alberta. It has been a fabulous century! May we enter the new millennium with strength, confidence and courage.

Margaret Henderson

Home Economics
One Size Does Not Fit All

IN THE 1940s, the School of Household Economics was located in the South Lab, a building designed to house engineering classes. It had huge skylights, metal window frames and noisy radiators—nothing that suggested gracious living. After all, the University considered this a temporary location (it continued to be "temporary" for the next two decades!).

It had been the custom for many years that the second-year students entertained the graduating students (third year) at a buffet dinner. Early in the spring of 1948, Miss Hazel McIntyre, foods instructor, asked the class if we'd like to prepare the dinner. As we were the first post-WWII class, we had a very democratic discussion of the question and decided that no, we were not interested in entertaining the third-year class. When we told Miss McIntyre of our decision, she seemed startled, but didn't say anything.

A short time later, she asked the class how our planning was progressing, and had we elected a chairperson yet. Apparently, one didn't ask a class if they would *like* to do something when you really meant that it *was* to be done!

So we got organized to prepare food for about fifty people. Our menu was greatly influenced by the available amenities—about thirty single electric burners. We decided on salmon à la king, as we could cook this on the hot plates. Several students were kept very busy vigourously stirring the pots to keep the salmon from burning.

The class had decided to finish the meal in style, with homemade after dinner mints. Two pairs of students prepared batches in adjoining small kitchens. There was much going back and forth, as the two groups attempted in vain to achieve the same shade of green. Someone finally discovered the problem—they were using two different brands of colouring.

The party was a success. A good time was had by all—and the third-year class did graduate.

Elizabeth A. Donald

My experience at the U of A began in 1940 when I enrolled in the undergraduate program in Household Economics. I obtained a B.Sc. (HEc) in 1943.

After an internship, plus three years of practice in commercial diatetics in the restaurants of the T. Eaton Company, Toronto, I returned to the U of A as a member of the academic staff. For seven very happy years (1947-1954), I directed the food service operation for the three residences: Pembina, Athabasca and Assiniboia Halls. Working closely with Reg Lister was an education and a delight. The University was expanding rapidly, and many who arrived (with their spouses) to join the academic staff stayed in the residences while they searched for suitable housing in the city. They were close to my own age, and as I ate with them in the dining halls, I formed friendships that I still treasure.

After five years (1954 to 1959) at Cornell University obtaining my master's and my Ph.D., I returned to the U of A to teach in the School of Household Economics. A year later, I was appointed Director. I took on the assignment with trepidation, since I was succeeding Miss Hazel McIntyre, who was retiring after being a greatly admired favourite for many years. The University was still expanding, and for the next decade or so a mood of excitement and optimism prevailed. Our school had always been in the Faculty of Arts and Science. When they became two separate faculties in 1963, we elected to stay in Science, and in 1966 we became an autonomous school with three divisions and our own Council. Then, in March 1976, we became the Faculty of Home Economics, with three departments, and my title became Dean.

Beth Empey

Long before it was in vogue for departments and faculties to hold retreats, the School of Household Economics used staff development seminars for the continuing education of its faculty. This marvelous event, valuable both as educational and community-building tools, served our school and faculty for nearly thirty years.

The seminars were usually scheduled after classes were out, in some distant location where we could discuss important issues without being interrupted by our research and teaching responsibilities. They also gave us a chance for informal fun and fellowship. We did occasionally try to hold the seminars on or near campus, but it was the "getaway" ambiance that gave the events their real allure. All faculty members were invited, and most decided to participate even though they paid their own way. I guess we all worried that if we weren't there, we were fair game to be a subject of conversation!

At my first seminar, in 1970, I was the "new kid in administration" hired to chair the Family Studies division. That year's seminar was held at the Banff School, at a time when the dormitories were very basic and the meals were still served family style. Before most of us had a chance to finish eating, we would hear the call, "Scrape!" and were expected to respond by scraping our dishes and passing them to the end of the table.

We discussed administration and student-related issues each morning and evening, but the afternoons were reserved for recreation. I chose horseback riding, along with Judy Strange, Thelma Dennis, Mike Stiles and a few other brave faculty members, most of whom had little or no riding experience. We all wondered why Ruth Renner (Chair of Foods and Nutrition) wasn't there to advise us, given her expertise in ranching! The horses moved pretty slowly up the mountain, but the homeward stretch was frightening for this novice.

In later years, when the Faculties of Agriculture, Forestry and Home Economics merged, we faced the tremendous challenges of developing a shared academic culture. We scheduled one staff development seminar focussing on cultural issues. It was held at Nakoda Lodge and featured a memorable session led by a Cree Elder. It taught us the importance of nurturing each other so that we could refocus our energies on continuing our leadership roles in research, teaching and administration, while facing such major changes in the structure of our programs, departments and indeed, our faculty.

Dianne Kieren

To design clothing for people with special needs, you must carefully study the individuals themselves. This is definitely not a field where "one size fits all"! A garment must be easy to put on, washable and comfortable in both style and fabric. It also must be fashionable. Looking strictly at people's physical needs, without considering their socio-psychological needs, does little to help them.

For our research project, we held numerous conferences with various groups to discuss relevant issues, ask questions and listen to what this population had to say. Following this we altered, modified and designed clothing to meet expressed needs, and then held more conferences. Eventually, we developed a wardrobe of over 250 garments, using them for discussion with those with disabilities and those in charge of their care. We gave presentations throughout Alberta, Canada and the United States, and some foreign countries. Often we made two or three local presentations per week.

The topic was extremely well received by men and women, young and old, disabled and non-disabled. The University of Alberta Press published a book which was reprinted four times and translated into German and Japanese. The study prompted a number of universities to launch their own investigations of clothing for special needs, each approaching the topic in a slightly different direction.

Anne Kernaleguen

Over the years, our faculty and its departments had undergone countless moves and renovations in an attempt to accommodate our expanding programs and what, by that time, was an incredible increase in both undergraduate and graduate enrollments. Still, in my opinion, space anywhere was not the same as space together. Only within a single facility could we come to understand one another's research, the courses being offered in each department and the underlying philosophy of an emerging discipline with its own body of knowledge and its own professional requirements.

I looked on as buildings were constructed for Mechanical Engineering, Humanities, Fine Arts, Agriculture and Forestry, Business and the Rutherford Library. I felt unbelievable frustration as I pleaded our case in the various committees. Moreover, since I was sometimes a member of these committees and not just a visitor, it was difficult to see our fortunes rise until we were on top of the list, only to be pushed aside by what seemed to be a more pressing need for space from another sector.

When I retired in 1990, my goals had not been accomplished—of uniting the faculty members and programs under one roof and one mission, and of bringing about a true focus on the development of a home economics knowledge base through our research and teaching. That's not to say that my twenty-three years in the faculty were not rewarding. We had tripled our enrollment, added graduate programs and increased staff research. We had truly grown into an integral part of an institution dedicated to both research and teaching.

The intervening years have also contributed to our history. The faculty of Home Economics became a Department of Human Ecology within the Faculty of Agriculture and Forestry. One of our three departments chose to join Food Science within that faculty, thus resulting in a further loss of the full mission of the programs and the profession.

The story, from School to Faculty to Department—from Household Economics to Home Economics to Human Ecology—from one location to four locations and back to one, ended in the fall of 1998. The two remaining areas of Human Ecology were united at last in a newly redesigned Human

Ecology Building (formerly Printing Services). The Household (Home) Economics Building, so proudly opened in 1965, has been refurbished to become the Environmental Engineering Building. Is it now possible for me to say, "Mission Accomplished"?

Doris Badir

Steve Hunka

The IBM 1500
1968-1980

THE ARRIVAL IN 1968 of the IBM 1500 computer-assisted instructional system marked the beginning of a revolutionary era in teaching at the U of A. During the peak of its operation, the IBM 1500 provided over 20 000 student hours of instruction and was visited by over 2000 children per year from surrounding schools. Of the thirty IBM 1500 systems produced, ours was used for the longest period of time and was the last to be returned to IBM.

From today's perspective, the system's technical specifications seem astoundingly modest. The main computer contained only 64 KB of memory (today, an average bargain-basement PC has 500 times as much). Its four large platters, housed in two disk drives the size of washing machines, initially totalled 1 MB, considerably less than the capacity of a single modern floppy disk. However, the IBM 1500 controlled twenty student stations, each comprised of a video terminal and light pen, a film projector and an audiotape play-and-record unit.

The system's acquisition was made possible by the faith and foresight of a number of administrators who sensed the coming importance of computers. It successfully served students for twelve years, thanks to the dedication of operational staff and academic staff from many different faculties.

BACKGROUND

During the late 1950s, Herbert Coutts, Dean of Education, worked with his department chairmen to develop a graduate program and facilities for educational research. To support this effort, they acquired various mechanical calculators, a key-punch machine and an IBM card-sorting machine.

At about the same time, through the efforts of Dr. Don Scott, the Department of Physics purchased an LGP-30 electronic computer. I used this machine as a graduate student, and eventually submitted a report to Dr. Russ MacArthur suggesting that it had some potential for educational research.

When I returned from the University of Illinois in 1961, after gaining some programming experience on their "home-made" computer, the Illiac 1, I encouraged Education staff and graduate students to shift from mechanical to electronic computations, using the University's IBM 1620 and IBM 7040 systems.

By the early 1960s, the Department of Computing Science had acquired a core staff, chaired by Dr. Scott. Professor Bill Adams and Dr. Keith Smillie developed a keen interest in the APL language, created by IBM's Dr. Ken Iverson (who grew up in Camrose, Alberta). When they brought APL to my attention, I envisaged how it could be used to teach mathematics.

Not long after that, we brought Dr. Iverson to the campus. While he was here, he gave a presentation to about 100 local school teachers, demonstrating how APL could be used to teach high school mathematics. Unfortunately, the idea failed to capture the interest of local teachers or the Faculty of Education's academic staff.

The tide began to turn in 1965-66, when Professor Adams went to Chicago to work at SRA (Science Research Associates), an IBM subsidiary that developed tests and curriculum material for public schools. He told us that IBM was about to introduce a new system designed specifically for instruction, the IBM 1500.

Together with VP Academic Dr. Max Wyman, Dr. Scott and I made a presentation to the Board of Governors for the acquisition of an IBM 1500 and an IBM 360 computer. President Johns phoned the very next day to tell us that both requests had been approved.

THE IBM 1500 ARRIVES

After some delays in delivery, IBM engineers from California installed the IBM 1500 in March 1968. Even though it was small, relatively speaking, the computer needed a large air conditioner. The air conditioner generally worked very well, but one Saturday morning it started to leak water. Fortunately, Dr. Fred Enns happened to come in to work. He had a key to the utility room and turned the water off quickly, but not before a considerable amount of damage had been done. Water-soaked ceiling tiles collapsed onto desks and filing cabinets in the Student Records office, directly below the computer room. The water also filled the electrical conduits embedded in the concrete of the 8th and 9th floors and was beginning to appear on the 7th floor.

With the computer up and running, we began training staff and students so that they could begin developing computer-delivered courses. After watching a demonstration of some of the IBM 1500's capabilities, one staff member of the Faculty of Education complained to the Dean that a poker game should be removed because it was not in good moral taste.

The first formal program for graduate students was the result of luck

Steve Hunka

rather than academic planning. While visiting the campus, a trustee of the Canadian Donner Foundation happened to ask Art McCalla, Dean of Graduate Studies, about projects the Foundation might support. Dean McCalla suggested to the trustee that the Foundation might consider supporting the development of computer-based instruction using the IBM 1500. We gave the trustee a demonstration of the computer's capabilities and informally discussed the need to train course developers. The Foundation responded with a $52 000 grant to be used as scholarships for graduate students. One of the first recipients was Dr. Eugene Romaniuk, current Director of the Faculty of Education's Division of Educational Technology.

USERS OF THE IBM 1500 SYSTEM

Although we expected to be inundated by academic staff eager to develop courseware, this was not to be. Initially, the greatest interest came from Education staff members who taught elementary statistics, and from the Faculty of Medicine.

Under Dr. Walter Mackenzie's deanship, the Faculty of Medicine was reviewing its academic program. In the process, the Department of Internal Medicine, chaired by Dr. Don Wilson, was actively reviewing new methods of evaluation.

Dr. Allan Gilbert was particularly interested in simulating clinical encounters. Such tests, developed at the University of Illinois Medical Faculty, required students to obtain patient histories and then decide on appropriate laboratory tests and treatment. They recorded their decisions by scratching paint off of multiple-choice forms, much like today's "scratch and save" coupons.

This formal, precise structure was ideally suited to computers. Dr. Gilbert provided the medical information I needed to develop the first simulation, of a hypertensive patient, using APL on the IBM 360. We soon moved the simulation to the IBM 1500 to take advantage of its audio and visual capabilities.

Dr. Brian Hudson, a visiting Australian medical Professor, also became intensely interested. Personable, witty and excited about his discipline, he also proved to be a natural programmer. Courseware development spread rapidly within the Faculty of Medicine. Dr. Dick Rossal developed a successful course in cardiology and, using one of Pennsylvania State University's mobile vans, had it presented at medical conventions and the Mayo Clinic. IBM was so impressed with the cardiology course that it used it to form the basis of a full-page advertisement in *Time* magazine.

In the Faculty of Education, Dr. Tom Maguire, Dr. Eugene Romaniuk and I developed an applied statistics course which ran for many years on the IBM 1500, later on a Digital Equipment Vax computer and right up to today on the Macintosh. Dr. Madelaine Monod and Dr. Nellie McEwan designed a course for teaching French, and Dr. Don Richards in Educational Administration developed one in educational finance. Dr. Milton Petruk and Dr. Craig Montgomerie programmed courses in electrical theory for students in industrial and vocational education. Special Education staff frequently used a course produced at Pennsylvania State University.

The system was also used by NAIT, the City of Edmonton Police training program and gifted students from local schools. It ran twelve hours per day from Monday to Friday, eight hours on Saturday and four on Sunday. Early on Saturday mornings, we often found students waiting to get in.

We hired students for programming tasks or to operate the system during off hours, and many of these went on to make names for themselves in computer-related fields. Dr. Andy Liu of the Department of Mathematics and Dr. Greg Kearsley, a recent Distinguished Visiting Professor, were both student operators. Norman Margolus, who went on to earn a Ph.D. in cellular automata at MIT, helped develop an interactive system to create graphics. Up until then, we had to enter graphics into the computer using punched cards, each hole representing a single pixel of light on the screen! We distributed this new software to other IBM 1500 installations.

The system attracted many academic and non-academic visitors. The IBM Board of Directors (Canada) toured the installation one day. The visit was planned and executed with military precision. IBM account representatives had timed the trip to the Education Building, arranged to have an elevator for their sole use and even purchased (heaven forbid today) ashtrays to be placed at each student terminal. I don't recall whether cigars were also provided!

A Chinese medical delegation made a special trip to Edmonton after meetings with President Nixon. The visit went well, although some delegates were reticent to try the patient simulations. At an evening banquet graciously hosted by the Faculty of Medicine, Dr. Collier of Biochemistry spoke fluently to the delegation in their own dialect.

In addition to the ongoing presence of our Australian Dr. Hudson, we accommodated extended visits by Dr. John Huntington from Miami University and Dr. Bruce Hicks, a former graduate student of Dr. Linus Pauling, from the University of Illinois. We also had short-term visitors from England, Germany, Russia, China, Cuba, New Zealand, Australia and Egypt.

The Canadian Armed Forces dropped by on a number of occasions in anticipation of using computers in their own training. Dean Myer Horowitz, who was always supportive during budget crises, often showed the installation to his guests, and David King, then Minister of Education, dropped by from time to time "to see what new was happening" in computer-based instruction.

In April 1977, IBM announced that they would discontinue support for the IBM 1500, effective April 1980. In a meeting at the Pentagon, representatives of the U.S. Armed Forces, Pennsylvania State University and the University of Alberta failed to persuade IBM to change its plans.

The U of A released its IBM system and replaced it with a PLATO system in Computing Services and a Digital VAX 750 system in the Faculty of Education. These new systems had much shorter life spans than the IBM 1500 for a number of reasons. Many courses had to be dropped because the new computers didn't support audio and film projection. In Education, new and less formal research paradigms were gaining prominence, and the support of the Dean and Department Chairs steadily waned. On top of everything else, relatively inexpensive microcomputers came onto the scene.

Eventually, Dean Patterson disbanded the Division of Educational Research Services, and the era officially came to an end.

Today, the U of A's IBM 1500 exists only in memory, in a three-ring binder of newspaper articles and photographs and on a videotape of the system in action and scenes from the closing ceremonies (when the power was shut off for the last time). We saved one complete student station in anticipation of a computer museum wished for by Henry Ewaschecko of Computing Services.

The IBM 1500 was an impressive little system for its day. More impressive, however, was the dedication and cooperation among academic staff from many different faculties who shared its use.

When I arrived in 1973 to direct the Division of Health Sciences Audiovisual Education, I went looking for the Media Library. I found none. I soon found that there was sufficient need and interest to establish one, but I had to find a place to house the audiovisual materials (and someone to look after them) before I tried collecting them.

Locating an unoccupied room was not easy. The Dean told me that aside from the classrooms, they were each under the authority of some department of the faculty. He said that he had no control of the space beyond the hallways and the washrooms, and that he wasn't certain that even the hallways were available for him to install rooms. (In the late 1990s, this happened in both the Clinical Sciences and Medical Sciences Buildings.)

I went on a hunting mission. In talking to the building manager (maintenance and cleaning staff know more than anybody what goes on in a building). Eureka! I discovered a men's locker room on the second floor that seemed to be scarcely used.

Charles Bidwell

PAULINE KOT

Launching a Computer Course in Nursing

I N 1981, I GOT THE CHANCE to take part in a brand-new teaching technology. Peggy Anne Field, the acting Dean of Nursing, asked if I would work with the Computing Service Department to develop a Computer Managed Learning (CML) program. It would replace the twenty-six hours of lecture in a health assessment course.

I was excited by the opportunity, and so were many of my colleagues. I gave everyone in the faculty the opportunity to join me in the project, and six took up the challenge: Marjorie Anderson, Rene Day, Joan Ford, Louise Jensen, Lynn Skillen and Marilyn Wales. By inviting their participation, I hoped to avoid the skepticism and resistance many new ideas face. I had in mind the old Guinness Stout ad: "I know I don't like it, because I've never tried it."

The CML course would allow us to use a more flexible approach in teaching our post-RN students, who varied widely in age, experience, educational background and assessment skills. It would also increase our teaching efficiency, an important consideration at a time of rising enrollment and shrinking budgets.

At that time, the University delivered a variety of courses using the Programmed Logic for Automated Teaching (PLATO) system, run off the mainframe. For our health assessment course, the CML design would let the students study independently on the computer, and at the same time allow us to monitor them and identify any learning problems. We developed and presented a few lessons directly on-line, but the students relied mostly on conventional instructional materials, including articles, textbooks and audiovisuals.

The course was perfectly suited to CML. It required the students to take concrete knowledge, which could be readily gleaned from the literature, and apply it in theoretical situations. It released us from the repetitive burden of presenting the material in lecture format. At the same time, we still had plenty of personal contact with the students in the weekly assessment laboratory, where they practised their skills.

In the PLATO CML system, students progressed through the course modules at their own pace. After reviewing the objective for a particular module, a student could take a pretest, or stop to review off-line study materials. After studying, the student would return to the computer to be tested on the objective. At the end of the test, the computer indicated whether the student was ready to proceed to the next module. If not, the student could either immediately retake the test or ask for suggestions for off-line study. Because we were constantly receiving progress data, we could intervene any time we detected particular learning problems.

Computing Services helped design the course and managed the computer programming. We had an educational psychologist on the team to help us develop the tests and an artist to produce illustrations. Each work station had an extra screen, which could display images on microfiche simultaneously with the text on the computer terminal.

Because the Faculty of Nursing had outgrown its space (on the third floor of the Clinical Sciences Building), the nucleus of the CML nursing team (Lynn Skillen, Marilyn Wales and me) moved into one of the university-owned houses on 90th Avenue off 111 Street. Although this meant having to rush to the Clinical Sciences Building, often several times a day, we were quite happy in the rustic atmosphere of our quaint new offices.

Our one computer was located in the garret, where the slanted ceilings, musty odour and the spewing and hissing of steam from a defective radiator provided a surreal atmosphere. I remember one searing summer's evening when one of our team members was cloistered in the eerie space. Suddenly, a bolt of lightning lit the sky, a clap of thunder boomed and the computer crashed, taking with it some valuable data. The poor woman, who was nervous around the computer at the best of times, sat at the keyboard like Chicken Little, whose sky had just fallen.

Dr. Mike Szabo competently guided the course design, and his programmers, Bill Jensen, David Fudger and Bob Fedun, showed inordinate patience while we nurses struggled to untangle the mysteries of the computer. After ten months of hard work, the program was ready to be pilot tested, and in the fall of 1982, it was officially launched.

The first offering of the course inevitably uncovered a few problems, but the course was a great success. Students loved having the flexibility to fit the course into their individual schedules. Before long, students in other health sciences showed interest, and a few (who could fit the course into their schedules) enrolled.

In 1986, the University retired the PLATO. A computer technologist, John Lung, helped us revise the course for use on microcomputers, but in many ways it was a step backward. Because we couldn't display text and visuals simultaneously, students had to flip through an album to find the photos and illustrations for particular test items. More importantly, we could no longer exchange notes with students, responding to their individual queries. With microcomputers, we were able to deliver the course off-campus (for instance, we took it to Red Deer and Fort McMurray), but staff and students alike missed the PLATO. Gradually, the course approval rating declined.

In the long run, however, CML has stood the test of time. In a study, students taking the computer-assisted course performed just as well on examinations as those who were taught in lectures. We received inquiries from universities across the country, as well as some from overseas. To this day, the assessment course follows the CML format.

When I was offered the project back in 1981, I thought that it might change the way health assessment was taught. It's exciting to think that it has done just that.

JULIA BOBERG

A Dream, a Hot Tub and an Institute

THIS IS THE STORY OF A DREAM realized at the University of Alberta. As a boy, Einer Boberg could not talk to anyone but the farm cats and dogs. When he tried to say his name, his speech muscles seized up in a rigid grimace, with jaws locked, eyes asquint, breathing cut off. There was no speech therapy in rural Alberta at that time, and those who attempted to work with stuttering were often baffled by it. The family doctor's advice was that the patient would grow out of it. The Camrose Lutheran College high school counsellor suggested prayer.

Still unable to say his name on graduation from high school, Einer figured it would take more than prayer to conquer his disability, and rode the Greyhound bus to Minnesota for a summer speech clinic. This gave him a few months of fluency for the first time in his life. He relapsed after returning home, took a second clinic a year later, sailed to Europe to study the violin and then had another devastating relapse.

Desperate to recover the fluency he had gained and lost, Einer quit music and Vienna. He enrolled in the speech pathology program at the University of Iowa, vowing to devote his life to the study and treatment of stuttering. His dream was to found a clinic to help others overcome the condition that had dominated his life ever since he had begun to talk.

Eleven years later, in 1971, with a Ph.D. and relatively secure control over his speech, he arrived at the University of Alberta to head the new Department of Speech Pathology and Audiology. The department shared Corbett Hall with Occupational and Physical Therapy and the Departments of Extension and Drama. Paintings and drawings from Extension art classes adorned the walls, and drama students practised fencing in the corridors. Beds of marigolds, salvia and petunias brightened the lawns amid the mountain ashes in summer. Professors' offices were little cubicles cut out of the former classrooms. It was a colourful place, though lacking the comfort and glamour of the modern renovated building.

During his first summer in Edmonton, Einer offered an experimental three-week intensive clinic for stuttering through the University Hospitals. With the help of two student clinicians, he led six clients through very intensive morning, afternoon and evening sessions. At the end, the clients and clinicians celebrated their mutual achievements together over dinner with family and friends at a nearby restaurant.

Each summer Einer ran further clinics. He constantly refined the program based on previous results, and incorporated new ideas and techniques from various clinics in Australia and North America. One of the early student clinicians was Deborah Kully, who played an important role in developing the program and with Einer, wrote *The Comprehensive Stuttering Program* (College Press, 1985). She became clinic coordinator in 1980.

As word of the program's success spread, the waiting list grew to over 100 names. By 1985, it was clear that demand exceeded available facilities. Einer approached the University Hospitals and the University to request space and funding for a year-round program. Both endorsed the idea, but had neither space nor funds to offer.

Nursing his disappointment, Einer retreated to his time-share villa at Fairmont Hot Springs to mull over his next step. After a day of vigorous hiking in the mountains, he was soaking in the hot tub when another man joined him. It turned out to be Don Fowler, a member of the Alberta Elks Association. The Elks have long made communication handicaps their special interest, so when Einer described his dream of founding a stuttering clinic, Don was very interested.

Several meetings later, a start-up grant was in place, along with a five-year pledge to cover the rent for the fledgling Institute for Stuttering Treatment and Research. Not a single Elks member at the national convention voted against the proposal. In those days, the provincial government matched donations, making the grants doubly valuable.

The Institute was registered as a non-profit society in December 1986, and two months later it moved into its first premises in the Noble Building on 109 Street. Its mandate is to provide the best possible therapy for stuttering, to conduct research into the causes and nature of stuttering, to provide advanced training to clinicians and to promote public understanding of stuttering. The institute is formally affiliated with the University but has its own bylaws and Board of Directors. The Elks continue to give wise counsel and to donate major grants, without which the Institute could not continue its work.

Since 1986, hundreds of stutterers of all ages and from many parts of the

The first Board members of the Institute for Stuttering Treatment and Research (ISTAR) at the opening ceremony, February 1987. L to R: Robert Manning (Past president, Alberta Elks; Dr. Einer Boberg (Department of Speech Pathology and Audiology, U of A and Executive Director of ISTAR; Deborah Kully (Clinical Director of ISTAR); Dr. Lois Stanford (Department of Linguistics, U of A); Don Fowler (Past president, Alberta Elks)

world have transformed their lives through therapy at the Institute. Trainee clinicians, both from the University of Alberta and elsewhere, have carried their expertise far beyond Edmonton's borders. The Institute's studies in brain function were among the first to suggest a neuro-physiological cause for stuttering. Through publications in professional journals and workshops at conferences, the staff have shared their expertise with colleagues in North America and abroad.

Einer Boberg died in 1995, just as the Institute was preparing to move to a larger and brighter space. Though his loss was a severe blow, the Institute has continued to flourish under Deborah Kully's and Marilyn Langevin's directorship, and to expand its international reputation as a centre of excellence in stuttering treatment and research.

The dream that began with a relapse into severe stuttering in Vienna in 1960 is now fully realized with the University of Alberta, thanks to a chance meeting in a hot tub at Fairmont Hot Springs. Don Fowler is currently Grand Exalted Ruler of the Elks of Canada. Considering the hundreds of clients who have benefitted from the vision he shared with Einer Boberg, it is an honour richly deserved.

On Teaching

The art and rewards of teaching

RALPH NURSALL

Lecture Theatres of the Absurd

I HAVE ALWAYS RELISHED the challenge of lecturing to first- and second-year undergraduates. Who among us cannot remember superb teachers, keeping us intrigued by the developing subject matter, or wretched ones, damning a subject forever for us? The University of Alberta has provided examples of both, plus all kinds in between.

During my years as a lecturer, I experienced a wide range of working conditions. I began in the Med theatres—steeply banked rows of fixed seats with tablet arms. In times of crowding, such as immediately after the war, these were supplemented with additional rows of chairs in front. I lectured in a stride space, behind a long workbench, equipped with water, sinks and bunsen burners, presumably a demonstration platform for esoteric, exemplary experiments. I suppose chemists used that equipment; for zoologists it was a surface on which to stand specimens and spread out notes. Behind me was a wall of giant slate blackboards (with a whole religion of cleaning). The upper boards moved up and down on pulleys. And the complete lecturer had a box of coloured chalk.

Ah, coloured chalk! Biology always had lecturers with artistic pretension who needed coloured chalk. They could simultaneously draw, with two hands, symmetrical reproductions of the inner workings of some exotic organism. These things were never seen on the prairies, but many of them were destined to live in memory, and to be greeted with a cry of recognition if come across on a visit to Hawaii, or the Mediterranean or a Chinese restaurant.

In zoology, we used custom-drawn wall charts to illustrate our favourite topics, again usually the innards of something or other. Professor Rowan himself made some; others were drawn by talented students earning small change and the rest were hired out. Whenever we were assigned new lecture space, we always planted wall hooks for our precious charts. Our lab walls gradually became covered with hooks, highly irregularly placed, as one person after another staked out suitable spots for particularly important demonstrations.

When Zoology moved from the Med Building in 1958, the familiar, old Med theatres became unavailable. There was a theatre in the Agriculture/Biology Building, but it was not tremendously large, and demands on it were great. We had a very difficult time finding lecture space for our ever-increasing numbers of introductory zoology students.

At the time, the University was beginning a period of rapid growth. The campus became awash in construction. One winter, a large paper box appeared on 89 Avenue, across from the Memorial Students' Union Building (now University Hall). In the spring, the box was removed and there stood the new Admin Building which had gestated inside. Its appearance relieved all sorts of pressure on the Arts Building, which had housed an incredible variety of departments and personnel. President, Registrar, Bursar, the lot, moved to Administration, freeing up gobs of space in Arts. And so, for about three years, the Arts Building provided Zoology with a solution of sorts.

On the first floor of Arts, where the Registrar's and Bursar's offices had been, walls were removed. A long, gun-barrel room was made, jammed full of tablet armchairs, probably not more than about eight per row. Lecturing there was both odd and unnerving. If there was a podium to stand on, it was very low. The narrow rows seemed to disappear in the distance, into uncharted territory. Sometimes you could almost see the curvature of the earth. For the first time in my career, I needed a microphone. I was never sure what was taking place at the other end of the tube. Bridge? Poker? Another class? I am pretty certain that the people back there did not really know what was going on at my end either.

One year later, we were "promoted" to Convocation Hall. That elegant room presented challenges of its own. Try to visualize hanging wall charts in Con Hall, or darkening it for slide projection! The Hall also had one memorable idiosyncrasy—the music practice rooms were behind the stage. Sometimes our earthworms were accompanied by Elgar, malaria by Mozart, birds by Beethoven. There were scales for everything, not only fish. One day, as I was in full tongue, Tom Rolston wandered out onto the stage with a fiddle under his arm. He stopped, stared in deep astonishment at the assembled throng, then dove for cover behind the curtains. We were met in a cultural adventure!

Large lecture theatres began to appear in new buildings as they arose. Those in Physics and the Tory Turtle were the most useful to Zoology. I say "useful" in a very restricted sense. The rooms could hold masses of people, but they were appalling places to work. They must have been designed by specialists in packing. Certainly the designers had no idea of the requirements for educational lecturing: lines of sight; ease of access and egress; accessible, comfortable controls for visual and auditory aids; appropriate facilities for projection of various sorts. Invariably, they even placed the clock on the wall above and behind the lecturer. Who, did they suppose, would be timing the lecture?

Shortly before I retired, I made a short video for a teaching committee, using Tory II to illustrate the worst features of big lecture rooms at the University (though Physics was worse). One commentator described my video as "theatre of the absurd." I guess that was a compliment. The tape is still on file in Edmonton. I wonder if anything has improved?

No matter what the setting, however, I always found it immensely satisfying to teach undergraduates. It was fun. It was hard work. And there was always something further to be done.

A. K. HELLUM

Learn by Teaching

WHEN I REFLECT ON MY YEARS in the U of A's Forest Science Department, it becomes clear that I have gained far more than I could ever hope to give. As a teacher, my ongoing exposure to bright young minds has enlivened my life and helped me develop clarity in my own understanding of forestry. At the same time, had it not been for my position at the U of A, I doubt that the wider world of consulting would have touched my life as it has over the years. Travelling and working in so many places (particularly in Asia) has changed my view of the world irrevocably, and for the better.

FIELD TRIPS

When I first joined the department in 1976, my students thought I should be punished for planning weekend field trips. No one had done that before, and I had no business interfering with their personal commitments.

Nevertheless, I forged ahead. We went to Slave Lake in mid-winter to observe site preparation and stand tending. The Slave Lake forester had laid out work about half an hour's walk from where the bus dropped us off. About half of the class was hungover from the night before. Some were paying a dollar a pill for 222s, others flaked out in the snow on the way to the project, and all of them were glassy-eyed and unable to concentrate. Fortunately, the other half of the class showed more individuality and interest.

I have told you very few details of this embarrassing trip. The rest of it is too painful to recount. I remember telling the students that I was too appalled at their behaviour to ever recommend them for employment with the Alberta Forest Service, my former employer. Some of them felt their punishment had worked and that I wouldn't have the nerve to plan more field trips. I proved them wrong.

While that first term seemed like a nightmare as it unfolded, I can now look back very fondly at those students for their spirit, even if it lacked positive direction. Many of them went on to make important marks for themselves in their chosen specializations. The experience showed me how vulnerable students are, how governed by authority. I never forgot to listen to them after that. For their part, they soon stopped complaining

The infamous field trip, 1977

about field trips because they did appreciate all of the planning that went into them and how much they learned from them.

Even now, ten years after retiring, I still maintain contact with many of my old graduate students. One is working with me in Thailand to publish a small field guide to tree seedling identification. Another, in Malaysia, contributed a considerable sum of money to help me publish a book. I get letters about marriages, family additions, publications, professional concerns and ethical dilemmas. This ripple effect, this ongoing sense of community, still sustains my love of teaching.

If I have one twinge of sadness, it is that I wanted each and every student of mine to become passionate about silviculture and nature conservation. I tried to instill in them a knowledge and appreciation of how ecosystems function. However, once people leave university, the compromises they face deadens their professional zeal. As a result, I do not see enough of this passion in Alberta or western Canada today.

If I had this life to live all over again as a teacher, I would try to burn with an even brighter flame than before, in the hope that students would understand how fragile this world is and how careful foresters must be not to compromise too much.

My life has become richer than I could ever have imagined because of students and their search for reality, honesty and understanding. My respect and my thanks go out to them wherever they are.

CONSULTING

There is no better way to visit another country than to work in it for a while. On short visits, flitting about on sightseeing tours, you do not have the opportunity to dig deeper, to improve your understanding and humility, and develop compassion for other ways of solving common problems. "Our way" rarely provides the right way for someone in another culture.

Every problem has so many possible solutions. Unfortunately, aid organizations (for whom I have worked) think that foreign solutions can be pasted onto local problems. They simply write up the project and send the people in to get the job done. They fail all too often because no one took the time to seek local advice. Sometimes, by remaining ignorant of local customs or wisdom, they end up doing more harm than good. Let me cite two examples.

In the West, we see the land as a resource that can be tilled to grow crops, cleared to build houses and highways, logged to provide wood or scarified to allow new forests to grow after logging.

In Bhutan, however, forest soil is sacred. It cannot be ripped up to seed and plant new trees, the way we scarify our forests in Canada. Bhutanese foresters, believing in the natural forest and natural regenerations, had only begun to dabble in the "exotic" practice of planting. Like the North American Indians, they feel that soil must be treated with reverence.

As a consultant in Bhutan, therefore, my bag of tricks was useless. I had been weaned on the need for scarification. If I could not scarify, what could I do?

The answer was simple. Study the natural rhythm of seed fall in various forest types and observe how rapidly new seedlings become established.

Hellum in Bhutan

Take time to match harvesting to this cycle in order not to take too much and too quickly. "Listen" to the land.

In Alberta, this is frowned upon as passive, descriptive forestry, something that belongs to a bygone era. Here we demand more from our forests than they can naturally provide. With hyped-up egos, we manhandle nature to suit ourselves. Eventually we will learn—maybe when we have gone too far—that nature will always prevail. The devout people of Bhutan have it right, even if western thought dismisses them as being 200 years "behind us."

Another consulting experience taught me more about the meaning of self-worth. I went to Vietnam in 1986 to help the Forest Seed and Planting Materials Company deal with the problems of postwar reforestation. Agent Orange had destroyed much of the country, and the remaining forest could not provide enough seed for the huge job at hand.

To make matters worse, the people had been isolated for so long that they had no appreciation for their own abilities. In fact, I had never before encountered such ingenuity, industriousness or determination to succeed.

One man was fluent in Chinese, Russian and Czech because he had studied in those three countries. He also spoke excellent French and English. He felt strongly that he had to travel to the West to learn how to properly test, store and study seed. I could not convince him and his fellow foresters that they would be much better off looking at their neighbours rather than trying to emulate the world's most sophisticated labs.

In those days, Vietnam had poor sanitation, an unreliable power supply and no means for repairing complex equipment, including photocopiers and electronic weigh scales. I sent eight of the foresters on a tour of Indonesia, Thailand and Australia to show them how techniques could be adapted to suit specific situations.

They came back unimpressed. When I advised them to use Gestetners rather than photocopiers, or to avoid plugging sensitive electronics into their gyrating power grids, I made them feel like second-class citizens. The first chance they had after I left, they flew to the U.K. and Sweden and came home with the high-tech equipment they wanted so badly. I would be surprised if any of this equipment worked past the first few months.

I wish I could have found a way to make them recognize their own capabilities and to convince them that just because something is "modern" or "sophisticated" doesn't mean it's better.

Working abroad has taught me some much-needed humility. For most of my life, I was so full of western ideas and western solutions. Had it not been for teaching, I would never have been able to tap into this world school of learning, and would have been much poorer for it.

Thank you, U of A.

I'll never forget my first day in office as Chairman of Medicine in 1954, when Dr. John Scott (who was retiring) showed me the budget for the department. It should be noted that at that time, the Department of Medicine also included what ultimately became the Departments of Psychiatry, Pediatrics, Preventive Medicine and Public Health, and Physical Medicine and Rehabilitation. The total budget came to $10 000 a year, which included Dr. Scott's salary of $4000. Such was the clinical research picture in those days, when clinical teaching was done entirely by part-time staff.

I wondered at the time how the clinical staff had carried their teaching burden during the war years because there were so few of them. Dr. Scott told me that his teaching load had been twenty hours a week! When the war ended, it was no wonder these old-timers welcomed the returning veterans with open arms.

When I took office as Chairman, I became one of the first geographic full-time members of the staff, along with Dr. Bob Fraser, who was then on a medical scholarship program. Believe you me, we were very lonesome people for whom the part-time staff had no particular love or affection. One very powerful member of the staff told me quite frankly that he would make it his personal business to destroy the concept of geographic full-time positions in the faculty. Fortunately, this never came to pass.

Donald Wilson

JOHN OSTER

Earl Buxton
Exemplary Teacher

IN THE LATE 1960s, while working as an English instructor at the University of Saskatchewan, I had to decide where to go to take my Ph.D. I studied calendars from universities across North America and was fortunate enough to win a travel scholarship that allowed me to visit a number of leading universities in eastern Canada and New England. When I visited the University of Alberta, however, I knew at once that I had found the university for me. The decision was easy once I met Earl Buxton, the man who was to become my program advisor, thesis supervisor and mentor.

By 1970, when I started my program, Dr. Buxton was in the last half-dozen years of his career and had established an almost legendary reputation as a teacher. In Edward Sheffield's *Teaching in the Universities: No One Way*, an entire chapter is devoted to Earl Buxton. This book examines the teaching practices of twenty-three Professors from across the country who had been identified by their students as exemplary teachers. Dr. Buxton was the only person from the U of A and the only person from a Faculty of Education to be represented in this collection.

In writing these reflections about him, almost a quarter century after his death, I am fortunate to have that chapter in Sheffield's book. In it, Dr. Buxton describes the development of his teaching, from the early days in one-room country schools, to teaching in city high schools and the University demonstration school, to his work as a Professor of English Education at the U of A. Even more valuable is Phyllis LaFleur's thesis, *Three Alberta Teachers: Lives and Thoughts*, in essence an oral history of Alberta education based on the reflections of three outstanding teachers, one of whom was Earl Buxton.

One of Earl Buxton's great strengths as a teacher was that he was a gifted raconteur. Some of his best stories were about his early teaching experiences in rural Alberta. He told one of my favourites to Phyllis Lafleur, colourfully describing his difficulties in attaining and retaining employment during the Depression.

Earl had been teaching for four years at a country school, apparently successfully. He felt quite secure in his job because two of the three school board members were strong supporters of his work. However, the chairman of the board had a daughter who needed a teaching position. At the school board elections, Buxton suddenly found that one of his supporters had been replaced. Rumours indicated that the election results had been influenced by a change in ownership of fourteen pigs.

Even though he lost his job, Buxton received an enthusiastic letter of reference from the board. Had he wanted, he could have used the letter as evidence for an appeal before the newly formed Board of Reference (brought in by the government in response to strong pressure from John Barnett of the Alberta Teachers' Alliance). However, despite the strength of his case, Buxton felt a little unwanted. He went into Gibbons to drown his sorrows.

"In the beer parlour there, I met two fellows. We had a few beers together, and I told them I had been fired by my board. They said, 'Well, our teacher's just quit so if you'd like the job, why we'll go down to Joe MacLean's store and we'll sign the contract.' It was about ten o'clock, the beer parlour had closed, we staggered down to Joe MacLean's store, and we signed the contract. And I've said that it took fourteen pigs to fire me and fourteen beers to hire me and that my value as a teacher seemed to be somewhere between fourteen pigs and fourteen beers" (Lafleur, p. 106).

His first teaching position, attained after sending out sixty-seven applications, was in a one-room country school with forty-eight students in grades one to eight. He earned $800 per year, providing he also acted as janitor. He felt that the deciding factor in getting the job was that he had been both welterweight and middleweight boxing champion of Alberta, so the school board felt he would be able to keep the older boys in line.

During the first six weeks, he recalled, "I struggled with a task that seemed to be about as frustrating and unproductive as the labours of Sisyphus," trying to teach reading, writing, arithmetic, spelling, literature, history, geography, art, science, and health to eight grades. "Then I found an answer to my problem: instead of trying to teach everybody everything, I encouraged them to teach themselves and each other" (Sheffield, p. 61). This tactic will be readily recognized by all the undergraduate and graduate students who took classes from him in later years.

"I need not dwell at length on the conclusions that resulted from my initiation to teaching at Cloverdale School. I suppose the most important ones were that learning is most effective when the teacher reveals his faith in his students' interest and ability; that pupils like to share their learning with others; that many students have creative talents that will emerge when the environment is favorable; and that the most valuable 'teaching aides' that any teacher can have in the classroom are the students themselves" (Sheffield, p. 62).

Thirty years later, the undergraduate students who responded to Sheffield's request to nominate outstanding university teachers obviously recognized the same teaching attributes he had developed as a rural school teacher.

Teacher trainees who worked with him described him as exuberant, friendly, humourous, genial, approachable and genuinely interested in every one of his students. He obviously loved literature and teaching. "He often got carried away quoting a passage, tapping out a rhythm, or otherwise responding to something in a poem or story. His knowledge of English

Earl Buxton

literature was amazing—he could quote from any work that any of us in the class ever mentioned" (Sheffield, p. 69).

One undergraduate student claimed Dr. Buxton "not only encouraged rousing discussions, he created them" (Sheffield, p. 70). Dr. Marg Iveson, currently a Professor of English Education at the University of Alberta, took one of Buxton's undergraduate English Education courses. She too recalls his uncanny ability to lead stimulating discussions and to draw non-participating students into the conversation. She remembers being amazed that whenever he called upon a student for an opinion or contribution, that student would not be embarrassed or hesitant, and would invariably have something interesting to say. When she asked him how he did this, he said, "You watch their eyes. Their eyes tell you when they have something to say."

Agnes Lynas, herself a legendary high school English teacher, recalls, "One time when I was at the University of Alberta, I taught a lesson for Dr. Buxton. His class was exciting and wonderful. When Dr. Buxton asked me what mark I expected to get, I said I didn't care. I'd had such a good time that if he failed me, it would still be the best lesson I ever taught" (Lafleur, p. 60).

I knew Dr. Buxton as a graduate teacher and thesis supervisor. I now see that one of his greatest attributes was that he was a great listener. He would thoughtfully stroke his chin, nod occasionally and lead you to explore thoughts more deeply than you had ever intended when you first ventured to speak. Then, somewhere during the conversation, he would extend your thinking even further by summing it up with a striking metaphor, relating it to research or theoretical literature on the topic or throwing in an extensive quotation from Shakespeare, Plato or Aristotle. Often you would leave his office with a book or two he had pulled off his shelves, for further study on the topic.

Earl Buxton's contributions to education were not limited to his work as a teacher and scholar. He was elected as an Edmonton Public School Trustee on three occasions and served as Chairman of the Board during 1967-68.

He once told me an interesting anecdote about a delegation from the

Chamber of Commerce who complained to the Board that high school graduates lacked proficiency in grammar and, therefore, would not be prepared for success in business. They brought their concerns to Dr. Buxton, not only because he was Chairman of the School Board, but also because he was the senior person in charge of preparing English teachers at the University of Alberta.

"Well," said Dr. Buxton, after listening carefully, "your arguments seem to rest on the assumption that there is a strong relationship between ability in grammar and success in business. You folks are all very successful in business, so I assume you have strong backgrounds in grammar. I just happen to have a set of grammar tests in my briefcase that I was planning to give my students tomorrow. I'm sure you wouldn't mind spending a few minutes right now taking this test to see if the correlation really is true." He immediately took the tests out of his briefcase and started to distribute them.

He never did find out if the correlation existed because members of the Chamber of Commerce are extremely busy people and they all had to rush off to attend to other urgent business.

Dr. Buxton's contributions have been widely recognized. Both a school and a scholarship now bear his name. His real legacy, however, has been the inspiration he provided for generations of teachers and educators. I spent only three years working closely with Dr. Buxton, two as a Ph.D. student and, later, one as a colleague. However, his example profoundly influenced me during my two decades in the very position he had occupied so brilliantly. I can only hope that I passed on a little of this legacy to another generation of English teachers.

When I came to the University of Alberta to teach European politics, our students had little interest in the subject. Thus, I did more and more teaching in Canadian politics. In those days, it was easy to be an expert on Canadian politics because there were so few in the field. This circumstance probably led to me becoming President of the Canadian Political Science Association the year I retired.

Fred Engelmann

The Joys of Academe

Adventure, passion, commitment—it's the academic life!

Ernie Ingram

Teaching, Scholarship and Service
Fusing the Pillars

PREFACE

Throughout his seventeen years at the University, until his retirement in 1989, Ernest J. Ingram was a leader in education, in the eyes of teachers throughout Alberta. From within the Department of Educational Administration, his contributions and accomplishments are so many that it would be hard to single out examples. He devoted his considerable energy towards looking for ways to improve his Faculty's contribution to the teaching profession, through its services, its research and the practical impact of that research.

He has had a profound positive impact on every organization he's been involved with. He has a gift for envisaging better ways of doing things and then developing the means to bring them about. If I were to summarize his career in one sentence, I would say that Ernie Ingram is one of Canadian education's great visionaries and developers.

The following article has been edited from a conversation I had with Ernie. We discussed his years at the U of A, his career before that and his overall outlook on life.

Gordon McIntosh

I HAVE NEVER REALLY SEEN MYSELF as a visionary. However, since my retirement ten years ago, I have given a lot of thought to why I have done the things I have, and to examining the values that guide my actions.

Although I might not class myself as a visionary, I certainly have always put a high priority on helping organizations and institutions to contribute to the betterment of people's lives. I've never been an "organization person," supporting an organization, right or wrong. I've always looked for ways to make them work better.

Individualism is a healthy and necessary value to have, provided it is appropriately melded with the value and pursuit of the common good. I strongly believe that realizing oneself in cooperative ventures with others is the most healthy approach, both from the perspective of individual and from societal development. This value has been a major driving force in my life.

Much of this stems from my background. Growing up during the "dirty '30s," I developed a strong concern and empathy for the plight of people and a desire to improve the human condition.

I was a member of a very caring family. My father, particularly, was very active in the cooperative movement and helped create the CCF party. These early experiences undoubtedly influenced my tendency to view things in terms of pursuing the interests and the welfare of people, both as individuals and as groups and communities, and to do so in a collaborative and cooperative way.

I forget which philosopher coined the idea, that "cooperative self-realization" is the most productive approach to human development. I have always tried to make this a guiding principle in my life. It is what motivated me to take an active interest in politics in my early years. I am still very interested in these kinds of philosophical issues and the political avenues through which they can be pursued.

My father also saw education as vital for the development of individuals and society as a whole. When my older sisters were nearing the end of grade eight, the age when most kids in our area quit school, my father fought to establish a small high school in the community so that they could continue their education. I remember the lively debates in our household. Our neighbours would drop by and argue with my father. "High school will only make our kids lazy," they said. "They're needed on the farm."

We were the first family in that small community whose children all went on to high school. I was the first boy from that little rural community, near Bentley, Alberta, to graduate from high school. Thinking about it now, those experiences probably shaped my belief in cooperative self-realization, and in the need for a good, well-rounded education for all.

Naturally, then, I decided to become a teacher. I began my career as a teacher in a one-room rural school. I started the job after just four months' training and went back for summer session to complete the one year needed for a teaching certificate.

From the beginning, I knew that this was not nearly enough professional preparation. I quickly completed my first degree by attending summer sessions and taking a one-year leave of absence to attend university full time.

I also believed that teachers deserved to be treated with much more dignity and worth—including dollar worth. So I became active in the Alberta Teachers' Association, not necessarily just for salary purposes, but to try to push those things that would give teachers the dignity and respect they deserve as providers of vital people services.

For two or three years, I was President of the ATA local in the Lacombe School Division. I then became chairman of the negotiating committee and helped break the provincial ceiling in teacher salaries. This caught the attention of the ATA, and they invited me to become a professional staff officer in Edmonton.

I made the move for the same reason I made many of the biggest moves in my career. I'm rather a subservient type, and when people ask me to do something, I generally try to comply. One Saturday morning in Bentley, where I was teaching, I got a call from McKim Ross, President of the ATA. "Ernie," he said, "we need another executive officer for the Association, and we think you are the one for the job. Could you come up this evening? We want to talk to you about the position. Bring your wife up, too; we'll pay for it."

Now I'm not one of those people who talk about how tough things were when they were starting out. On the contrary, I had it easy. When I met the ATA Executive Council in Edmonton, it wasn't for a job interview. They were persuading me to accept the job. I would get nowhere in today's dog-eat-dog system, with everyone competing for scarce jobs and clawing their way up the career ladder. I would be relegated to permanent unemployment.

One reason I went to Edmonton was to get a free supper. I knew the ATA fed their guests well; I'm living proof of that. The Executive took us to the Mayfair Golf and Country Club and paid, of course. For the first time in my life, I had a liqueur after a meal. We were put up in a fine hotel; there were even clean sheets on the bed. Best of all, we didn't have to get up early in the morning so that the hotel staff could use the sheets for tablecloths at breakfast.

On the way home the next day, I told Jennie, "You know, I really have to take the job. They want me to."

I don't think I have ever aspired to any particular position or career path. That's not how I look at life. I always viewed what I was doing as helping people. If I did create new opportunities for myself, it was to keep from getting bored. I couldn't confine myself to one position for thirty years with little or no challenge. But I never thought in terms of promotion or moving up the career ladder.

When I joined the staff at the ATA, it was still split between those who saw it primarily as an economic welfare organization and those who viewed it more as a professional association. Up until that time, its major thrust was economic. McKim Ross, who was President at the time, took me aside and told me, "We want you to help us emphasize the professional aspects of the Association's work."

After investigating other teachers' organizations and other professions, I thought of several ways of providing professional development opportunities for Alberta teachers.

In those days, as now, many teachers focussed on their specific subject disciplines. Although I personally do not like this to be the primary emphasis, I realized that organizing teachers into subgroups and specializations would be a good first step.

So we established specialist councils in subject areas such as mathematics, science and social studies. Others, such as the Guidance Council and the Council on School Administration, were not subject oriented. We started with six councils and added more over the years. Their sole role was to advance the professional growth of their members.

We also created a core of fifteen to twenty professional-development consultants who helped organize and conduct a variety of professional development programs for teachers in the regions. We established professional development committees and officers throughout the province so that locals could initiate their own programs. In addition, we prepared and published a variety of professional development resource materials. With this integrated approach, we not only developed better teachers, we provided them with the means to develop themselves.

These initiatives are still alive and well in one form or another. Another that I take a bit of pride in, and which I think is still operational, is the professional initiation of new teachers. When new teachers enter the profession, the ATA holds a formal initiation ceremony. This fosters a sense of belonging to a profession that cares for its new members.

The next step in my career was to return to the U of A to study for my Ph.D. I'd like to say that I thought this out very carefully when I was a boy on the farm and decided that one day I wanted to be the proud owner of a Ph.D. However, that farm boy had no idea what a Ph.D. was. Like my move to the ATA, I pursued my Ph.D. because I was asked to.

For two or three years, I had been working closely with Art Reeves, the first Chairman in the Department of Educational Administration, helping to train short-course leaders. During that time, we had many lengthy discussions. During one of these, he turned to me and asked, "Ernie, you are just finishing your master's degree. Have you ever thought about coming in for your Ph.D.?"

I had never planned on this, but you really have to have known Art Reeves and the influence he could have on people. By the end of the conversation, he told me (and I mean **told** me), "Ernie, maybe this fall is a bit early to start, but I want to see you in the program the fall after that."

It may sound funny today, but when Art Reeves told me that, I took it as an order. So when I came home, I told Jennie—"I have to go into the Ph.D. program."

Stan Clarke, the ATA's Executive Secretary, was very pleased that I had made this decision and recommended that I be given the necessary leave of absence and financial support. I started the program in 1963 and received my Ph.D. in the fall of 1965. I returned to my position at the ATA in the fall of 1965 and remained there until the spring of 1967 when I accepted a position with the Ontario Institute for Studies in Education.

Once again, my move to the OISE was a case of following orders. During an ATA Executive Council meeting, I received a call from John Andrews, the Assistant Director of OISE. He said, "Ernie, we need someone here who can help us give a development thrust to our efforts. We are supposed to be conducting graduate studies, research and development, and we have a spin off called Field Services. The position of Head of Field Services is open. I see that as being closely tied to development, and we think you are the right person for it."

John asked if I could come to Toronto to discuss the offer with them. So I told Stan Clarke and Jennie that I had to go to Toronto because John Andrews had asked me to. I'm being facetious, of course, but that is close to how it happened. Again I was brought to Toronto not to be interviewed for the job, but rather to be convinced that I should accept it.

During my years at OISE, I worked with John to integrate its three functions—graduate studies, research and development. One of our first initiatives was to develop a system of field development offices.

After trying various strategies for getting OISE staff to collaborate directly with local school systems, we had to come up with a new system outside of the departmental structure of OISE (which followed the academic university tradition). We decided to create field centres throughout the province, integrating research, development, instruction and service in order to help regional educational communities improve. Before I left OISE, we had three of these operational. There are now several of them, and from what I hear, they are functioning very well. In fact, their success may be one of the reasons that OISE has continued to survive in this era of cutbacks.

In 1968, I was commanded (yet again) to come west to join the new Alberta Human Resources Research Council. The HRRC was a broadly based educational research and development centre. Lorne Downey was named the HRRC's first Director. Tim Byrne, Deputy Minister of Education, was on the Board of Directors. I don't remember who called me first, but both Tim and Lorne invited me to come back to Alberta.

Although the HRRC lasted for only four short years, we were involved in a number of important projects. One that stands out is a self-help program called SEARCH (the Selection of Educational Alternatives for Rural Change).

At that time, Alberta had many tiny rural high schools scattered across the province. Each was organized the same way as a big school, as an independent entity doing everything on its own. SEARCH looked for ways in which schools in neigbouring communities could cooperate to provide greater educational opportunities. The pilot involved two fairly small high schools in one county. They experimented in several collaborative projects, sharing staff, community involvement, students taking some courses in both schools and so on.

By 1972, we heard from reliable sources that HRRC would be closed down. Apparently, Ontario Premier Bill Davis had advised Peter Lougheed not to let an organization similar to OISE exist unless he had control over its research and development programs. This, plus the fact that HRRC was a left-over program from the Social Credit Government, led to its demise.

The initial impact was devastating for many staff members, myself included. For the first time in my life, I had lost a job. What was worse, I had to take the initiative in finding another one.

This time, my orders came from Jennie. She informed me, in no uncertain terms, that I was too young and too poor to retire. I phoned Dean Myer Horowitz and said, "As you well know, Myer, HRRC is going down the drain. I was wondering if there were any openings over there. I'll do anything—type, or be a janitor, or whatever."

Gordon Mowat, Chairman of Educational Administration, phoned me a day or two later and said, "Ernie, we do have a position, and you can have it." I asked whether it was an academic position or one in the secretarial pool. He replied, "Well, academic, of course." The process of recruiting and appointing staff is certainly different today. I would never make it, not even as an unskilled clerk.

It was a little difficult working in an established university academic community after the excitement, innovation, change and development during my years at the ATA, OISE and HRRC. I do not mean to be critical of the department. In fact, it was the first department of its kind in a Canadian university and played a leadership role in its field for many years. However, a university department's structure doesn't lend itself to radical change.

For a short period of time, I thought this was great. I had gone through a lot of turmoil and excitement over the past several years and was ready for a bit of relaxation. Gradually, though, I looked more and more for ways to change things, to create a more integrated, dynamic atmosphere within the department and the faculty as a whole.

The first innovative activity I can remember was working with Gordon McIntosh to update and modify two of the department's courses. We developed these into a set of two courses on the change process itself. Before we can make serious inroads into improving education, we must first research and understand the processes involved in change and development. The courses we developed helped educational practitioners effectively improve their programs.

I was also heavily involved, with Gordon Mowat, Ed Seger and others, in developing and organizing the Administrative Development Program (ADP). The ADP allowed educators to pursue and complete an M.Ed. in Educational Administration without having to take a leave of absence. Two or three years later, we initiated (with special funding from Advanced Education) a similar outreach program, the Extended Campus Program (ECP), for students who could not conveniently come to Edmonton each week.

Both these programs were based on the kind of integration philosophy I have pursued throughout my career—not just the general integration of teaching, research and service, but also the integration of many of the courses the students had to take. I coordinated both programs for most of my remaining tenure in the University. Frank Peters, Ken Ward and Craig Montgomerie were regular members of the programs, and several other staff members also participated. In another attempt to integrate across departmental boundaries, we generally had one or more staff members from other departments participate as well.

I always worked well with my colleagues in the faculty and made many good friends. However, some of them became annoyed with me at times because I was forever pushing for a more flexible and dynamic type of operation.

In the final years before my retirement, this philosophy culminated in two major initiatives. In 1986, I got involved in the Alberta Consortium for the Development of Leadership in Education, a forum for communication and cooperation among groups responsible for developing educational leadership in Alberta. It brought together Alberta's ten major educational organizations, including the four universities, the Department of Education, the Alberta Teachers' Association and the Alberta School Trustees' Association. I served as Chairman of the Board of Directors for a time. The Consortium sponsored several very productive conferences, workshops and seminars, focussing on the broad nature of leadership and on the collaboration necessary for developing it.

The Strategic Planning Project, which consumed all of my time during the last two years with the University of Alberta, provided the best opportunity I had during my tenure with the University to move toward realization of many components of my philosophy—integration of teaching, research and service; cross-departmental collaboration; collaboration with the profession and others we serve; cooperation rather than competition as the most effective approach to development; and wide involvement and consultation in the policy development process.

It was designed as a full-scale comprehensive planning project, including in-depth internal reviews. Practically all members of the faculty and many of our partners from outside the faculty were heavily involved over the life of the project. They were involved in many ways—as sources of information and ideas, as participants in seminars and feedback sessions, as members of task forces and as members of feasibility testing panels. Many of the ideas and approaches brought forward by the project have been adopted by faculty members, as well as by various units of the faculty. It was a very satisfying way to end my career with the University.

The basic loyalty of a faculty of education should be to search for the "truth" in teaching and learning, and to disseminate the results of this search to educators and would-be educators. Embedded in this basic loyalty, of course, is collaboration with others in the development and maintenance of an effective education profession and sets of specialties within this profession.

The faculty, and the departments within the faculty, pursue their responsibilities through three major processes—teaching, research and service. Sometimes these functions are integrated, and at other times they are carried out independently.

Universities have long been built upon these three pillars. Many academics, and those in the communities they serve, realize how important it is to blend these three pillars to support more integrated programs. However, the traditional university culture, structured around specific academic disciplines, sees scholarship as the primary pillar.

Professional schools, as they became incorporated into the universities, also took on this traditional academic structure, with scholarship as their major goal. They saw this as the means to achieving academic respectability. Research, teaching and service tended to become separate pillars, with most of the prestige reserved for research.

As professional schools grew in prestige, the fusion of the three pillars grew more feasible. By this time, however, faculty members had become accustomed to traditional academic roles.

Within the Faculty of Education, University of Alberta, the struggle for acceptance and academic respectability, along with efforts to integrate the research, teaching and service functions, began on the day the faculty was created in 1943 and continues to the present. Although the faculty has gained acceptance and academic respectability, its struggle to fuse the pillars has been less successful. Overall, the fusion process has slowly advanced, but it has experienced periods of retreat along with periods of advancement.

If I had any advice for my faculty as the new millennium approaches, it would be to use the event as a catalyst to initiate another process of review, visioning and planning. Whatever shape this might take, the primary emphasis should be on integration of teaching, research and service; cross-departmental collaboration; collaboration with the profession and others we serve; cooperation rather than competition as the most effective approach to development; and wide involvement and consultation in the policy development process. I would also recommend that the process be driven by the basic value of providing for the betterment of mankind through the provision of the best educational services and opportunities possible.

During the 1990s, our entire world has been dominated by the drive for efficiency, competitiveness and individualism. While these can be positive goals, they should be kept in balance with other key values. In the 1990s, we have lost that balance. In the education profession, and in the world as a whole, we must bring these factors back into balance with the drive for human development (individual, societal and environmental), cooperation and effectiveness in improving the human condition. Values and effectiveness, rather than efficiency, should be our major driving force.

In 1958, my first year in the Chemistry Department, I had to teach general chemistry to engineers. Rube Sandin was still on the faculty (he was an extremely popular professor), and I asked him for advice on teaching. He told me, "When you go into a class, always remember there is someone out there smarter than you."

Rube retired in 1962 but continued research well into the '70s and remained a source of inspiration to many of us. Rube disliked most administrators and often said, "A Dean is a mouse practicing to be a rat."

When I arrived, Harry Gunning had just begun to build up the Chemistry Department. He had tried to hire my Ph.D. director, Karel Weisner, away from the University of New Brunswick. Weisner turned him down but reported that he had a good young prospect at Harvard, and I got offered the job. I already had two offers from pharmaceutical companies, and I really wanted to be a rich industrial chemist. However, Dorothy and I decided we would try the U of A for a couple of years. Forty years later, we're still here.

I enjoyed teaching organic chemistry very much, both introductory and advanced courses. Many of the chem majors I taught are now staff members at Canadian and American universities. I also taught Gary Horlick, the current Chairman of the Chemistry Department. I first began to feel old when my students started telling me that I had taught their parents.

Bill Ayer

Service to Agriculture, at Home and Abroad

I was raised on a farm near Kindersley, Saskatchewan, and my boyhood days had a profound effect on me. I still have vivid memories of the prairies during the "dirty 30s." Soil drifting was rampant, and many farms were abandoned. Fortunately, my parents' farm was on productive soil. We always had enough to eat, although yields were lower than normal. We were even fortunate enough to take short camping trips to a lake in northern Saskatchewan. In contrast, families farming on sandy, less productive soil were devastated. This experience helped me choose soil science as a career, and to this day I have no regrets.

Gordon Webster

My most unusual experience at the University of Alberta was "The Great Amaryllis Caper" of 1987, near the end of my twenty-five-year career.

Bert Knowler, University Comptroller, had the novel idea of presenting each of his staff of fifteen with an amaryllis bulb, in appreciation of their faithful service. He promised a Christmas dinner as a reward to the person who produced the best blooms. To keep things on the up and up, he recruited me, as Professor of Horticulture, to act as judge and jury.

Now it so happens that the amaryllis is a very finicky and unpredictable individual. It may begin growing immediately, or it may wait for months before showing any signs of life. Furthermore, once it does decide to move, it might produce a lovely flowering stalk right away or leave you with a magnificent stand of rich green leaves, the flower making its grand entrance any time up to a year later. Bert's gifts were distributed on desks throughout an entire floor of the Administration Building, under widely varying growing conditions.

In record time, one of the plants, blessed with a southern exposure, produced a beautiful stalk crowned with a cluster of large red blooms. The plant's thrilled caregiver practically demanded that she receive the prize without delay. With my misguided encouragement, others, whose plants were in various stages of growth or nongrowth, argued just as vigorously that we should wait until all the plants had strutted their stuff.

January came and went, and February, too. I faithfully continued my biweekly trips from the Agriculture and Forestry Building to take my measurements and make notes on flower quality and attractiveness. But as time went on with still no end in sight, morale sagged and we decided to call a halt. I must have presented a report of sorts, but I don't recall its contents.

A tea party was held in lieu of declaring a winner, and the whole mess was brought to some kind of closure. I don't believe I was invited to the party; in any event, I didn't attend. Both Bert and I retired shortly thereafter, with a hard-won appreciation for the vagaries of the amaryllis.

Edgar Toop

The Department of Plant Science, originally the Department of Field Husbandry, was established in 1917, nine years after the University was founded. Professor G. H. Cutler was named first Head of the department. That year, he and Carl Scholl made surveys and plans for the Saskatchewan Drive, Campus and Investigation Fields for crop research programs. Freckles, a spirited grey gelding, provided one horsepower for the buggy and the lorry used for transportation to the three experimental fields.

Today, what used to be the Saskatchewan Drive Field is almost entirely given over to a parking lot. Campus Field is now the site of the Students' Union and Physical Education Buildings. The Jubilee Auditorium, Aberhart Services Building, the Nurses' Residence and other buildings stand at the site of Investigation Field. Departmental field facilities are now located at Parkland Farm, established about 1945 on an acreage west of 113 Street and south of 70 Avenue, and at another University Farm two miles west of Ellerslie, acquired in 1961.

In 1946, I was appointed Assistant Professor of Plant Science to help instruct the large classes of veterans. That year saw the beginning of the tremendous interest in the development of selective herbicides, arising out of the wartime discovery of the herbicidal properties of 2, 4-D and MCPA.

William Corns

As a farm boy growing up in Manitoba, I was fortunate to have parents who believed in education. I was able to attend the University of Manitoba for undergraduate study in Agriculture and, following a brief period working for Agriculture Canada, continue graduate studies in nutrition and biochemistry at Washington State University and the University of Wisconsin.

Between my arrival on the Faculty of Agriculture's academic staff in 1949 and my retirement in 1985, the University of Alberta experienced major growth. I refer not only to the increase in student and staff numbers and in programs, but to the outstanding research which earned the University international recognition. Edmonton grew a great deal, too. When my wife and I came here, it was a provincial city of under 100 000 population, with few paved streets and limited amenities.

I enjoyed and was invigorated by teaching undergraduate courses, particularly Principles of Nutrition, which I taught for over twenty-five years. The large number of war veterans in my first two years offered a special challenge, as these students were dedicated and, in most cases, were older than me.

John Bowland

We asked district agriculturists of the Provincial Extension Service to suggest farmers in their areas who would be interested in having us place some fertilizer test plots on their land. We then contacted each farmer and discussed the research project. The farmer would give us free use of about a half acre to place plots, using the farmer's seed and our seeding and fertilizing equipment, to compare three or four different fertilizers at various rates. At harvest time, we did replicated sampling and threshed the samples to determine yields. Over the year, the farmer was able to observe the effects of the various fertilizer treatments, and after our statistical analysis, he received a copy of the results.

Our cooperative test plots often suffered from the same hazards that all Alberta farms face—drought, weeds, hail, frost, insects, disease—all possible unfavourable growing conditions. However, over a period of twenty years, with tests spread throughout Alberta and on many different kinds of soil, we gathered some very useful information.

John Toogood

My particular responsibility in the Department of Soil Science was soil fertility, that is, the processes and properties that control nutrient supply. I took over much of the field plot work started by Drs. Fred Bentley and John Toogood. Our ongoing project sought to determine the best amounts of commercial fertilizers to add for various crops under varying conditions in central Alberta.

I met many farmers, and it was a great learning experience for me, if not for them! I could recite many interesting or amusing (now!) events from that time, such as running out of gasoline in the middle of nowhere, sharing a sagging Winnipeg couch with my summer assistant, getting drenched during harvesting as we tried unsuccessfully to beat the first fall snow and many others. I remember being particularly amused by one farmer's comment after he had watched us jog across our plots as we worked. He said that he had never seen government workers (as he considered us) move so quickly.

In more recent years, I've been asked by farmers why I, or my colleagues, are now only seldom seen in rural Alberta. They had (have?) expectations that Agriculture Professors ought to be more involved in the farming community. Unfortunately, Faculty Evaluation Committees and granting agencies are not always sympathetic.

Throughout my career, I've emphasized looking *at the soil*, not simply at what's growing on top of it. In general, people see soil only as a medium to grow crops, not as a natural body in its own right. I have always said, "To see soil, you must dig a hole."

Jim Robertson

"To see soil, you must dig a hole."
(Jim Robertson)

I graduated from the University of Alberta with a B.Sc. (Agriculture) in 1950, with emphasis in agricultural economics. My first job was with the Alberta Department of Agriculture. At that time, the Alberta Public Utility Board regulated the retail price of milk. To do this, they required annual production cost analyses from dairy producers and fluid milk processing plants.

In the fall of 1962, I was seconded to the Faculty of Agriculture as a Farm Business Management instructor. Two years later, I joined the Department of Extension, and in 1966 I moved to what was then called the Department of Agricultural Economics and Rural Sociology (the name was later shortened, mercifully, to the Department of Rural Economy).

Alf Petersen with Mount Hanang in the background, about 175 miles from Kilimanjaro

During my time in the department, I became quite interested in international rural development through the work of Ottawa's International Development Research Council (IDRC). Our first project was to develop and test a small village-sized flour mill that could dehull the indigestible bran on sorghum, a major food carbohydrate in Africa's sub-Sahelian countries. This was traditionally done by hand with a mortar and pestle.

The first prototype mill was tested in the large town of Maiduguri in northeast Nigeria. A small Canadian health food company had developed a dehuller made out of used hacksaw blades, cast into two metal grinding wheels. It worked well, but if local workers adjusted the wheels too closely together, the hacksaw teeth were broken off in a matter of seconds.

The final prototype was the essence of simplicity, thanks to Canadian ingenuity and the help of the National Research Council unit at the University of Saskatchewan. It was simply a rotating shaft with grindstone wheels spaced at short intervals, all encased in a rubberized metal enclosure about three feet in length. It could be easily adjusted to accommodate almost any type of grain and proved extremely durable, even in the hands of novice workers.

Alf Petersen

Travis Manning, fondly known as The Chief, was a superb leader and facilitator. He inspired and helped young faculty get established; he provided excellent counsel; his office door was always open; he listened to others' problems with care and provided needed support; he was always positive and upbeat.

Under his guidance, the Department of Rural Economy soon gained a reputation as one of the friendliest, warmest places on campus. Staff turnover was low and spirits were high, thanks in large part to the family-like atmosphere he fostered. He and his wife, Bobbie Jean, hosted many legendary social events.

Dr. Travis Manning (1921-1996), first Head of the Department of Agricultural Economics. His research contributed greatly to Alberta Agriculture, particularly in the areas of marketing and irrigation.

His friends and colleagues appreciated his unpretentious manner and wry, dry wit. Some of his humour was self-directed. He once commented to a colleague about a decision he had made and later regretted. He said that if he had kicked himself every time he thought of that mistake, he would be to the moon by now.

He took pride in his academic and professional roles and gave unselfishly of his time and energy. He often spoke of the pride and joy he felt to see the ideas he shared evolve and flourish through the efforts of his students and colleagues. His scholarly contributions went well beyond his own individual efforts.

Bill Phillips

Robert E. Follinsbee

A Brush with Billions in the Barrens

There is an evocative description of the barrens in Guy Blanchet's story: A priest told his Native Indian congregation about the beauties of heaven, and a Native man responded, "Tell me, Father—is it more beautiful than the land of the musk oxen in summer where the mist lies on the water and sometimes the wind blows and the loon cries very often?"

ONE COLD, BRIGHT SEPTEMBER DAY IN 1947, at the close of field season, I led a Geological Survey of Canada canoe party along the south shore of Exeter Lake, Northwest Territories, to our rendezvous point. We had a day to wait for our pickup, so I went for a stroll along the beach. Suddenly, an unusual sand deposit caught my eye. It glittered red with garnets, black with ilmenite and green with olivine and chrome diopside (but *not* white with diamonds). It had been winnowed out of esker sands by 6,000 years of postglacial wave action. I collected a sample bag full, labelled it F125-47 (for Folinsbee sample #125 of 1947) and added it to our summer's take.

The summer, if you could call it that, had been a savage one. Cold front after cold front had swept the barrens with forty mile per hour winds. Horizontally driven rain and temperatures hovering near freezing kept us huddled in our Mount Logan tents. Windbound and wet, we met the bare bones definition of a field geologist—a wet ass and a hungry gut.

Our crew of seven had landed in Yellowknife from Edmonton in June, and we spent the next month practising traverses, portaging and paddling and studying the 2.7 billion-year-old rocks around this gold mining town. I taught the crew how to bake bread with a reflector oven to ward off the dreaded bannock belly, the result of a diet of underdone baking powder biscuits. The town of Yellowknife was still in a frenzied state from the opening of the Giant gold mine and a wave of postwar prospecting that had lured crews 300 miles out onto the barrens to the northeast.

The trapper Gordon McLennan and his wife overwintered at Lake Providence right at the point where Franklin had started his journey down

R. E. Follinsbee at a triangulation post, Mathews Lake, Northwest Territories, 1948. With no timber available, the topographer, Eric Fry, used an Inuit assistant versed in erecting Inukshuks to create an equivalent.

the Coppermine River in 1821. McLennan reported over his radio in early July that there was enough open water at the river's mouth to land float planes.

So we loaded supplies, took off on a pontoon-equipped aircraft and landed where we had left our three canoes in the fall of 1946 (two seventeen-foot Freighters and a sixteen-foot Prospector for inland reconnaissance trips). Most of Lake Providence was still frozen solid seven feet thick, as it was when Franklin slid his canoes over the ice.

We followed his example, mapping the shoreline geology from the ice for the first ten days, and eventually got through to the open Yamba River, a strong tributary of the Coppermine that flowed in from the great esker system to the north. Then we began struggling our way up the narrow and rocky Yamba River. Often we had to portage or "line" — dragging the canoes over rocky rapids in waist-deep freezing water with rope at the bow and stern.

After three days of paddling, lining and portaging up the river, we approached the exit from Yamba Lake at a narrows through Daring Lake, an old Inuit and Indian hunting spot and caribou crossing, now an ecological station.

The caribou migrate along the great east-west esker system, a vast stretch of gravel deposited by ancient glacial streams. At spots, the esker lies below the present lake level, forcing the caribou, young calves and all, to swim the open passages. With their buoyant insulated caribou wetsuits, they have no problem.

For us, wading in the river in jeans, it was a different matter. As we approached Yamba Lake, the water, which had been only extremely cold, turned icy, and we heard the tinkle of candled ice which had drifted downstream from honey-combed Yamba Lake floes. We pulled out and set up camp. Our cook thawed the crew with our emergency rations of tinned oxtail soup.

It was a desolate area. Like Franklin and Back, we noted small glaciers where overflowing streams in winter built into ice sheets up to twenty feet thick, lasting all summer, foreshadowing the next ice age. On the beach at Yamba Lake, we found a black sand concentrate rich in magnetite, garnet and monazite (a slightly radioactive thorium-bearing mineral). It went into our sample bags.

The caribou cross at the point where Yamba Lake feeds into the river. All around us were big, black, lichen-covered boulders, scratched territorially by barren land grizzlies. Since time immemorial, they have hunted caribou at this crossing, dashing from rocks to ambush the passing herd. For six thousand years (the end of the ice age in this area), man has done the same, Inuit and Indian. Strange to say, in all my five seasons on the barrens, I saw only a few bear paw prints, and no bears.

That summer's travels took us across some of the most desolate but beautiful country in Canada, a chain of lakes named for Naval vessels—Ajax, Exeter and Achilles—and ultimately to Contwoyto Lake, headwaters of the Great Fish River that Captain Back descended in 1835, now named after him. The Thlee Cho Desseth (Great Fish River) empties into the eastern Arctic and was the goal of Franklin's remnant crew in their doomed dash to escape the Arctic ice in the late 1840s. None made it. Back lost no men in his great descent; Franklin lost all.

Unloading our orange canoes roped to a pontoon-equipped aircraft at Courageous Lake, 1946

Happily, none of the thirty men who were my assistants from 1946-1950 died or had accidents. The chief geologist of the Survey insisted that you only had adventures when you made mistakes.

Only one of my assistants, Dr. Walter Fahrig, went on to make a career of mapping for the Geological Survey. The rest, forsaking the barrens, became oil or mining barons—like Arne Neilsen, my assistant in 1947, later CEO of Mobil and Superior Oil of Canada.

Franklin tells the story of meeting Chief Akaitcho (Big Foot) at his tent in Yellowknife. (*Akaitcho* was an honourable name; it meant that, like a wolf with its big paws, the Chief could walk immense distances over snow.) Franklin greatly impressed the Indian Chief by gently blowing off a mosquito that landed on his hand, saying, "There is room in the world for both thee and me." In contrast, my assistants always squashed mosquitoes with glee, exclaiming, "There *isn't* room in the world for thee and me!"

It was a lonely land—particularly if you have a pregnant wife waiting at home. In the fall of 1947, I flew directly to Edmonton from Yellowknife, not having heard from my family all summer. I called my wife, Catherine, as soon as the plane touched down at the airport and eagerly asked how the pregnancy was coming along. Very coldly, she answered, "The baby arrived a week ago" (our third son, Terry). The Arctic blasts that blow forever over the barrens are no less icy.

Catherine and I made up (and I did stay behind for the arrival of Caty in June of 1950, my last year in the barrens).

During those five years (1946-50), I mapped an area now being drilled for diamonds in a thirteen million dollar program by De Beers on behalf of Mountain Province. Our Geological Survey of Canada budget was $5000 per summer, including my salary, all provisions, bush flying and salaries for my student assistants and cook. The Survey did cover our travel to and from Yellowknife and threw in an extra $500 if my reports and maps were delivered by Christmas.

Because there was no room in my busy schedule to study the two esker samples, they remained in storage in the old Arts Building at the University from 1947 to 1954. Finally, in the fall of 1954, I left for Berkeley, California, on the first sabbatical granted (at half salary) in the history of the Geology

Department—created in 1912 by Dr. John Allan. Packed in my wife's old family Chrysler were four kids, my wife and the two beach concentrates from the great Exeter esker.

I studied esker samples all winter, extracting and dating the monazite at Yamba Lake as 2780 million years in age, the oldest Canadian Precambrian date at that time. I described the minerals (which I now know to be diamond indicators) in a paper duly published in the Transactions of the Royal Society of Canada for 1955.

Twenty years later, on sabbatical in South Africa, I was invited to a Director's lunch in Kimberley after a visit underground to one of the diamond mines. Barry Hawthorne, chief geologist of De Beers, presented me with a poke of pyrope garnets, byproduct of the diamond extraction process. It looked suspiciously like the sample I had collected at Exeter Lake in 1947.

A caribou bull in velvet fording a break in the esker highway

Another fourteen years passed before I finally put two and two together, when Diamet announced their diamond pipe discovery in 1989. I bought into Diamet stock on the way up, a stock that they had difficulty flogging at thirty-five cents, and which eventually sold for nearly sixty dollars a share.

Forty years after my Exeter Lake sampling, Chuck Fipke of Diamet saw the same esker concentrate at Exeter Lake, recognized the Gurney G 10 garnet diamond indicators and started staking his claims. Fipke had been following a trail of diamond indicator minerals from Norman Wells on the Mackenzie River. A De Beers prospecting team had discovered the deposits eight years earlier, but failed to find their source.

Fipke and his partner, Stewart Blusson, deservedly made millions. Blusson donated fifty million dollars to the University of British Columbia. For my studies, I was inducted as a fellow of the Royal Society of Canada in 1956 at the University of Toronto. Society fellowship came easier then!

The Earth Science fellows of the Society were invited to tea at the elegant red brick home of Dr. J. B. Tyrrell, FRSC, who early in his career discovered dinosaurs in Alberta. (The Tyrrell Museum in Drumheller is named after him.) Tyrrell also made an epic traverse across the barrens from Lake Athabasca to Hudson's Bay, then down to Winnipeg. He identified the centre of the great ice dome at Dubawnt Lake, which spawned the trunk esker system of Exeter Lake. Tyrrell later made his fortune in the gold mines of Kirkland Lake and became President of one of the richest mines. That Christmas of 1956, at 94, he sent all the Earth Science fellows cards, inscribed in a shaky hand, "Getting old, J. B. Tyrrell."

Survey personnel were not allowed to stake their discoveries. Fred Jolliffe, my GSC party chief at Yellowknife from 1938-1941, reported the finding of a gold vein on the west side of Yellowknife Bay to prospectors at Fort Smith in the fall of 1935. This triggered a staking rush which led to the discovery of the Con (Cominco) and Giant gold mines, which yielded ten million ounces of gold.

I never had to make an ethical decision as to whether I could stake at Exeter Lake after resigning from the Survey because Fipke was ahead of me in realizing the importance of my chance discovery.

I still have Tyrrell's card and my esker diamond indicator sample, and I am going to make my fortune in Winspear Resources, now exploring for diamonds at Camsell Lake, south of Lac de Gras, also one of my old stamping grounds. I have left writing these notes until late in life, almost into the millennium. Like Tyrrell, I am getting old, but I can still dream.

I was accepted into the hallowed halls of the U of A in 1957 as a lecturer at a salary of $4400 per year. My first office was in the old Gas Lab, just west of the present-day Business Building. I've often thought that the Gas Lab should have been preserved as a historical site, for the name if nothing else. Cynics might also suggest that it was an appropriate locale for one such as myself.

In December of that year, I had a rude awakening to the realities of academia. A chap named Ben Lindberg had been brought in from the States in order to broaden the scope of the School of Commerce (which was, for all practical purposes, a School of Accounting). A council meeting was called to discuss the future direction of the School.

A report had been introduced, proposing substantial changes to the program, including the addition of a wide variety of new courses. The proposal was voted on and turned down. Ben turned to Andrew Stewart (President) and said, "Gentlemen, thank you for your cooperation over the past three-and-a-half years. Mr. President, what I said to you last August is now in effect. The meeting is adjourned."

With that, Ben walked out, went downstairs and submitted his letter of resignation that same day. Some time after the meeting, it was pointed out that the report had been turned down by one vote, which included that of a non-eligible voter!

As a result of that episode, two others (also from the States) handed in their resignations. Since we only had about six full-time people on staff, yours truly ended up becoming an Assistant Professor.

Bill Preshing

BALDER VON HOHENBALKEN

Peeling a Polyhedron

WITHIN THE ACADEMIC COMMUNITY, we mathematicians are often considered overly cerebral. Those in the Arts fail to see the beauty, passion and poetry of our profession. Those in Business and Engineering tend to shroud our pristine structures with empirical data. I would, therefore, like to give here a heartfelt glimpse into our rarified work.

To the indulgent reader: a better part of this piece is about mathematical research. This a risky undertaking, like skating on thin ice—gliding gingerly over the surface might get you to the other side, but dig just a little bit too deep and you land in complications up to your neck. Thus, at the peril of my collaborators finding this account imprecise and obvious, I tread very lightly, using as little jargon and notation as I can manage. This will not prevent others from giving up over the remaining mathematical gobbledygook. Maybe it's just right for you, if you skim appropriately.

When, and from where, does one get one's predilections? Those warm and pleasant feelings that are attached to certain activities, be they manual or mental? The French say *tous ce jou avant six ans*, and I tend to believe that.

There is, for one, your heredity. More than one thing comes to us via the genes, including attitudes. The marital misfortunes in my family produced a revealing example of that. My younger brother Gerndt was born just a few months before his (and my) mother left our home, and he spent his whole childhood, save a few holidays, with her and her new family. I, seven years older than him, remained with my father. But what did I observe when I visited Gerndt later in life in his own domain? The same fastidious pack-rat habits, of the same items (tools, nails, screws, wires), stored and displayed in the same fashion my father did, and I do myself! Down to the same way of coiling electrical cords, and making clever little inventions!

And then there obviously are the things you learn at your parents' knees. In my case it was mathematics—nothing fancy, nothing high-powered, simply neat little tricks and brainteasers that my father liked to do with me. Hard, severe and demanding as he was otherwise, he became soft and happy when he saw me eagerly lap up these simple games.

Even before my father's involvement, though, I loved mathematics. When I was in kindergarten, I asserted to my grandmother that there must be negative numbers. She dismissed with shocked certainty the very suggestion.

In high school (the Austrian *Gymnasium*), I was sufficiently bright to contain the mathematics taught there in my little finger, but I never made it to whiz kid status because of a rather weird attitude of mine. I felt it would be an unbearable sign of intellectual deficiency to study hard and then not be first; therefore, I did not study at all! Using only the knowledge I soaked up in class, I usually made it to second or third place, to understandably only lukewarm applause from father and teachers.

Well, university time came around, and I still marched to the same drummer. Oh, I disputed and haggled intricately with my fellow students, I read what I liked and I made *Gedankenexperimente*. But sitting down and cramming I would not do. In Munich, when I should have been studying business administration, I spent all the extra time I had ardently courting a girl. Later in Vienna, where I went for a doctorate (in political science), I found plenty of time to dance fancily at society balls.

What finally made a man out of me was the work on my thesis: "Can Productivity Be a Measure for Wage Policy?" Somehow, the warm glow of the problem-solving sessions with my father enfolded me again. I started to dig with alacrity into the literature around my not exactly earth-shaking topic (to which the ultimate answer was "yes"), and enjoyed the feeling of justified satisfaction after a day with the major and minor lights of economics.

Then I ran across the gently mathematical models of Tinbergen and Frisch. They provoked in me a sort of heart-thumping internal combustion. I read with hot cheeks, and I was hooked. "Research," an enterprise which I had regarded as beyond my reach at best, and as a pretense of pompous academics at worst, started to have true emotional meaning for me.

From this point on, I served the goddess of knowledge with enthusiasm. I started spending my days in the reading room of the departmental library, pursuing the best way of making a point. I finished my dissertation a little late, because of my perfectionism, and it received excellent marks. (I did not do as well in sociology and constitutional law, which, following my old tenet, I found not worth the bother.)

I was already deep into my studious period when I met Gerhard Tintner, the *éminence grise* of econometrics in those days. He was visiting the University of Vienna and was lecturing on von Neumann's theory of games. After his classes Tintner took his small audience *ins Kaffeehaus*, where I got to know him personally. A few months later, he invited me to become his research associate at Iowa State University, where he taught economics, mathematics and statistics.

Clearly this honour was undeserved, if only because of my lingering cavalier attitude toward earnest scholarship. There was also the woeful deficiency of economic curricula at German and Austrian universities, where a derivative was still considered abstruse mathematics. When I arrived in Ames, Tintner pretended that I knew all about these things, and this time I had no choice but to throw myself into harness.

It turned out to be a happy experience because my intellectual horses pulled very well—in fact, ahead of most of my fellow students. For the paper that Tintner proposed we write together, I already had done some nice econometric footwork, and after my two years at ISU were up, Dean Smith at the University of Alberta offered me a rather princely salary ($6000 per annum, in 1961) to come north and be their mathematical economist.

That was all nice and dandy, but I was still miles away from sustaining and fruitful research adventures. In particular, I lacked the feeling for what was "do-able"—that critical insight into what is neither trivial nor impossible.

It took years of frustrated dabbling, until I returned to Ames for a year and there found a new mentor, Paul van Moeseke (the *Meister*). I started to work with him on the theory of portfolio selection, but what really fascinated me were the associated computational methods. Back in Edmonton, I had learned APL (the then dominant programming language at the U of A), and soon I was swamping poor Paul with new methods, so-called "algorithms," which I developed on our powerful mainframe.

This was in the late sixties, and that "algorithmic fixation" lasted for twenty years because these logical machines, which can do almost anything, are amazingly addictive. My time and my love belonged to constructing algorithms, many of which got published over the years. Despite my thralldom, however, I was not eaten alive by the computers, which happens to more people than one thinks (they used to be called "terminal cases"). I did manage to lead the usual life of a Professor, with teaching and exams and committee work.

Oddly, my earlier lack of devotion to straitlaced scholarship often turned out to be an advantage. I thought that subjective originality was just fine, and so, instead of steeping myself first in the already known methods, and thus narrowing my horizon, I remained ignorant and free to explore ways of doing things far from the beaten path.

Such freedom, if it is to lead to anything, requires constant and ardent cogitation. But I happen to like thinking, and in many situations it is a liberating joy to do so. For instance, sitting in a dentist's waiting room, together with bored people reading yesteryear's magazines, one can balance in one's head the most amazing and intricate structures, gently nudging them this way and that, sometimes supporting them with involuntary hand waves. It's exhilarating, and difficult, and one starts over many times erecting this glowing edifice until, with luck, two or more components click and lock together in intracranial space. With glee, one tests this new solid plank and, convinced, one climbs onto it and tackles the next story up.

It was this way that my "simplicial-decomposition algorithm" was developed (non-mathematicians, prepare to skim!). It serves to optimize a nonlinear objective function subject to linear inequality constraints. The geometrical counterpart of the latter is a (n-dimensional) polyhedron. Now, rather than moving along its surface from corner to corner, as the accepted paradigm of pivoting would have you do it, my dreamt-up algorithm selectively triangularizes the polyhedron, and consecutively optimizes the objective function on those "simplices." The last simplex will then contain the solution of the problem. Had I toed the conventional line, this weird and wonderful construction would never have occurred to me.

The simplicial-decomposition algorithm turned out to be a modest theoretical and practical success. It was discussed and favorably compared with other methods in programming journals and used for portfolio selection, against a handsome fee, by some brokerage houses on Bay Street and Wall Street. Some fellow in Los Angeles even became a millionaire by selling a stock selection package, whose heart was my algorithm (by now in the public domain).

The next challenge came from Bruce Clarke, a colleague and friend, and a theoretical chemist. His problem was (the d-dimensional analogue of) the following: given the corners of, say, a cube, find the 12 edges and the 6 facets of that cube.

Perceiving that the decomposition principle was applicable here, I spent the next several months in cognitive euphoria developing the algorithms that could solve such problems in all dimensions and for any arbitrary set of corners. My addiction to these wonderful puzzles was so strong that I had to tear myself away at the very last minute to give my classes. I thought about them morning and night, while watching TV, whether sober or well oiled.

My completed methods were again rather unconventional and skinned my friend's polyhedra nicely. When a published version came to the attention of the eminent mathematician Victor Klee, he invited me to Seattle to give a talk about them. I was absolutely thrilled by this because in earlier years, I had regarded Klee like I do Newton or Leibniz—as a timeless demigod. My acquaintance with Vic led later on to most interesting joint research.

In subsequent years I collaborated with several younger colleagues on statistical estimation (the "wedge method"), on game theory (generalized Shapley values) and on Voronoi diagrams (interpreted as catchment areas of supermarkets). I usually played the mathematical fiddle while my friends tooted the economic and empirical horns. The music we made was nice and unconventional enough to yield a dozen papers. The hot ears while chasing these things were still very much with me.

Back in 1961, I had become Assistant Professor (to the great pride of my father), and I have now been a Professor for many years. For some reason, this was the extent of my career ambitions. I never aspired to be really rich (except during my penurious youth), nor famous in the shallow sense (like a movie actor, which I once was), nor powerful like a big-shot politician or administrator. I hewed to the values of my doyen Tintner. To be at a university, with intellectual stature and a serviceable income, was all that I wanted.

Then, in 1989, I became ill to the death. For weeks on end I vehemently refused to think or hear about my job, my past exploits, my former goals. In fact, I didn't want to live at all, the way I was, and the way I was going to be.

But one is an animal of habit and despite various miseries, the siren song of thinking led me gently back to the old pastures. Dispensed from teaching, I rekindled my interest in the things my friend Vic in Seattle and I had thought about some years earlier. I corresponded with him, and he and I and Ted Lewis, a new mathematician friend of mine from the U of A, wrote a paper together.

Yet more excitement was to come. Consider the following. Three eggs in triangular formation on a table are clearly commonly supported by the table from below, and a piece of cardboard laid on top of them commonly supports the eggs from above. Ted and I were looking for a nice proof that this is also true in all other dimensions. For instance 1000 eggs in 1000-dimensional space would also share two commonly supporting hyperplanes. We started again with algorithms to find such planes and did a lot of the typical lateral thinking about that, examining and discarding in the head and on paper the wildest ideas and constructs.

And then, on a nice summer morning, still in bed out at my lake cabin and examining common supports on the ceiling, the solution occurred to me. The algorithm I had devised to calculate such planes could in fact be regarded as a fixed point, whose existence could be shown with the help of a powerful fixed point theorem (which says that for certain mappings some point lies in its own image). I lay there transfixed, running over my argument again and again, with joy and pride washing through my heart. I started laying out the plan for the paper to go with this idea, and then called friend Ted in Edmonton, who understood immediately.

A month later, we sent the finished paper away for publication and received positive reports, even accolades. But at the second go-around, a new referee discovered a seemingly minor flaw in one of our proofs, fixable possibly within the hour. After seven weeks of hard work, the flaw was still unrepaired and then, adding insult to injury, Ted found a counterexample to the lemma itself, rendering it false, and a proof pointless.

We had to make a new start, possibly using another fixed point theorem. Since Ted and I were only vaguely aware of what was available, I appealed to Vic in Seattle for help. He immediately liked the fixed point approach and, amazingly, produced in two days a new version of the paper, using a fixed point theorem for "null-homotopic mappings." With Vic added to the impressum, the paper was soon accepted by Geometriae Dedicata, a respectable geometry journal.

But then came a final twist. While considering other support structures, I discovered that Vic's proof could be turned inside out. Instead of mapping the unit sphere into itself (which required a rather advanced fixed point theorem), one could self-map the convex Cartesian product of the bodies to be supported (e.g., the Cartesian product of two perpendicular line segments is a rectangle). To guarantee a fixed point here required only the classical Brouwer theorem. Vic found the new proof so much better that we decided to retract the already accepted paper at Geometriae Dedicata and replace it with the new version. It was even said that this last demonstration would be a candidate for Paul Erdoes' *God's book of the most beautiful proofs*.

Being nicely warmed up, the three of us turned our attention to the situation where the supporting structure is a (hyper)sphere rather than a hyperplane. The 2-dimensional case of this has been known since antiquity as the problem of Apollonius, which concerns a circle touching three disks. We set out to generalize this, whereby it is apparent that d+1 bodies are now required to well define the spherical problem in d-space, rather than the d bodies for the general planar problem.

The work on this kept our computers humming, as hundreds of e-mail messages and manuscripts flew back and forth. Clearly the fixed point approach was again central for the existence proofs, for both Euclidean and non-Euclidean supporting spheres. Vic applied himself to the bodies lying inside the sphere (which can touch the sphere in more than one point and thus pose most intriguing problems) and to various arcane generalizations. Ted and I both ran support and supplied separate (ingenious!) proofs that there is at most one supporting sphere in the most important Euclidean case.

The beautiful main theorem reads (bear with me, non-mathematicians) as follows: If B = B′ union B″ is a family of d+1 compact convex sets (e.g., bodies in d-dimensional space), and B has no hyperplane transversal (i.e., there is no plane that cuts all bodies simultaneously), then there is a unique Euclidean sphere that supports each member of B such that the members of B′ lie inside the sphere, and the members of B″ lie outside the sphere.

In November 1995, our finished paper was accepted by Discrete and Computational Geometry. The reports of the two referees were rather unusual. Both warmly recommended the paper, but No. 2 went furthest: "This paper is a delight to read: it is very well written, the topic is of interest to a wide audience, and the arguments are clear and concise. Although the proofs use standard techniques, there are occasional subtleties through which the authors gently guide the reader. In short, I liked everything."

Is there any moral to all this? Well, yes, it's "Do mathematics!" It is a lofty and spacious occupation, not a crowd scene like selling real estate. And the goal is not the further dismemberment of this earth, but to find jewels that belong to the stars.

In 1986, a Canadian Forces gun was brought in (arranged by Bob Middleditch) to provide a dramatic starting signal for the President's Walk.
"As a starting signal the cannon shot was useless. Nobody started. Everyone stood dazed and shaken. From the north came a tinkling sound like glass falling ... far away."
Art Burgess

Leadership
How to run a university

JEAN B. FOREST

A Decade to Remember

ELECTION TO SENATE

IN 1972, CHANCELLOR LOUIS DESROCHERS asked if I would allow my name to stand in nomination for election to the Senate. I agreed, and was duly elected.

As one of my first duties, I served on a task force that inquired into the value of the Senate. I was amused that one of the options being considered was abolition, and so soon after my arrival! Happily, a good case was made for the Senate's value, particularly as a link between community and the University—between "town and gown."

Louis Desrochers and Jean Forest

This task force was the first of many commissioned by the Senate during my term of office, and over the years, the valuable, well-researched reports that they produced on a wide variety of University issues added immeasurably to the credibility of the Senate on campus and beyond.

In 1973, I was elected to represent the Senate on the Board of Governors. During the ensuing decade, I learned a great deal about the governance of a large university—entrance requirements, quota faculties, tuition fees, academic standards, foreign students, research grants, facilities and many other issues. I remember my utter confusion over the use of abbreviations for the names of the countless committees on campus and my initial difficulty in sorting out the function of each.

PRESIDENTS AND STUDENTS

Soft-spoken President Max Wyman quietly introduced direct student participation, having them appointed as voting members to all advisory and decision-making committees as well as to the Board of Governors. The students contributed significantly, and the initiative helped the University escape the student unrest and rioting which plagued a number of campuses at that time. Just as a footnote, one of our most active grad students at the time was Tim Christian, who later went on to become our esteemed Dean of Law!

President Harry Gunning, who succeeded President Wyman, was also very supportive of the students. He did not, however, endear himself to the members of the provincial government (nor to the Chairman of the Board) when he joined the students in a protest march on the legislature over funding and tuition fees.

His successor, Myer Horowitz, continuously demonstrated great confidence in the students and their capabilities. During his term of office, he became so revered by them that the student theatre was renamed "The Myer Horowitz Theatre."

I loved the students for all of their antics and I recall being rather sad, at the end of my term, to sense a change in the student body: from the idealism and social consciousness of the '60s and early '70s, to the more pragmatic, professionally oriented students who followed. Many of the latter seemed too preoccupied with personal achievement and material success to become involved in the socio-political issues of the day. No doubt this represented a swing of the pendulum, gauged necessary in response to the signs of the times, but because of it, campus life lost a little of its spirit and passion.

Still, they had their fun—on the playing fields, in the lounges and frat houses—and most faculty and staff members indulged them. I recall roaring with laughter—staunch Catholic that I am—over the anecdote related by my daughter Karen, who was a grad student at the time. She had been enjoying an evening at the Power Plant when the news came over the radio that a new pope, subsequently named John Paul II, had been elected. The bartender on duty announced free beers for all the students present. When asked if he might not be in trouble with administration over such a generous gesture, he replied in a thick Polish accent, "What da hell! Once in two t'ousand years? No problem!"

On the Board of Governors and on the committees, the student members served diligently and conscientiously, bringing their unique insights to the decision-making process. I greatly valued their contribution.

APPOINTMENT: CHAIR OF THE BOARD OF TRUSTEES OF THE ACADEMIC PENSION PLAN

Even though it's a volunteer position, membership on the Board of Governors presents its share of difficult assignments. Shortly after I became a member, Chairman Fred Jenner asked me to chair the Board of Trustees of the Academic Pension Plan. I protested that I knew nothing about pensions, investment portfolios or the academic plan, but he insisted that I was quite capable of "learning on the job." Despite the steep learning curve, we did well with our investment portfolio—even though, upon the recommendation of our investment counsellor, we sold all our stock in Bombardier, which has long since gone through the roof!

In addition to ongoing discussions over the level of benefits, we faced perennial complaints from the faculty at Calgary, who wanted to split off from the plan. I will never forget the meeting at which the trustees voted to allow them to do so. Murray Roussel, the Comptroller of the University, was absolutely aghast at such an unprecedented departure from policy and practice, as were a number of U of A faculty members. Their concern, however, eventually came to naught when the provincial government decided to take over the entire plan. After much hard negotiating, the Board of Trustees was dissolved, relieving me of my concerns over faculty members' pensions.

THE BOARD OF GOVERNORS: DEBATES AND DISCUSSIONS
Of the countless debates and decisions during my years on the Board, I will relate only two: one for its effect on the physical campus and one for its effect on the University per se.

1. Restoration of Original Residences
First, the renovation/restoration of the three old residences on the west side of the Quad—Pembina, Athabasca and Assiniboia Halls. There was little controversy over the restoration of Pembina Hall, the most beautiful building and the one requiring the least amount of repair. Athabasca Hall needed more extensive repair and renovation but still fell within the funding allotment. Assiniboia Hall, however, was in such disrepair that it would be cheaper to demolish and replace it. We vigourously debated the pros and cons of the two options.

Concerned that we were losing the battle to save the old building, I met with the architect to find some compelling argument to sway the more fiscally minded Board members. He pointed out that preserving the building would also save the beautiful, mature trees around it, worth many thousands of dollars. This could well offset the additional costs of renovation. I placed the argument before the Board. Many others made passionate pleas of their own, and we did win the day. We witnessed with great pride the restoration of all three residences, and the University received the Heritage Award for the project.

2. Integration of Collège St.-Jean as Faculté St.-Jean of the U of A
I had long been associated with Collège St.-Jean, a French-speaking liberal arts college owned and operated by the Oblate Fathers and

affiliated with the University of Ottawa, and I had been active in promoting French-language education within elementary and secondary schools. I believed it would be of great advantage to have the Collège more closely affiliated with the University of Alberta.

After negotiations among the college, university and provincial government, Collège St.-Jean was purchased and incorporated into the University as Faculté St.-Jean. Remaining on its own campus, on Rue Marie-Anne Gaboury, aided by the injection of funding from the University, the federal and provincial governments, as well as the private sector, Faculté St.-Jean has developed into a distinct yet well-integrated component of the University. Offering French-language programs in arts, science, education and business, the Faculté makes a unique contribution to the education and culture of western Canada. The University takes great pride in the Faculté, and I share that pride.

NOMINATION AND ELECTION TO THE POSITION OF CHANCELLOR

Six years after being elected to the Senate, I was nominated for the position of Chancellor. After having had nothing more than one interview with the Selection Committee, I was advised that I had been elected. Elections at the University were conducted on a much different level than at the school board, where I had three times "campaigned" for the position of school trustee.

I recall the pride with which my husband, Rocky, and our children received the news, as well as my own trepidation over how the public would receive the news that the new chancellor would be a woman—and one without a university degree!

I was, however, quite unprepared for the headline published in the *Edmonton Report*: "From One-Roomed School Teacher to University Chancellor: It's Been a Long Hard Climb!" What a laugh! I'd never dreamed of holding such a position, and if, indeed, the "climb" had been long, it had most certainly been enjoyable.

Concerned, however, about the reaction of academia, I determined that prior to my installation, I would meet with each Dean on his or her own "turf" in their own faculty, as well as the Presidents of St. Joseph's and St.

Stephen's Colleges on campus. Happily, I was warmly welcomed by all.

Preparing for my installation, however, provided its own challenges. I was lost in the Chancellor's gown, which had been handed down from one Chancellor to the next—all men! So I was directed to "Stewart and Pateman, Gentlemen Tailors" to be measured and fitted for a new one. When it was completed, no one could be found to fashion the hand-made University crest that adorned the original gown. Our affable registrar, Alex Cairns, offered the services of his wife, Helen, and—voila!—the crest was added in exquisite needlepoint. Over dinner recently, I told Helen how much I have always treasured it.

Next, we discovered that the Chancellor's Chair was far too high. When I perched upon it, my feet dangled most inelegantly (and I might add, uncomfortably) in mid-air. Rocky, a skilled carpenter, built me a little footstool which, tucked invisibly beneath my flowing gown, made sitting through years of lengthy convocations much more comfortable!

MARY TOTMAN, EXECUTIVE DIRECTOR OF SENATE

Throughout those years, I marveled at my good fortune in having Mary Totman as Executive Director of Senate. Chosen by my predecessor, Ron Dalby, Mary was an absolute gem. Her appreciation for the role of the Chancellor and the protocol associated with the position, her sense of the appropriate for every circumstance, and her meticulous attention to detail saved me (and probably the other four Chancellors whom she served) from many a possible blunder. Mary turned out to be my real "right hand"—very important to a left-handed rookie! With her able assistance, the first meeting of Senate that I chaired came off very successfully, as did every other meeting—including the out-of-town meetings that we pioneered and she arranged.

Mary defended her Chancellors to the hilt. I recall hearing her on the phone one day, deflecting a caller who was critical of my inaction on a certain issue. In her precise, impeccable English accent, Mary replied, "The Chancellor chooses her fights!" End of conversation.

THE WORLD UNIVERSITY GAMES

As Chancellor, I had the opportunity to meet many fascinating people and participate in many exciting University events. One such event was Universiade—the World University Games. I was so thrilled to be involved in the delegation that travelled to Madrid to present our bid for the games.

I also recall the ever-meticulous Mary Totman taking pains to advise the host committee that the Chancellor of the U of A was a woman, even though in French "Jean" is a man's name. To no avail—at the closing banquet, our hosts presented the other women with beautiful Spanish mantillas, while I received cuff links and tie!

No matter; our presentation was successful and the Games lived up to our highest expectations. Provided with excellent venues, beautiful weather and warm western hospitality, athletes from all over the world competed before throngs of cheering spectators. We were so proud of everyone involved, especially our volunteers, and were happy to host Queen Elizabeth, Prince Philip and other members of the royal family, as well as many foreign dignitaries from around the world.

CONVOCATION

Our University "did us proud" on many such occasions, but never more so than at convocations, where students reaped the rewards of years of hard work and sacrifice. For me, these occasions provided the "icing on the cake"—seeing the pride and relief of the students, as well as that of their families who'd helped them through.

I have many poignant memories, as when the oldest woman ever to convocate received her degree, when a blind student received his and when an aboriginal student held aloft a symbolic feather as she triumphantly left the stage. Other memories make me chuckle: a family of small children calling out "Way to go, Mom," a mischievous male student bowing to the Chancellor while carefully balancing a live budgie bird on his mortarboard or the day I looked out to discover husband Rocky—who faithfully attended all convocations—sitting with earphone in place, listening to a Grey Cup broadcast rather than a dull convocation address.

One of a Chancellor's most cherished functions is the conferring of honourary degrees. With great pride, I had the opportunity to honour luminaries from around the globe, as well as local people whom I had known and respected. I think particularly of mentors like President Max Wyman, Chairman of Alberta's first Human Rights Commission; Dr. Harold MacNeil, long-time Superintendent of Edmonton Catholic Schools; and Archbishop Joseph MacNeil.

MOTHER TERESA

My most memorable convocation was held in St. Paul, in honour of Mother Teresa. Because of her schedule, the arrangements had taken a great deal of time and effort, and the logistics of moving everyone and everything to the cathedral in St. Paul proved more daunting than expected. However, Mary Totman was up to it. When she admitted, though, that she was having particular trouble transporting the Chancellor's chair, I jokingly said, "Not to worry, Mary—I always wanted to sit in a bishop's chair!"

Myer Horowitz, Mother Teresa and Jean Forest at the conferring of Mother Teresa's honourary degree in 1982

Apart from the awesome experience of being in the presence of this remarkable woman, four details stand out in my memory:

- the crush of the crowd, which I found quite claustrophobic until Mother Teresa commented that to her, Canada seemed so "empty" of people
- her humble reluctance to don the doctoral gown and hood (we agreed she need not do so)
- Premier Lougheed flying in to present Mother Teresa with the million-dollar cheque that Albertans had generously donated to her charities

- slipping off my shoes when the ceremonies were over and sitting down on the grass beside the Schlossers' motorhome, to a cold beer with them and other friends and colleagues

PRINCE CHARLES

During my term of office, the Honorary Degrees Committee had also chosen Prince Charles as a recipient. He accepted, but he couldn't come until 1983. So Chancellor Peter Savaryn had the honour of conferring the degree. I recall sitting directly behind the Prince as he was about to begin his convocation address. Suddenly, he turned to me, handed me his certificate and said, "Excuse me, ma'am, but I'm in a bit of a bloody mess. Could you hold this for me while I speak?" I did, and he spoke. I also noted with surprise all the hand-written notations in the margins of his typewritten speech. It was the Prince of Wales at his best!

LAST CONVOCATION AND FOND FAREWELLS

In the spring of 1982, I presided over my last convocations as Chancellor. How well I remember the concluding act! John Schlosser, Chairman of the Board, and President Myer Horowitz dashed from their chairs and twirled me around the stage in a "gig" which, with long gowns a-twirl, was worthy of any "Troika," as we had been aptly dubbed!

We were wildly applauded by our three spouses, Patricia Schlosser, Barbara Horowitz and husband Rocky who, after faithfully attending all those convocations, doubtless looked forward to a respite.

The Board of Governors hosted a fun-filled farewell, including a hilarious "roast" sung to the tune of "My Beautiful Alice Blue Gown." At another fond farewell, the Senate presented me with two bound volumes of all the speeches I'd given while serving as Chancellor, a bound volume of all the task force reports commissioned by Senate during those years, plus an album of the photos from the convocations during my term.

The pièce-de-résistance was the Garden Party at University House at which (surprise of surprises) Ernest Dahlwood and his Convocation Band played. I was presented with my Chancellor's Gown and advised that the Jean B. Forest Scholarship had been established thanks to the generosity of all my friends on campus!

Thus ended a decade of involvement in the governance of the University—for me, one of the most rewarding experiences of my life.

For two decades since then, I have followed with great interest the Univerity's continued growth and development. With great pride, I have noted its increasing international stature in teaching and research and its growing involvement in local community service. These have been achieved through the dedication of its volunteer Board of Governors and Senate, its renowned faculty and competent administration and staff working together with its illustrious student body. With the support of government and the private sector, the University of Alberta has become an institution of which the founders would be proud.

In 1964, funding for higher education in the prairie provinces had never been greater, particularly in Alberta, where oil and gas revenues appeared to be without limit. University libraries were rapidly expanding, creating an ever-increasing need for professional librarians to build and manage collections and to serve the information needs of a growing student population. At the same time, public library systems were undergoing rapid growth of their own.

However, the picture was not completely rosy. The three then-accredited English-language Library Science schools, McGill, Toronto and British Columbia, could not supply enough graduates to meet the demand, and the gap was widening yearly.

Therefore, on January 31, 1966, the General Faculties Council approved the establishment of the School of Library Science at the U of A. A budget was approved, and administrators began a search for a Director.

In 1967, Sarah Rebecca Reed was appointed Director and Professor. She set about her work with what proved to be characteristic strong will and great energy. In addition to her, the first faculty for the School included Associate Professors David W. Foley, Gurdial S. Pannu and John G. Wright, as well as Visiting Professor Frederick G. B. Hutchings. Trude Pomahac joined the staff on September 1 as Professional Officer. With a class of forty-four carefully selected aspiring librarians, all was in readiness!

Robert E. Brundin

When I was elected Chancellor of the University of Alberta in 1970, the Senate's future was in serious doubt. Many in the academic community questioned its value and wanted it abolished. Dr. Max Wyman (President of the University and Chairman of The General Faculties Council) felt that we should seriously study the Senate first, rather than simply doing away with it.

He and I brought together a very powerful committee of academic and non-academic members, with a mission to determine what a Senate could and should do for the University. The committee's report, eventually adopted university-wide, argued that the Senate had a valuable role to play, both as a deliberative body and a public conscience.

The committee reccomended that the Senate have its own executive staff. William G. Thorsell, presently the Editor-in-Chief of *The Globe and Mail*, was hired as the Senate's first executive officer. Bill proved very effective, helping the Senate form a number of task forces to study questions of interest to the University and to the community at large.

I advocated strongly that these task forces not take any formal positions, but rather serve as prestigious "soap boxes" for the discussion of each issue. The task forces then reported to the open Senate, and the entire University followed the reports with great interest. Each stakeholder group then decided on its own what action, if any, it would take in respect of the issue debated.

That philosophy renewed confidence in the Senate's value. I'm proud to say that this approach, and the Senate itself, remain in place to this day.

Louis Desrochers

W. E. HARRIS

Looking at Ourselves
The President's Advisory Committee on Campus Reviews

AN INVITATION

I HAD BEEN LOOKING FORWARD to retirement at the end of the summer of 1980. However, in April, President Myer Horowitz asked if I would chair a steering committee for a couple of years to help start the review process for the University. Before I could agree, I wanted to learn more about what a review would entail, and I wondered if I had the appropriate background.

I studied "A Report to General Faculties Council on Proposed Terms of Reference for a System of Reviews of Academic Programs," which was the joint report of the Dean's Council and the Academic Development Committee. After a couple of weeks of further background reading and thought, I accepted the invitation to chair the committee.

By June 1980, the steering committee for the reviews had been formed: W. E. Harris (myself), Chairman; G. Baldwin (VP Academic, the President's representative during startup); J. Forster (Dean of Graduate Studies); G. Ford; and Ms. Florence Watters, Committee Coordinator.

IMMEDIATE OBJECTIVES

The steering committee needed a clear understanding of the purpose of a review. It had to develop sound procedures quickly and establish a favourable climate for reviews on the campus. Inevitably, we would also have to expect to make mistakes and to learn from them. The three main objectives were:

1. The reviews should have positive goals. In a *Folio* article, President Horowitz had made it clear that the reviews were not to be a policing action. They were to help us help each other and would involve scholars from within the University as well as from outside. I welcomed this kind of approach, having observed it first hand while serving as an external reviewer for the Chemistry Department of the University of Saskatchewan.

2. We should take advantage of the experience of other universities and adapt the best of their procedures. In that same article, President Horowitz stated, "We are absolutely determined not to repeat the mistakes which have occurred in other institutions." For example, a review system a couple of years earlier at the University of Calgary had collapsed.

3. We must quickly gain the support of the University community, who were understandably wary. An effective review would be impossible without the cooperation and acceptance of the academic staff.

GETTING STARTED

On July 9, the steering committee of the President's Advisory Committee on Campus Reviews (PACCR) held its first meeting. We set out to obtain information from other universities about their experience with reviews. Accordingly, we arranged for a day-long session in September with Dr. Blaine Holmlund, the long-time director of reviews at the University of Saskatchewan. He gave us a wealth of advice.

As soon as possible, I spent three days at the University of Saskatchewan to obtain first-hand comments from those who had gone through their successful review process. For more background, I attended a conference at the University of Guelph. F. Watters and I attended a major conference on academic reviews sponsored by the University of Illinois.

The PACCR committee met with Dr. R. Miller, a consultant who had written several books on the general subject of evaluation. Dr. Rick Harpel of the University of Colorado visited us and told us about his experience. He said that they had initiated nine departmental reviews in one year and nine more in the next, and that they now needed a year off just to catch up.

We were advised to start the review process slowly, with small, well-run units so that we could develop our procedures under favourable conditions. After that, we were strongly advised to limit reviews to about ten units in any one year, and certainly never more than fifteen.

Because of the diversity among departments and faculties across campus, the Joint Report of the Dean's Council and the Academic Development Committee recommended that the procedure should be flexible. It would be a mistake to develop detailed standard operating procedures that would presume to fit all units. Rather, we encouraged each department and each review team to tell its story in its own way. Broad general instructions rather than detailed directives were appropriate for the units and for the reviewers.

We attempted to keep the university community informed about our activities and philosophy from the beginning. At the end of October, the President's Advisory Committee of Chairmen invited me to meet with their group and talk about the objectives of the reviews.

Although we were inexperienced, it was important to talk to this group at an early stage. I described in detail the attitude and the common-sense approach to the review process we intended to use. Although most members of the Chairmen's Council simply listened, Dr. T. Nelson and Dr. G. Marahens appeared determined to stop the review process. VP Baldwin and President Horowitz addressed their concerns as best they could and assured them that the reviews would proceed.

That meeting proved crucial. During the weeks that followed, several chairmen quietly approached me and volunteered their departments for review during our second year. These included Dr. G. Prideaux of Linguistics and Dr. T. Burton of Recreation Administration. Their cooperation was extremely important for the development of our procedures.

I welcomed the opportunity to talk with anyone interested in our philosophy since it helped to clarify my thinking. I gave an invited talk to the Faculty of Education in the auditorium with about 250 present. I welcomed the request of the capable *Edmonton Journal* reporter, Ron Chalmers, for an interview. After a few minutes, it became clear to him that our aim was not "blood on the floor" and he visibly lost interest. No item subsequently appeared in the newspaper. I suspect a positive, non-policing approach was not deemed to be newsworthy.

We decided that during the first year we would initiate the reviews of five departments that would represent some of the diversity within the University. Dr. Westlake, Chairman of Microbiology, met me on the street one summer day and volunteered his small, well-administered department as the first one to be reviewed. It proved to be a stroke of great good fortune. His positive attitude helped us develop some procedures and ensured that our startup errors did not hurt us too much.

The Microbiology Department quickly produced a self-study, and the Unit Review Committee (URC) was on site in mid-February. The Department of Rural Economy was next, and it was also a fortunate early choice. By December, the next three reviews had been initiated: Anatomy, Pediatrics and Romance Languages. Also by December, General Faculties Council broadened the mandate of PACCR to include reviews of non-academic units. For such reviews, we had to develop procedures with little or no advice from outside sources.

A PREDICAMENT

It would be misleading to imply that the reviews started smoothly and without difficulty. By December, there was a stressful atmosphere within the PACCR committee. It was evident that George Ford's perceptions of the process differed fundamentally from mine. Clearly we did not see eye to eye on matters of principle and practice. I believed that the process should not be a policing action, that we should take advantage of the advice we had received, and that we should start slowly and be non-confrontational. I had been wrong back in April 1980 when I had confidently told Dr. Horowitz, "I can work with anybody," and that he should feel free in his choice of other committee members.

By the end of the year, it was clear to me that the climate in the steering committee could not lead to the development of a satisfactory review process. I was not certain how to develop a sound process and I needed good advice and amicable discussion. Finally, I concluded there was now no alternative, and so with a sense of relief and regret, I submitted a letter of resignation to Dr. Horowitz. A couple of hours later I received an emergency call from VP Baldwin: "Dr. Horowitz and I have to leave for Lethbridge today. Don't do anything!" Two days later he and the President called me in and told me, "We refuse to accept your resignation. Dr. Ford has stepped down [from the PACCR committee]."

THE PACCR COMMITTEE

The PACCR steering committee (L to R): Walter Harris, Chairman, Henry Kreisel, Fred Enns, Bill Jopling

VP Baldwin asked Dr. Fred Enns to talk to me concerning the possibility of filling the vacancy in the PACCR steering committee. When we met, he immediately remarked that he thought a flexible, humanistic review process should be developed. I responded with a "hooray." Fred Enns told me later that he had been wary at our first meeting.

As the months progressed, it was an ongoing pleasure to work with him as an intelligent, positive, constructive colleague for the remainder of all of the reviews. Dr. Forster became increasingly ill. After he died, President Horowitz asked former academic VP Dr. Kreisel to join the steering committee. Dr. Kreisel was a wise, congenial colleague to help "light the fire" of positive reviews during the years that followed. When the non-academic units were included in the review system, W. H. Jopling was added to the PACCR committee. Bill Jopling was a perfect choice to handle much of our initial interactions with non-academic units.

The single committee to oversee the reviews of academic and non-academic units worked well. During the remaining decade, the four of us (Enns, Harris, Kreisel, Jopling) had well over one thousand amicable, forthright productive meetings.

In the spring of 1981, the PACCR Coordinator, Florence Watters, was transferred to another position. Dee Budd in the President's office filled in for the next few months, but the additional workload became excessive. In December 1981, Lorrie Pearson was appointed as full-time coordinator and was assisted by Lu Ziola for a couple of years. The PACCR headquarters was moved to the Chemistry Building, physically and symbolically separated from central administration. When Lorrie Pearson retired, Shirley Moore was appointed to the position of Coordinator.

In 1980, I agreed to undertake a two-year commitment as Chairman. As time went on, President Horowitz asked me to extend my commitment several times. Finally our arrangement became open-ended, with either of us able to terminate my involvement with six month's notice. Near the end, when dealing with some large and some difficult units, it seemed inappropriate to turn the direction over to a new steering committee, and I continued until all of the 127 units had been reviewed during eleven years.

DEVELOPMENTS AND COMMUNICATION

In the second year of the PACCR review process, we gained more experience and refined our procedures under a full load of fifteen units. We became involved with units from all major faculties as well as non-academic departments. To start a review of a unit, PACCR met with the members of the unit. After about a fifteen-minute presentation, we invited questions and comments. For a unit self-study, we made available some examples of earlier self-studies. We offered any other help that we could reasonably give. Dr. Ted Holdaway of Institutional Research and Planning provided academic departments with basic data for use in their self-studies.

A PACCR review of a unit entailed three major reports: the unit's Self-Study, the report of the Unit Review Committee (URC) and the Unit Response. The URC normally consisted of four members. The unit was asked to provide nominations for two members from outside the University but from the discipline and nominations for someone from a related unit within the University. PACCR nominated the university-at-large member to act as a surrogate for the interests of the wider university.

The members of PACCR prepared a summary of the three reports for the President. Before we met with the President, we met with the Head of the unit for an oral exchange of conclusions and perceptions. We then met with the President who then met with the Head of the unit along with the appropriate VP and the Dean. PACCR also wrote a confidential letter to the members of the URC to give them our perception of the results of the review. It was clear from the responses we received that the members of the URC had more than a transient interest in the unit they had reviewed.

PACCR met with and reported annually to several groups; the Priorities and Planning Committee, the Deans' Council and the Chairs' Council. We also met once with a Senate committee. Reports were published in *Folio,* and a booklet entitled *Campus Reviews* was made available to departments, reviewers and others interested.

Before each on-site visit by URC, we sent a notice to *Folio* inviting input from any who wished to provide information or comment to the URC. The Students' Union and the Graduate Students' Association were also kept informed. Students associated with academic departments provided scheduled input directly to the URC.

After our seventh year, President Horowitz asked us to review the PACCR process. In our seventh annual report, we made the following recommendations for consideration and discussion:

1. The PACCR process should be repeated and built into the administrative structure of the University.
2. The crucial role of the President should be recognized and maintained.
3. The Advisory Committee for steering the reviews process should be made up of senior members of the University community who have wide experience and sound judgment, but who do not currently hold administrative positions.
4. The Deans of academic units and Vice Presidents for administrative/support units should have the main responsibility for monitoring progress towards achieving agreed-upon recommendations arising from reviews, with the Vice President (Academic) or Vice President (Administration) retaining overall monitoring responsibilities.

5. The President should have a reasonable sum of money each year to be used to respond to the findings of the reviews.
6. Program improvement should continue to be the major objective of reviews.
7. The reviews should be carried out as part of a process in which a unit examines its current strengths and limitations with a strong forward-looking emphasis.
8. The reports of Unit Review Committees should continue to be treated with confidentiality.
9. Single review teams, typically two external and two internal reviewers, should continue to be the norm.
10. Practices and procedures currently being used should be carefully re-examined and adapted for the longer term.

An example of a review team. This review team was for the microbiology department. (L to R): R. Colwell (former President, University of Maryland, now President of the National Science Foundation), R. Wolfe (University of Illinois), B. Wilkinson (Economics Department), L. Milligan (Animal Science Department)

Near the end of the reviews of all the units, the PACCR steering committee wrote a major final report entitled "President's Advisory Committee on Campus Reviews, Tenth Annual Report." In one section of the Tenth Annual Report, the PACCR process is described in detail, including the self-study, the time problem, reviewers, URC reports, unit responses and the PACCR process in perspective. In another section, the major issues addressed by reviewers are described. One appendix is the third edition of *Campus Reviews*. A second appendix lists all the units that were reviewed along with the names of the reviewers.

RESULTS

The results of the 127 PACCR reviews cannot be given in detail in a page or two. From my prejudiced point of view, I think every unit received benefits—but not always in the economic sense. How much benefit depended in part on the attitudes of the people in the units. When there was a will to bring about important changes, particularly within the leadership of a unit, then much could and did happen. The reviews helped to identify major problems and point the way to their solutions. The URC report provided a focus for important discussions and served to encourage change, renewal or reconstruction. The continuing interest of the President contributed much to the success of the review process.

The reviews encouraged serious and systematic consideration of the total work of a unit and acted as a catalyst for program improvement. As a result of a review, many changes took place that would not otherwise have occurred. Sometimes serious problems that had been allowed to fester were resolutely dealt with. Most units saw a review as an opportunity to examine the past, evaluate the present and consider directions for the future.

The following is a condensation of major issues addressed by unit review committees.

1. *Departmental renewal.* The reviews found that departments may go through something akin to a life cycle of initiation, growth, plateau and decline. Appropriate action needs to bring about a process of renewal before decline sets in.

2. *Administration.* Unit Review Committees often concluded that insufficient attention was paid to the administrative component of a unit's operations.

3. *Aging equipment.* There are substantial problems and costs relating to the upkeep and replacement of equipment and buildings.

4. *Communication.* Many review teams commented on the inadequacy of communication as a factor in internal and external problems and relations. I believe that studies have shown more broadly that lack of communication is a common problem.

5. *Graduate studies.* Reviewers indicated that often the time taken for students to complete their studies was too long. Not all departments clearly enunciate admission procedures, and they often fail to monitor the progress of their students.

6. *Transition to research and teaching.* The modern university places increasing emphasis on scholarship and research. The transition from a mainly teaching institution may require reorientation of staff.

7. *Teaching workloads.* Especially during the first three or four years of the reviews of academic departments, a case was sometimes made for more resources on the basis of a heavy teaching load. It seemed not to matter whether the teaching load was really heavy or not. For example, one zealous chairman of a department that had a teaching load that was almost certainly lighter than all but two in the University was able to persuade his Dean to assign more resources and obtained a teaching load lighter than all but a single department in the whole University. Departmental instructional duties are diverse and an indicator of teaching load must include lecture hours, number of students, laboratory instruction and teaching assistants. Are teaching loads directly proportional to the number of lecture hours? No. Are they directly proportional to the number of students taught? No. PACCR had to come to grips with the issue of teaching loads and encourage departments to use valid numerical comparisons of loads as an aid to common sense. Arguments based on teaching loads were used in a less manipulative way in the last few years of the reviews. A validated indicator of teaching load is described in the Tenth Annual

Report beginning on page 41.

8. *Teaching and research.* The workload for academic personnel includes undergraduate teaching, research, professional responsibilities and administrative duties. On the matter of teaching and research, teaching can be a source of research ideas and research a source of teaching content. However, a common perception is that undergraduate teaching duties inhibit research activities. Another perception is that high competence in research endows one with high competence in the teaching function. PACCR studied the question of teaching and research and found that the correlation coefficient of the relation of research productivity to teaching competence is neither negative nor positive and is actually zero.

9. *Diversity.* Early in the review process, I concluded that there is a sorting mechanism in society that somehow causes individuals to gather into groups with unique and different characteristics from other groups. Once formed, the members of the group tend to understand and support each other. For example, consider groups of chemists, lawyers, pathologists, accountants or surgeons. Each group differs from each of the others—not that they are better or worse, but different. On a broader scale, those in the arts units differ from those in sciences. Review teams for Arts units needed more time for discussion than did units in Science. Contrary to what I first had assumed, I think that those in Arts strive to attain and have more faith in numbers than those in Science, who approach numbers with a skeptical attitude.

COMMENTARY

Additional material with respect to the PACCR review process is available in the University Archives as follows:

1. The draft of this article (12 pages)
2. The Tenth Annual Report of PACCR (58 pages)
3. The President's Advisory Committee on Campus Reviews, Annual Reports, 1981-1990 (300 pages approx.)

An article entitled "Reviews: Catalysts for Improvement" in the *President's Club Newsletter*, May 1988, described the PACCR review process and stated:

> *This [review] process brings together the best minds to concentrate on recommendations for each department or administrative unit. In addition, it tends to be a positive force in creating awareness of our University beyond the urban, provincial, and national boundaries.*

> *One example of program improvement involves the Registrar's Office. The Unit Review Committee identified problems with students' registration. Mr. Brian Silzer, who had just been appointed registrar, used the analysis and recommendations as the basis for the development of telephone registration.*

The success of the PACCR review process was recognized by other universities contemplating campus-wide review programs. Requests were received to describe and make recommendations about initiation of review programs in other institutions. They include University College of Cape Breton, University of Montreal, Guelph University, University of Calgary, Agriculture Canada and an Arts and Science Deans meeting in Victoria.

The Tenth Annual Report was circulated to many interested persons. The report prompted a number of unsolicited comments including the following:

> *There is no doubt in my mind that your personal integrity, coupled with your patience and perseverance in emphasizing a positive approach to program improvement, were the key factors in the acceptance by the University community.*
> *Florence Watters (PACCR Coordinator during the first year)*

> *Your contribution to the University has been enormous. You have brought wisdom, judgment and the voice of reason to what in all probability has been the single most important review the University of Alberta has had or will ever see.*
> *Peter Meekison (former VP Academic)*

We have just entered the fourth year of our program. In general, we are still following your procedures with a few changes to fit into the Guelph scheme of things.
Stanley (University of Guelph, Internal Review Committees Coordinator)

Dr. Fred Enns kindly read and reviewed the more extensive draft of the PACCR millennium project report and gave valued advice. Dr. Enns gave me permission to include the following personal comment.

I enjoyed all my work at the University of Alberta over the years, but I count the time working on PACCR as the most fulfilling and satisfying. To work with colleagues like Walter Harris, Henry Kreisel and Bill Jopling was a rare privilege. Because the reviews got us into all parts of the University, both academic and non-academic, I gained an appreciation of the University's stature and made me proud to be a part of it. The opportunity to meet eminent, world-renowned authorities from all the disciplines, who formed our Unit Review Committees, is afforded to few people. I am grateful to have been one of those few. And the feeling that we were making a significant contribution to the University of Alberta was like icing on the cake.

There is not the slightest doubt that a successful review process could not have been possible without the contributions of many individuals. I do not attempt to name them all.

It was an enormous pleasure to work closely on a day-to-day basis with Fred Enns, Henry Kreisel, Bill Jopling, Florence Watters, Lorrie Pearson, Lu Ziola and Shirley Moore. The continuing interest and contributions of Dr. Ted Holdaway are appreciated. The advice of Dr. Blaine Holmlund at the beginning was crucial to the startup. The interest and dedication of President Horowitz was of decisive importance. It was a delight to get to know and work with numerous others including Vice Presidents, Deans, the Heads of all the units in the University and with students.

The cooperation of 250 of my University of Alberta colleagues was heart warming. They accepted my invitation to act as reviewers and gave loyal service (with no honourarium) to units under review and to the University. It was stimulating to meet and work with 290 scholars who were our reviewers from outside the University in the diverse fields of learning. The cumulative advice received from this group of more than 500 scholars has been priceless for the current welfare of the University. Their names are listed in the Tenth Annual report.

To end on a personal note, I have been privileged to have had three careers at the University of Alberta during forty-four years. First was a decade as a teacher of about 500 students per year. Second was two-and-a-half decades with a career in teaching, research administration and professional responsibilities. Third was the decade of involvement in the reviews of all the units in the University. Each of the three careers had its special rewards and enriched my life.

GEORGE FORD

On Being a Head, and Staying a Head

I N 1959, AFTER SEVENTEEN YEARS of teaching at the U of A, I was appointed Head of the Department of Mechanical Engineering. Being a Head represents a particular challenge when there's no "Body." The department had only just been established, but by the time I left the position to become Dean of Engineering in 1971, it had become a cornerstone of the faculty.

Our beginnings were humble: no program, no lecture rooms, no labs and no money. So, we changed the rules and improvised, making our home in offices scattered throughout the Departments of Civil and Electrical Engineering.

At the outset, our department was largely shaped by what we didn't know. Traditionally, Mechanical Engineering emphasized the thermosciences. Because our expertise was thin in this area, we shifted our emphasis from machine shop practice to metallurgy, from heating and ventilating to fluid mechanics and heat transfer. Applied mechanics became our specialty, and from that basis evolved one of Canada's most dynamic mechanical engineering programs.

We had inadvertently placed ourselves at the cutting edge of the field. Within five years, machine shop practice had disappeared from Canadian mechanical engineering programs. Clearly, adversity had its reward. Our limited budget forced us into new directions, and our young, eager and energetic staff compensated for our lack of funds.

For equipment, we also had to make do with what we could afford. In 1959, our budget for lab equipment was just $2000. So we accepted all gifts, the good and the bad, and adjusted them to our needs. We inherited a Keith Fan, a one-cylinder diesel engine, and a viscosimeter that seized and whipped around almost killing the operator every time it was used.

Thank goodness for the war surplus and for Miss Bidgood in Ottawa! She sent us endless lists of surplus material on which we made blind bids. Often she would wire back messages such as, "Received your bid. Raise it to $25 and it's yours." We got carloads of useful junk to make more equipment.

Sometimes, though, we were burned, and burned badly. Once we were so determined to get three fast-acting cameras that we went all out and bid $35. When the shipment arrived and we opened the box, we discovered that the cameras did not have lenses. Screams could be heard all the way to Ottawa!

We were convinced—perhaps too convinced—that our first class of twenty-one mechanical engineering students was exceptional. One February morning in 1960, I strolled into my eight o'clock lecture. All the students were there (they always were; it was too easy to be missed in a crowd of twenty-one). There was a mountain of books piled at the front of the room, with a white flag flying from the top and a message on the blackboard: WE SURRENDER! We listened to their concerns, relaxed our expectations a little, and nineteen of them went on to become the first of many successful graduates from the Department of Mechanical Engineering.

As the program mushroomed, so did the hunt for new staff. We were extremely fortunate to build a compatible staff who enjoyed working together. Our young instructors radiated enthusiasm and brought with them diverse skills that were woven into the courses. They breathed new life and spirit into the department, even if the old guard watching over their shoulders sometimes shuddered at the changes they made.

As our program grew and matured, we were allotted more funds. We were also raising more money through our research and contractual efforts. Gradually, we took on an aura of affluence. We could now boil water in many diverse and fancy ways. We acquired wind tunnels with hot and cold running fluids and surrounded ourselves with instruments and gadgets that screeched all levels of noise (which we then duly measured).

As the power requirements for the expanding University rose, so did the necessity of power-producing equipment. By stealth and guile we acquired equipment. Budget preparation became a game of wits; we had to specify every piece of equipment and price it down to the last dime. It became a guessing game. How much would we get? How much would be cut back?

Every budget had a "white elephant," a request that could be shot down when the budget was announced, leaving us with enough to buy the things we really needed. Our "white elephant" was a portable package steam boiler. We shot that great beast for five years. Then one day, the President called and told me, "Your department has been trying to buy a steam boiler for the past several years and you have always had to forego it in order to get other much-needed items. I have recognized the seriousness of your case and have obtained a special warrant from the Board of Governors to purchase a boiler." All of a sudden we had a "live" white elephant. It is still in use.

Throughout those years we remained without a permanent home. Like the prophets of old, we wandered the desert, going from building to building and shack to shack seeking a place to set down our equipment. We dwelt first in the Power Plant, down with the steam boilers and the cracked smoke stack (we had our home in the sheep shed) and then in the South Power Plant (half the campus still doesn't know where that is, and doesn't care). Eventually we moved north into the new Chemical/Mineral basement which, like the bowels of the earth, never saw the sunshine.

Still, the initial struggle was over. We had plenty of students, we were a little richer and we were beginning to get some reasonable equipment. We had our first Ph.D. student (Don Bellow). With his thesis project, he sought to determine when a beam becomes a plate, or vice versa (it related to the fundamental frequency of vibration in wing sections of an airplane). To do this properly, he needed a device that could read and record the output of a hundred or so strain gauges in a matter of seconds.

While visiting a high-tech establishment in the eastern United States, we spotted a wide-carriaged typewriter with no secretary, busily recording vast tables of data without any errors. It was just the thing we needed! We jotted down the serial number and snapped a picture so that we could place an order when we got home.

A week passed, and then another (even though the mail was fast in those days) before we got our reply: there was no such machine! We phoned to give them the serial number again and offered to send along a picture. The head honcho in Toronto assured us that the machine didn't exist. Naturally, this slowed Don's progress with his thesis.

Then one day, two clean-cut, nattily dressed young men visited the department. We assumed they were IBM representatives sent to get further details on our order. "A visit wasn't necessary," we told them. "We would gladly have told you all you needed to know over the phone."

"We're not from IBM," one of them snapped. He whipped out his calling card, a shiny badge emblazoned with screaming eagles—the FBI. The other kid showed his—the RCMP.

What a mess! They wanted to know where we had peeked at the machine and how we had managed to get a close-up photograph. Countless questions poured forth, some relevant, some not. Finally, they informed us that we had violated something or someone, and that we were in big trouble. The FBI man said, "I'll report this to my people"; and the RCMP warned us, "Be careful where you take pictures."

Within a week, though, we got a letter from IBM in the USA saying that we could have a machine and that it would be delivered via their Canadian connections. We got our first robot, which now gathers dust in one of our labs. Don Bellow was able to complete his thesis, but the incident delayed his graduation for a few months.

In the late '60s, the administration gave us permission to begin planning a building of our own, but we were fourth on the list behind Chemistry, Law and Fine Arts. However, we had the advantages of knowing precisely what we wanted (plenty of windows, to make up for our years in the basement!), and of having everything in hand, including the architect and design engineers. We assigned one of our staff (the same Don Bellow) to ride herd on the planning, and we were well on the way while the others were still trying to compute their needed space.

We created a spacious, inviting building that teaches engineering as you walk through it. We broke most of the rules in order to get what we wanted, but by breaking those rules and coming up with creative ideas, we were able to show what good engineering is all about.

Just over a decade after its birth, the Department of Mechanical Engineering had built a permanent home at the U of A.

In 1956, a year after completing my program in Nursing, Dr. Andrew Stewart, President of the University, approached me to join the teaching staff. The following year, I was recommended for the position of Director of the School of Nursing.

In those days, there was no contract or job description. I knew little about the administration of the School, let alone of the University. Somehow, I muddled through and learned the ropes.

I spent nineteen years as Director, and later as Dean of the Faculty of Nursing. I am often asked why I stayed so long, and my answer is that I enjoyed my work and my association with members of other faculties. I appreciated the freedom of discussion and the lack of rigidity and red tape that often exists in other institutions.

Ruth McClure

H. T. G. WILLIAMS

The Department of Surgery
Taking the Chair

Author's note: In 1972, Dr. Bob Macbeth completed a fine early history of the Department of Surgery, and I have drawn heavily on his account.

WALTER MACKENZIE

D R. WALTER MACKENZIE was born in Glace Bay, Nova Scotia. After earning his M.D. at Dalhousie University, he took his surgical training at the Mayo Clinic. This was indeed a full residency training as we know it today. He could have stayed on the Mayo Clinic staff, but his father advised him to go west. He settled in Edmonton just before the second World War.

He volunteered for the Navy and saw much action as his ship took part in the supply convoys to Russia taking the northern route to Murmansk. After the war, he came back to Edmonton and built up a large referred surgical practice while maintaining close contact with friends that he had made during his days at the Mayo Clinic.

As Bob Macbeth points out in his account, Walter Mackenzie played a profound role in the department's growth during his time as Chair.

He firmly established a modern Residency Training Program, both in General Surgery and in the surgical specialties.

He also introduced surgical research. He persuaded the Alberta Division of the Cancer Society to fund the construction of the J. S. McEachern Cancer Research Laboratory in 1952. This building still forms part of the Surgical Medical Research Institute (SMRI). Most of the department's surgical residents were able to train for one or more years in the research labs, to their considerable benefit.

This effort was greatly helped by the establishment of a Research Fund with grants from the Edmonton Civic Employees Welfare Chest Fund. It seems that Dr. Jack Lees, a senior surgeon in the Baker Clinic, had a lakeside cottage next door to the cottage of the Fund's Chairman of the Board. When Dr. Lees heard that the board was anxious to help medical research, he passed the word along. Dr. Mackenzie, in his inimitable way, organized a luncheon for the board members, and the rest is history. Ever since then, the Fund has made very significant contributions to assist surgical research.

Dr. Mackenzie put the U of A's Department of Surgery on the map. He received Honourary Fellowships and Honourary degrees galore and had influential surgical friends throughout the world. He invited many of these to speak in Edmonton, and he and his wife, Dorothy, would host wonderful dinner parties for them.

I would like to share a couple of stories about Walter Mackenzie. His father ran an upscale hotel in Baddeck, Nova Scotia. This wonderful Cape Breton town, overlooking the Bras d'Or, was patronized in the summer by wealthy New England businessmen and their families.

Walter's father kept a diary with careful notes of any event that occurred, however trivial. So the next summer, he would be able to put his arm around the shoulder of a customer's young son and say, "I remember that wonderful fish you caught last year—it was 7 3/4 pounds, I believe. See if you can do as well or better this year."

Walter never forgot that lesson. One day, we were both in Atlantic City for an American College meeting. The Board of Regents was about to vote on the next President Elect. Walter said to me, "We must go along the Boardwalk to meet a few people."

The Boardwalk was the main pedestrian thoroughfare and an excellent place to meet people. For the next two hours, he and I would go up to chat with influential surgeons, and Walter always enquired after the health of the wife and children, mentioning them all by name. Whether he was correct every time or not I don't know—perhaps his friends were just too polite. In any case, it worked. He became the only Canadian that has been President of both the American College of Surgeons and the Royal College of Physicians of Canada.

When Dr. Mackenzie first became Department Chair in 1950, the big excitement in the surgical world was the development of cardiopulmonary bypass systems, which opened the possibility of carrying out open heart surgery. In 1952, he sent a young Toronto surgeon, Dr. John Callaghan, for further training under Russell Brock at Guys Hospital, London, and Frank Gerbode at Stanford University Hospital.

Dr. Callaghan arrived back in Edmonton in 1955, full of vim and vinegar after a year of intensive work in the laboratory. He carried out Canada's first successful open heart operation in Canada in September 1956, two years before any other centre in Canada developed a similar program. The program was very much of a team effort, with Dr. Eric Elliott and Dr. Morris Friedman in charge of the heart-lung machine, Dr. Ted Gain in anesthesia and the very important contribution of the cardiologists, Dr. Bob Fraser and Dr. Joe Dvorkin, Dr. Neil Duncan and Dr. Richard Rossall.

Since that first open heart operation, the Division of Cardiovascular and Thoracic Surgery has performed well over 17 000 operations using cardiopulmonary bypass.

In 1960, Dr. MacKenzie was appointed Dean of the Faculty of Medicine. He relinquished the Chair to Dr. Bob Macbeth, an Alberta graduate who completed his surgical training at McGill.

BOB MACBETH

During his fifteen years in the Chair, Bob Macbeth successfully completed the work that Walter MacKenzie had started. The department was comprised of five well-defined divisions when he took over, and the remaining three were added during his tenure.

Bob Macbeth consolidated all of these divisions with their training programs and arranged to formally affiliate all of the city's general hospitals within the teaching program. U of A residents rotated through the various hospitals, and many eventually took on staff positions. This did much to assuage town-and-gown animosity, even though a certain friendly rivalry was bound to persist. Surgical staff throughout the city have made a splendid contribution to surgical teaching.

Under Bob Macbeth's able, enlightened and honest administration, the

Department of Surgery achieved an excellent record in undergraduate and graduate surgical teaching. The residency training programs all had far more applicants than positions.

Nevertheless, before moving on, Bob Macbeth expressed certain concerns. Now that the specialty divisions had been established, there were fewer beds available for General Surgery. As the more aggressive divisions pushed to expand, the numbers could be reduced even further. Dr. Macbeth was worried about the deleterious effect this might have on the department's teaching, since General Surgery was responsible for most of the undergraduate training and a good proportion of resident training.

MY YEARS IN THE CHAIR

I (H. T. G. Williams) took over the Chair from Bob Macbeth in 1975.

I first came to Edmonton in 1957, after graduating from the University of Liverpool and completing six years of resident training. I spent one year in the research laboratory and another year as a Teaching Fellow in the Division of Cardiovascular and Thoracic Surgery.

I then joined Dr. Mackenzie and Dr. Willox in private practice for fifteen years—happy years of seasoning and experience. I am indebted to both my associates for all the things they taught me. Furthermore, I can honestly say that during those fifteen years, we had many frank discussions, but never a disagreement, argument or a cross word.

I had always been interested in teaching and welcomed residents and students into my operating rooms. In my experience, a three-person team of surgeon, resident and medical student, working with the nursing staff, could provide better patient care than a surgeon and nurses alone. Also, it is a great privilege, honour and obligation to be directly involved in the training of the next generation of surgeons.

Bob Macbeth had left the department in great shape, both financially and in terms of its organization and standing in the North American surgical community. If I could maintain this, I would do well.

In the mid -70s, much of our time was taken up by the planning for the new Health Sciences Centre, later to be named the Walter C. Mackenzie Health Sciences Centre. At times, the process was exciting, even exhilarating, and at others extremely frustrating. On more than one occasion, the designers and planners introduced so many changes that we virtually had to start all over again. If you missed a meeting, you might find that you lost space or facilities to another department. In the end, though, the effort was worthwhile.

The black clouds that Bob Macbeth could just see on the horizon were now very obvious. The number of surgical beds at the U of A Hospital had gradually dwindled, from nearly 1100 down to 800 in the new hospital. Distributing these bed cuts throughout the Divisions was not easy.

Furthermore, the governments were cutting grants to universities, and like every other faculty, Medicine had to do more with less money.

At this point, I would like to mention the tremendous contribution of the Alberta Heritage Foundation for Medical Research. Its fellowships have allowed many of our residents to train in specialized centres all over the world and bring their new skills back to the province. Other residents have been able to take one or two years of research training, and several of these have gone on to careers in academic surgery. In addition, the Foundation funded countless establishment grants and equipment grants. It really has been a wonderful success story.

BRYCE WEIR

Dr. Bryce Weir took over from me in the Chair of the Department of Surgery in 1986.

Dr. Weir, a McGill graduate who had completed his neurosurgical training in Montreal, came to Edmonton with very high credentials to join the Division of Neurosurgery. He soon developed an active and productive neurosurgical research laboratory. By the time he took the Chair, he was an international authority on cerebral aneurysms, subarachoid hemorrhage and the resulting vasospasm producing severe or irreversible brain damage.

He reorganized the department's divisional structure, allowing more city surgeons to become involved in department affairs. This has been to everyone's advantage. He also established the Departmental Councils, where all members of the Department of Surgery gathered once a year to discuss pertinent topics.

In 1987, Dr. Les Dushinski and Dr. Joe Mossey came up with the idea of endowing a Chair in the Department of Surgery in the name of Dr. Walter Stirling Anderson. Their campaign went forward with Dr. Weir's strong support. Contributions from friends, colleagues and grateful patients were matched by the government, and the sum now stands at well over two million dollars. The Chairman of the Department of Surgery is now called the Walter Stirling Anderson Professor of Surgery, a fitting tribute to a man of real stature and a wonderful surgeon.

Cutbacks and bed closures continued during Dr. Weir's reign, and he coped with them in a fair but determined manner.

Dr. Weir was enticed away from us in 1991 by an offer of a Chair of Neurosurgery at the University of Chicago, probably the most prestigious neurosurgical appointment in North America.

STEWART HAMILTON

In 1991, Dr. Stewart Hamilton took over the Chair.

He graduated in Medicine from McGill and completed his General Surgery training at the University of Alberta, followed by special training in Critical Care Medicine.

He is a clear thinker, a good speaker, a good organizer, and a very able surgeon, with special interests in managing trauma and all aspects of critical care.

But he has had a tough time from the start. The financial constraints have continued, and other forces—the regionalization of hospital care and the concentration of serious cases in the two main hospitals—have played havoc with both undergraduate and resident education.

We spent twenty-five years convincing Hospital Boards of the advantage of restricting surgeons to working in one hospital. This allowed three-person teams of surgeon, resident and students to work together, learn together and care for patients together.

Now surgeons spend a significant part of their time driving between hospitals, and the residents and students have little opportunity to talk to and examine patients before operating. They don't have the chance to properly correlate symptoms and signs with pathological findings and postoperative course. I doubt if the Health Authorities gave any thought at all to the effect these cuts would have on teaching.

Fortunately, surgeons, by their very nature, are flexible and adaptable. I hope that, with good will all around, the Capital Health Authority, the Medical School and the Department of Surgery can devise a better arrangement. If not, accreditation may be in jeopardy.

Behind the Scenes

Now it can be told!

ALBERT S. KNOWLER

The Great U of A Heist

SEPTEMBER 9, 1982, began as a beautiful summer day, warmed by our famous Alberta sunshine. It was the third day of registration, and a large number of students had already congregated in the centre of the campus when I headed to work at 8:30 a.m.

As I arrived at my office, on the third floor of the Administration Building, I began to reflect on a meeting from the previous day. My Associate Comptroller, Bob Leonard, and I had met with Gordon Perry, Director of Campus Security, and his assistant, Ralph Oliver, both experienced former members of the RCMP. We talked about recent armed robberies in Edmonton and in particular, the holdup of a Loomis Armoured Car courier while leaving the Students' Union Building the previous winter.

I was worried about the huge amounts of cash we handled during registration in the Butterdome and about the openness of our cashiering cage facing the foyer on the third floor. After a one-hour discussion, we arranged to meet again in a month or so, after the rush, to carry out a full review of our cashiering procedures.

In the interim, it was agreed that we should follow the established procedure during registration. Our insurance underwriters required two men from our staff to work together picking up tuition fees (cash and cheques) at the Butterdome and then carrying them in brown paper bags to our cashier. Sig Johnson and Ted Bialowas would make the pickups every two hours during registration, returning to the Comptroller's office using different routes and building entry doors each time.

At 9:03 a.m. I was working at my desk. Suddenly, my secretary, Ellen Kvill, burst through the doorway from her office, her face beet red. "There's

Ellen McLeod (Kvill) and Bert Knowler

a man in the reception area pointing a revolver at Sandy Obreiter and wearing a Howdy Doody mask (later recalled as a Raggedy Anne mask). I had gone to the doorway to see who was there because I heard someone come in. He pointed the gun at me and said, 'Don't move!' I told him to go to hell and then came into your office. He's still out there!"

My heart pounding with adrenaline, I told Ellen that I would call 911 and also phone to warn the Bookstore and Housing and Food Services to secure their cash and cheques, in case they were also targeted. Then I asked her if she could possibly go back through the doorway and just stand there and say nothing for the sake of Sandy's safety. I was afraid that Sandy, who was twenty years old and very upset, might say or do something to provoke the man into violence.

With great courage and presence of mind, Ellen walked back and silently faced the intruder. Sandy was sobbing at this point, obviously terrified, but remained seated at her desk for the next two or three minutes.

Meanwhile, a second masked robber approached the front counter of the cashier's cage. He pointed his gun at Bonnie Home, our Cashier, and yelled at her to hand him the large deposit bag on the floor against the front counter. Bonnie had just closed and sealed it, ready for pickup by the Loomis courier sometime in the next twenty-five minutes. The bag was about 30" high, stuffed to the top with approximately $1 200 000 in cheques and $65 000 in cash.

Bonnie had been working at her desk at the rear of the cage when the robber appeared. She stood up and yelled back at him, "God damn you!" She then ran out the back door of the cage and reported the incident to her supervisor, Sig Johnson, Accountant-General, Accounting Division. He immediately called the police.

The robber hurled himself over the counter, grabbed the deposit bag and burst into the reception area to rejoin his partner, who was still silently holding Ellen and Sandy hostage. Together, the robbers ran out of the room.

Having just put down my phone, I heard footsteps in the adjoining hall. The robbers seemed to be lost, running down one hallway, then retracing their steps to run down another. Ellen later told me that they kept returning to the reception area in their search for an exit route.

I decided that the only prudent role for me was to stay put and wait for the police. I hoped that the robbers would eventually manage to leave the building without harming anybody. I wasn't worried about the money because we were covered by insurance.

Ironically, the first police car arrived in front of the Administration Building while the robbers were still busy on our floor. The officer had to wait for backup, however, and by the time another car arrived, the robbers were gone with their loot. In retrospect, I feel the delay prevented what could have been a bloody confrontation.

Finally, the thieves located the exit door to the west side stairwell, and the sound of their running footsteps faded. Their commotion caught the attention of the two accountants in that area, Dennis Grover and Denis Fitzgerald. They followed the armed men downstairs and along the walkway towards their getaway van, which was parked on the north side of SUB. The accountants got there in time to write down the license plate number and the colour and make of the vehicle, in order to make a report to the police. Unfortunately, the robbers quickly abandoned the van in the Groat Estates area, just across the river from the University.

As soon as the robbers had left the third floor, Ellen brought Sandy into my office to try to calm her down. She slumped against the corner wall of my office and slid down to the floor, sobbing loudly and gasping for air. I sat on the floor beside her and put a hand on her shoulder. I told her that it was over, that the robbers were gone and that she was safe. Ellen and I told her to take the rest of the day off to recover, but it was obviously a terrible experience that she would remember for the rest of her life.

Ellen remained calm and remarkably poised throughout the ordeal. I've wondered since then whether she, as a part-time student raising two teenage daughters on her own, was an expert at managing stress!

The police arrived to begin questioning my staff and me, when we were suddenly inundated with the media. I immediately advised my senior staff to avoid disclosing the amount that was stolen in order to avoid attracting the attention of other criminals. Unfortunately, one reporter managed to wheedle the amount out and, of course, it was published in the *Edmonton Journal* the next day.

We were fortunate that years earlier, we had considered the possibility of armed robbery. In designing our machine receipting system, we made sure that we captured enough vital information at the input stage to allow us to reconstruct every single transaction. With this information at hand, we were able to recover replacement cheques from virtually everyone concerned.

My staff spent two months obtaining replacement cheques, and our insurance broker, Marsh MacLennan, arranged for claims to be reimbursed to the U of A during the winter of 1982-83. Our insurance carriers treated us fairly and expeditiously. We recovered every cent of stolen cash, as well as the interest earnings foregone during the recovery period. In addition, we were able to recover the cost of our staff members' time in calculating and documenting the loss. Our risk management program, which was the responsibility of the Comptroller's Office, stood us in good stead.

Once the dust and the paperwork had settled, we turned our attention to redesigning our cash-handling procedures. In the past, there had been two schools of thought among our senior personnel. The first was to keep it simple and not give the impression that we had anything to hide. The second was known as the "Fort Knox" approach—with cameras, time delay devices for opening safes and cash registers, bullet-proof glass and so on.

We had come a long way from the 1930s, when Billy Watson carried the daily deposit in a large purse, while riding the High Level Bridge streetcar to the main downtown branch of the Imperial Bank of Canada. My predecessor as Comptroller, Murray Rousell, had been aghast at this procedure when he started as a U of A accountant in September 1946. When Loomis opened a branch in Edmonton three years later, the University of Alberta Bursar's Office (it became Comptroller's Office in 1968) signed up as its first customer.

In twenty-eight year's service in the University's financial hub, leading up to 1982, I had never heard of an armed robbery taking place at a Canadian university. At the annual meetings of the Canadian Association of University Business Officers (CAUBO), the subject had never even been mentioned, to my knowledge.

Times had changed, and the University had grown. After much consultation with security experts, we decided to proceed with the Fort Knox concept. We launched an intensive consulting effort on this subject among specialists from our insurance broker, our bank (CIBC Main Branch, Edmonton), the Edmonton Police Department—Strathcona Division, Campus Security Services and the Physical Plant Department.

Our best and most complete advice on the subject came from Thomas Dunlop, Security Consultant at the CIBC Main Branch. A former RCMP officer, he walked me through our third floor quarters and didn't stop talking for an hour, pointing out weak spots in our layout and giving us a thorough risk analysis of our cash-handling system. I remember following him around with a notepad and writing down at least twenty-five recommendations for improvement. He freely offered his considerable knowledge and experience in his field, and he also made himself available for any questions that might arise later.

I carried out further consultations with city police officers and with

Mr. Perry and Mr. Oliver of Campus Security, all of whom gave me very good advice on how to tighten up our security. I received great help from Gordon Bulat, Director of Physical Plant; Dan Pretzlaff, Superintendent; and Russ Motyka, Project Manager.

The project was completed in a three-day blitz over Labour Day weekend, 1983—a remarkable feat, considering the scope and complexity of the task. By Tuesday morning, the cash cage was open for business. It would not be prudent to describe the changes in detail. Suffice it to say that the staff in Physical Plant referred to the project as "Fort Cox" due to the careful monitoring by Derek Cox, our Office Manager. There were a number of trades and technologies involved in the project and, thanks to a coordinated effort, the final result met our objectives with ease.

The police investigation concluded that the robbers were highly professional, that they were likely francophone (based on their accent) and that they had used .357 Magnum semi-automatic revolvers. No trace was ever found of the two perpetrators or their booty, and none of the cheques were ever cashed.

The thieves had certainly done their homework, probably during the two days preceding the robbery. At 9:03 a.m. Thursday, the foyer was not crowded with students, as it would be for most of the day.

One positive outcome of this upsetting ordeal is that there have been no other holdups at the U of A since then, and that my successors and others have maintained an alert vigilance whenever cash is involved.

If such an event took place today, we would bring in counsellors to help the staff overcome the shock of the experience. I wish we had thought to do so back then. Instead, each of us had to handle it in his or her own way when we went home at the end of that frightening day. I personally felt that my human rights had been violated and suddenly felt unsafe even in my own house. Not long afterwards, my wife, Claire, and I installed deadbolts on our entry doors.

I never formally thanked Ellen Kvill (now McLeod), Sandy Obreiter, Bonny Home and other staff for the bravery and cool heads that they displayed back on September 9, 1982. I do so now!

D̲OUGLAS̲ E̲NGEL̲

On Becoming Too Close to Grad Students

IN THE DIM DARK DAYS when audiovisual was evolving into media and new technology, two doctoral candidates were enjoying the camaraderie of our department and the independence that comes with having finished their course work.

With extra time on their hands, they devoted themselves to perfecting the art of mischief.

One evening, I returned to my office after a deadly dull conference. Despite my jet lag, I was not unaware of my surroundings. I eased my office door open with my elbow—my hands were full of carry-ons—and, reaching for the light switch, sensed something wasn't quite right. We had suffered a number of thefts that spring, so I cautiously backed off.

I found a custodian (yes, we had them in those days) and borrowed a flashlight. Back at the office, I confirmed my suspicions—the screw holding the switch plate was loose. A thin white wire stretched inconspicuously from the switch to the baseboard and behind the desk.

I eased the door open just enough to slip in, being careful to avoid what I expected—the old bucket of water trick. No water. Shining the flashlight about, I saw that a number of surprises lay in wait for my arrival.

My well-worn desk chair had been replaced by a bright, shiny toilet, obviously wired to trigger further delights should I sit down. Investigating further, I found a cassette player and a Polaroid camera, rigged to a delay switch (presumably to allow me time to get seated). Sitting on the toilet would trigger the music (our national anthem). The camera was set to take a picture of me standing at attention in the full glare of the flash.

The culprits would surely be lurking nearby to witness my initial reaction. I had to act quickly. I quietly removed the camera for my own use, raised the seat cover to start the proceedings and ducked down behind the desk. The culprits arrived right on their musical cue, crowding in for the anticipated last laugh. Instead they were caught on their own film.

Reverse blackmail is sweet revenge.

It is not easy to discuss the overall concept of Building Services at a large educational institution such as the University of Alberta. Every facility on campus has its own requirements. The various tasks involved in maintaining them all would form a list longer than a man's arm, and by the time you added the last item to the list, the first would have changed.

Every successful organization is a continuously evolving and expanding complexity of physical property and mechanical apparatus, with progressively better-educated people working and functioning within it. No such organization is the same as it was five years ago, two years ago or even six months ago.

The last fifty years have seen a dramatic change in the field of Building Services, as in almost every other field.

Kevin Moodie

Dr. Fred Conroy will be remembered for his good humour and wonderful stories. Once a year, in the 1940s, around St. Patrick's Day, he would host City Urology Rounds at the General Hospital. He would arrive at the meeting as an oversized leprechaun with green-dyed hair, green suit and shoes. He would then spike the morning coffee with Jamieson's Irish Whiskey. The residents (and, in fact, everyone) loved it! After the meeting and presentation of problem cases, Fred would make the rounds to soothe patients who were passing green urine. He had ordered methylene blue tablets with their St. Patrick's Day breakfasts.

Dr. Bob Francis became Chief of Urology at the Royal Alexandra Hospital in 1952, and for many years headed a very effective teaching unit at that hospital. He is a wonderful jazz trombonist and his five-piece combo of urologists—the Five Four Skins—had a notorious record.

W. H. Lakey

ROBERT FRASER

Simpler Times

T O THOSE OF US WHO WORKED in the past but now live in the present, the past seems to have been a time of fewer problems and simpler answers.

In the early 1940s, I was a medical student and then an intern at both the University and the Royal Alexandra Hospitals. The "old Royal Alex" was ruled by one supreme authority, Dr. A. F. Anderson, who simplified administrative matters by decreeing what would and what would not be tolerated.

Senior interns were scarce since most graduates were immediately posted to the Armed Forces. Six of us juniors, augmented by two or three seniors from the class six months ahead of us, covered the whole busy Royal Alex. We were continually on call, but revelled in the responsibility.

In 1945, an isolation hospital was attached to the Royal Alex to house patients with tuberculosis and other infections during mandatory quarantine. A truck owned by the Royal Alex served as an ambulance to transfer patients from home to the isolation ward.

The intern on duty drove this vehicle, accompanied by one of his confreres when necessary. I do not remember being asked whether I had a driver's license, and I have no idea whether anyone or anything was insured. The same vehicle made the occasional side trip past "the Vendors" to pick up beer, a pleasant addition to the hospital diet for those living in intern quarters twenty-four hours a day, and frequently thirty days a month.

One winter, just after the end of the war, the "ambulance" was sent out to bring in a discharged soldier who had developed scarlet fever. Deep snow flanked the road and pathways. We arrived at the man's door at the top of some rather steep front steps. An anxious-looking war bride, newly introduced to Canada, stood aside as we loaded her husband on a stretcher.

The two of us struggled to negotiate our heavy patient down the front steps. Perhaps we should have taken time to properly secure him. He abruptly left the stretcher to slide smoothly, head first, into three feet of Alberta snow.

It was difficult to pretend that this was a planned part of the transfer. While the tearful bride watched, we retrieved her hero and tied him securely to the stretcher. In response to our apologies, he replied with considerable sincerity, "Don't worry. This is the first time I have cooled off for two days!"

No incident report was required in those days, and no complaint ever reached the ears of Dr. Anderson. As I said, those were simpler times.

Bob Fraser

JAMES N. CAMPBELL

Memories and Misadventures

THE FOLLOWING EVENTS TOOK PLACE when the newly formed Department of Microbiology was housed in the south-west wing of the present Dentistry-Pharmacy Building.

THE CHRISTMAS PARTY

In 1965, during the interregnum between the departure of G. E. Myers and the arrival of W. E. Razzell as Chairman, the Department of Microbiology held the most famous in a long line of memorable Christmas parties.

As usual, we held the party on the last afternoon before the holiday, in the research laboratory adjoining the Chairman's office. The lab was located on the second floor of the present Dentistry-Pharmacy Building, directly over the elegantly appointed office of the Dean of Pharmacy.

On that particular day, a balmy chinook blew in. Given the building's primitive ventilation system, the large crowd, and the typically lively nature of our functions, this soon made the room unbearably hot. So, naturally, we opened the windows.

When we finally wended our bibulous way home, no one remembered to close the windows. That evening, in true Alberta fashion, the temperature plummeted to –30° and froze the pipes solid. Some time later, a janitor making his rounds noticed the chill, closed the windows and went on his merry way home for the holidays.

As soon as the room warmed up, of course, the burst pipes thawed, the flood waters began flowing, and they continued flowing because everyone was off celebrating Christmas. To make matters worse, the building was old and, to borrow a nautical term, "lacked watertight integrity." In other words, it was a leaky ship of a building, full of cracks and holes. The water poured straight down into the office of the Dean of Pharmacy.

The damage in our department was trivial, but by the time the flood was discovered, the Dean's expensive carpet was literally afloat, along with some of the lighter furnishings. As Acting Chairman at the time, I was nominally responsible. I was certain that my budding academic career, if not ended, was at least in mortal danger. Fate stepped in to save me, however.

The caretaker who had closed the windows neither spoke nor understood English at all well. When questioned by the investigating SWAT team, he assumed that they were trying to pin the blame on him. He categorically denied that anything untoward had happened on his shift. The more they grilled him, the more he stonewalled. Finally, the union representative was called in, and the whole thing degenerated into a loud argument about workers' rights.

The University eventually decided that this was leading nowhere. They wrote the mishap off as some sort of act of God, thereby letting both the hapless janitor and your humble correspondent off a very sharp hook.

The Dean of Pharmacy, in addition to being a scientist, was also an award-winning author and humourist. We thought that such a person might appreciate the lighter side to all these unpleasant proceedings, so we sent him a ribbon-bedecked umbrella, along with a sympathy card courtesy of the department. His secretary later told me that, to put it mildly, he did not find the gesture funny. It was a long time before his famous sense of humour returned, at least as far as the Department of Microbiology was concerned.

Now, more than three decades later, I bring to light the true facts of the "Flood of '65" in the hope that there exists in Canadian jurisprudence a statute of limitations that protects me from post facto prosecution.

THE CANTALOUPE WAR

In 1968, I had just come back from a wonderful sabbatical year at the University of Liege and was ruefully contemplating my return to the harsh world of teaching and administrative duties. My flagging spirits were cheered, however, by the following incident, which remains one of the memorable highlights of my time at U of A.

At the time, W. E. Razzell was approaching the end of his brief tenure as Chairman of Microbiology. He had recently granted a two-year appointment to one Dr. László Pipek (not his real name), with the option of converting it to a permanent post if everything worked out.

László, an expert in the field of bacterial sporulation, was born in Hungary and educated in Europe. He struck me as an astute, cooperative scientist, and a very likeable and interesting person.

He was also, however, a genuine character. He viewed himself as a person of impeccable taste and artistic awareness who had somehow found himself in a remote and culturally deprived backwater. He often said that Edmonton was like Siberia, only with more fast-food outlets and better central heating. His affectations and condescending wit soon put him on a collision course with Razzell. The Chairman, an ultra-pragmatist who wanted the spotlight for himself, expected unquestioning acquiescence from his departmental staff. A crisis was inevitable, and when it came, it was spectacular.

In those days, our department had to make do with only one walk-in cold room. Pipek, a recognized expert in bacterial sporulation, used his share of the room to store his prized collection of mutants of *Bacillus* spp., with defects at various stages of the sporulation process. In those days before gene-splitting, such a library of mutants could only be prepared by the laborious processes of mutagenesis, selection, screening, etc. This rare and delicate collection formed the very core of Pipek's research.

One day while shopping with his wife, Razzell spotted a mouldy cantaloupe in the supermarket. In 1941, in Peoria, Illinois, Kenneth B. Draper had used just such a cantaloupe to isolate *Penicillium chrysogenum* NRRL 1951 B25, the strain of fungus that made possible the first mass production of penicillin. With this humble cantaloupe, thought Razzell, introductory students could recreate Draper's original experiment and experience first hand the thrill of scientific discovery. He triumphantly bore his rotting treasure back to the department's cold room and stored it directly alongside Pipek's precious cultures.

László was understandably outraged at the prospect of having his precious mutant bacteria contaminated by the mould spores emanating from Razzell's little classroom project. In spite of his bravado, though,

László (like the rest of us) was a little afraid of Razzell. Rather than confronting the chairman directly, he chose to yell at Maxine Coombs, our talented but very gentle preparation room technologist, insisting that the offending object be removed forthwith.

Maxine relayed this suggestion to the Chairman who responded, also at the top of his lungs, that no one was to lay a finger on his beloved cantaloupe. Poor Maxine was trapped between two enraged academic pit bulls. Knowing that Razzell's bite could be even worse than his bark, she wisely decided to let the mouldy melon stay put.

Then, at approximately 3:15 p.m. one afternoon, the situation came to a head. Our department has a long-standing tradition of having coffee seated on the floor in the hall. On this particular day nearly the entire staff, including Razzell, were sitting at the end of the hall, about 30 metres from the cold room door.

Pipek entered the cold room and, seeing the hated object still there, let out a roar. The combination of his Hungarian-French accent and his outrage caused the message to be somewhat garbled, but the gist was, "I said I wanted this @#%& thing the *%## out of here!"

Finally, after an increasingly incoherent monologue, he took the mouldy cantaloupe and fired it down the hall, obviously aiming at the chairman. Given the distance and the awkward nature of the missile, it wasn't a bad attempt. The line was good, and the fruit held together in flight, but it fell about three metres short of the primary target.

However, when it struck the floor, it exploded in a most spectacular fashion, showering walls, ceiling, the chairman and assorted innocent bystanders with well-rotted cantaloupe juice and fragments of pulp.

The ensuing silence was hypnotic. We survivors, sensing an impending inferno, rapidly vacated the fallout area, lurking out of sight but within earshot.

Razzell was never hesitant to level a sharply worded criticism at any member of the department, if he felt it was warranted. To his credit, he delivered these critiques privately and never in front of other staff. In this case he made an exception. After an eloquent and precise summary of László's major character flaws and probable ancestry, he fired him on the spot.

202 Echoes In The Halls

Echoes In The Halls

László may have lost the War of the Cantaloupe, but he did manage to sneak in a very telling final blow. Razzell had a strong aversion to the presence of Playboy-type calendars in the laboratories, arguing that they detracted from a proper academic atmosphere. He had earlier circulated one of his forcefully worded memos demanding their removal.

Pipek, remembering this, quietly collected an impressive number of the more specific centrefolds. Sometime immediately prior to his departure, he secretly glued them inside drawers, cupboards, cabinets, incubators and so on, throughout the department. For the next several months, every time Razzell opened a new door he would be greeted by yet another full-colour cutie. This would, without fail, elicit the desired response. It was one of the most successful and longest-lasting practical jokes ever executed in this department.

The Student Law Society election campaign produced some highly salacious posters and pictures in the fall of 1969, hung throughout the reading rooms and stairways. One quite large sketch that I thought went too far depicted an aged, professorial-looking character clad only in brief running shorts with very puckered genitalia hanging past one hem. The sketch bore an uncanny resemblance to a certain retired Dean of Law. When I took it down, I was besieged by indignant female students accusing me of sex discrimination, since they had hung the poster in response to the male students' productions demeaning women. We let it stay, but when it was rumoured that an *Edmonton Journal* reporter might be on the way to view the exhibition, they all came down.

In 1973, Humanities and Social Sciences Reference migrated to the new North Rutherford Library. The building and its galleria had many beautiful features, but quite a few drawbacks as well. For example, somebody sited the main building air intake directly over the shipping and receiving areas for both the library and HUB Mall. Exhaust from delivery trucks was efficiently pumped into the second floor staff offices until Administration had *Turn Off Engine* notices posted outside. Even then, we sometimes had to go and accost careless truckers.

David Sharplin

Building the University

How today's U of A came to be

HARRY GUNNING

Emerging from the Hinterland

IN THE LATE '50s—the post-Sputnik era—the democratic countries were deeply concerned about the Soviet nuclear threat. Governments suddenly began providing increased funding for science and engineering research. At the time, I was a senior Professor of physical chemistry at I.I.T. in Chicago, with a large research team of doctoral and post-doctoral students. Much of my research support came from the U.S. Rocket Program and from the Atomic Energy Commission.

I had recently been visited in Chicago by the great Canadian scientist-statesman, Dr. E. W. R. Steacie, President of the National Research Council in Ottawa. I had been a member of his research group at the NRC in the late '40s before leaving for an academic appointment in the U.S.

During his visit, Ned Steacie explained in detail to me how the NRC was providing vital research funding to the Canadian universities for basic research in the sciences. Unfortunately, many provincial universities were not equipped for training students at the doctoral and post-doctoral levels. Ned hoped he could influence these universities to upgrade their academic capabilities.

His words were still fresh in my mind when he telephoned me, saying that I should prepare myself for an offer as Head of the Chemistry Department at the University of Alberta. He assured me that if I did accept, I could count on his complete support in building up the department's academic stature.

I must confess that at that time, I knew next to nothing about the Chemistry Department at the U of A. I had heard, however, of an outstanding staff member there. He was such a gifted lecturer in organic chemistry that he had convinced many students to devote their careers to that discipline. Many of these students are now senior scientists in major U.S. companies such as General Electric. As a consultant, I had heard them sing the praises of Dr. Reuben Sandin.

When the members of my department found out that I was considering an appointment in Edmonton, Canada, their reaction surprised me. After locating this city in their atlases, they concluded that I was headed for the frozen north. One morning, I found a booklet on my desk, issued by the U.S. Air Force, entitled *If You Are Trapped in the Arctic*. Though I can't remember all of the advice in the book, I do recall one page. In very bold type, it described how to say, "Where is the nearest Trading Post?" in East and West Eskimo!

In the spring of 1957, I made several visits to the U of A, with my dear wife, Donna, and our daughter, Judith, then thirteen. I gave lectures on

Chemistry Department staff, 1967, outside the Chemistry Building. L to R: H. E. Gunning, H. B. Dunford, P. Kebarle, D. Darwish, C. Bigelow, F. Birss, H. S. Frank (Physical Chemistry visiting speaker), W. E. Harris, R. N. O'Brien, G. R. Freeman, R. U. Lemieux, R. K. Brown (photo supplied by W. E. Harris)

some of my current research, and we were all royally treated by Vice President Dr. Walter Johns and his family, and by Dr. Walter Harris, a senior staff member in Chemistry.

I was very impressed with the quality of people that we met. Remembering what Ned Steacie had told me, I finally accepted the position. We became residents of Edmonton in the fall of that year.

At that time, the Chemistry Department's facilities, located in the old Medical Building, left a good deal to be desired. I had brought with me four of my doctoral students from Chicago, who planned on completing their Ph.D.s in my laboratory in Edmonton. Here, as in many other situations, Walter Johns was most helpful. I rapidly developed a great admiration for this distinguished administrator. His academic background was in Classics, and he was surprised to find a scientist who shared his great admiration for the Roman poets.

Naturally, one of my first priorities had to be to provide adequate research facilities for my four doctoral students. Central administration provided funds for me to order the necessary research equipment and supplies, and to convert some vacant space into a research laboratory.

At this point, I must confess, I experienced some serious frustration. In Chicago, all of the great scientific equipment houses were well-represented. An order placed there one day would certainly be delivered by the next. In Edmonton, scientific equipment had to be brought in from faraway places, often taking months to be delivered. I couldn't escape the mental picture that my equipment was being dragged across the prairies by a team of horses pulling a stoneboat. Fortunately, I convinced myself that frustration was really just another word for challenge and adjusted my expectations accordingly.

I soon learned that my department had an established custom of sending its best graduates away to complete their Ph.D.s and post-doctoral studies at major universities in eastern Canada or the United States. These students rarely returned to Alberta; in fact, the great majority of them ended up in the U.S. The pattern in other departments was exactly the same.

In other words, the University of Alberta, under policies dictated by the government-appointed Board of Governors, operated a sophisticated brain-drain system. Our best minds, so sorely needed for the growth and development of the province were, instead, enriching the intellectual resources of the United States! This conclusion, further strengthened by detailed discussions with Ned Steacie, convinced me to stay true to my goals.

In discussing the problem with other departments, I found a great deal of support for building the University into a research-centred institution, where students could pursue Ph.D.s and post-doctoral studies with internationally recognized staff members. It was painfully clear to me that the greatest obstacle to this goal was the attitude of the government-appointed Board of Governors.

Let me cite an example. After a great deal of planning and detailed discussion, the Chemistry Department had completed tentative blueprints for a new building to replace our antiquated facilities in the old Medical Building. With modern research facilities, the building would meet the needs of the department for the foreseeable future.

As the first step to seeking approval, I made an appointment to see the President, a gracious Scottish gentleman named Dr. Andrew Stewart. I already admired Dr. Stewart very much, as well as his charming wife, who was a gifted poet. In fact, I have collections of her verse in my library and I treasure them very much. She had a rare gift for making the ordinary, extraordinary.

After some preliminary discussions, Dr. Stewart took the blueprints from me and studied them very carefully. His first comment was, "This is a large building indeed."

Dr. Stewart listened carefully as I explained our objective of providing adequate chemical facilities up to the time when the University's total enrollment reached 10 000 students (at the time, enrollment was approximately 4500). I noticed that he kept looking in the direction of the adjacent room, where the Board of Governors held their meetings. Finally, he told me, rather sadly, that the enrollment at the University would never be allowed to exceed 5000 students!

This did not particularly disturb me, since I had already had a number of formal and informal meetings with members of the government. I felt that the Board was simply ruled by what I called hinterland thinking. By running a small four-year college and restricting it to 5000 students, they were promoting the export of gifted Albertans and assuring that we remain a backwater province. With oil royalties beginning to enrich provincial coffers, progressive members of the government were beginning to see a new, more important position for Alberta.

Some months after our meeting, Dr. Stewart left to become Chairman of the Board of Broadcast Governors in Ottawa (in today's terminology, a kind of non-digital CRTC). We very much missed him and his fine family. However, with Dr. Walter Johns as his successor, the University was now in very good hands indeed.

I continued to have many meetings with members of the government and the University staff. Dr. Steacie's goals for the Chemistry Department had overwhelming support in every intellectual discipline in the University. I sensed a new pride and enthusiasm among our best staff members. Building the University of Alberta into a leading intellectual centre, capable of giving Albertans the most advanced education available and equipped with the best facilities for adding new knowledge in all fields, became a very dynamic institutional objective.

With Dr. John's strong support, the move toward developing modern buildings gained momentum. A major complex was designed for the Physical Sciences, including a new building for Physics and Mathematics, and another for Chemistry, plus adjoining lecture theatres. With a full complement of specialized services, the buildings could accommodate advanced research in all disciplines.

Thus, the U of A began its transformation into a forefront intellectual institution. A similar change was occurring in the province itself. The increased emphasis on knowledge, advanced research and innovation, just beginning at that time, has now become a major driving force in our economy.

As Albertans, we can now say with pride that our province contributes its full share to Canada's growing intellectual and economic stature. The University played a key role in making Alberta what it is today.

GORDON MCINTOSH AND HENRY HODYSH

Portraits of Change
The Builders

FOREWORD

The two great educators portrayed in this paper are considered the "builders" of the Faculty of Education at the U of A. The paper is part of a larger project, which looks at the personalities and philosophies of all nine Deans who have led the Faculty of Education since its inception in the early 1940s.

We'd like to thank the interviewees—Larry Beauchamp, Fred Enns, Myer Horowitz, John Paterson, Bob Patterson, Wally Worth and Harvey Zingle—who were so generous with their time and insights. We also salute the support staff who contributed so much extra effort, and the readers who helped shape this project through its many drafts. Without everyone's support, we would not have been able to get it right.

A S YOU PASS THROUGH THE TURNSTILES at the entrance to the H. T. Coutts Library in the Education Centre, the faces of three men look down at you from their portraits above. How many students, staff and visitors have paused in this alcove to look at these portraits of the first three Deans of the Faculty of Education and asked themselves, "What were they really like?"

With this paper, we do our best to answer that question for two of those men, M. E. LaZerte and Herbert T. "Pete" Coutts. Only in passing will we talk about the accomplishments of the Deans. We write about them as interesting men with impressive qualities, and we describe the ways in which these qualities were expressed in their work.

MILTON EZRA LAZERTE: THE FOUNDER (1943-1950)

The study of education at the U of A dates back to the earliest days, when its home was the Department of Philosophy and Psychology. By the 1930s, students could earn Bachelor of Education degrees through the School of Education (still part of the Faculty of Arts) after completing a first degree in another faculty.

Dr. Milton Ezra LaZerte, the first Dean, faced a mammoth task. In 1945, just two years after the establishment of the faculty, it became entirely responsible for teacher education in Alberta. Until then, the vast majority of the province's teachers had trained at the provincial normal schools. Alberta was the first province in Canada to make teacher education the exclusive responsibility of the University.

Milton Ezra LaZerte was a powerful figure in Canadian education and an outstanding academic leader at the University of Alberta. He pursued, with vigour, a clear, groundbreaking vision (now taken for granted): that prospective teachers should prepare for their profession at the University, alongside students in the traditional professions such as medicine and law, taking many of the same courses and meeting the same standards.

Like his friend and colleague John Barnett (General Secretary of the Alberta Teachers' Association), he deeply believed that teaching holds supreme importance to society, and that teachers must be prepared in a way that supports and extends their professionalism. Symbolizing his commitment to this belief were his dual appointments—while Dean of Education, he also held the presidency of the Alberta Teachers' Association.

Even after retiring, he continued to work for teacher professionalism. Fred Enns talks about the LaZerte study on the status of the Canadian teaching profession, commissioned by the Canadian Teachers' Federation, and carried out after LaZerte's retirement from the University. "This was a landmark study," Enns recalls. "LaZerte did a lot of speaking about his findings and I attended a number of his lectures. I was impressed by many things about this study and his lectures but, most of all, by the obvious pride he had in the teaching profession."

Wally Worth describes Dr. LaZerte as the founder. "He was like a small

M. E. LaZerte

bulldog, dynamic and aggressive," says Worth. "Some people may even have said he was abrasive. He was full of enthusiasm for what he was doing."

We talked with several people who knew Dr. LaZerte well, and they all gave remarkably consistent descriptions of the man.

"In addition to all of his other positive characteristics, he was the right height," observes Myer Horowitz, poking fun at his own diminutive stature. "Pete Coutts introduced me to him, and in anticipation of my first meeting with someone whose work I had been reading for many years, I was very nervous. This may have clouded my memory, but I remember how nice it was to be able to look him right in the eye without straining my neck!"

"...He is a good example of the power of an individual as expressed through his personality and through his statements. This power seems to translate into physical terms, causing you to think he is bigger than he actually is."

Fred Enns describes Dean LaZerte as a person with "a reputation for being very abrupt. He was very strong and definite. He was not a very tall person, but he sure made up for it in presence. He spoke in rather clipped sentences. It was never 'Maybe this' or 'Maybe that.' He was very definite. He knew."

Wally Worth remembers Dean LaZerte as "very bombastic and intimidating. You walked very carefully around him as you did with Coutts. They were people with strong views and strong personalities. Deans were lifetime appointments. They had one heck of a lot of power. It was long before the days of staff selection committees. If there was a vacancy on the faculty, LaZerte hired whom he wanted to hire, and he did not have to go through a committee to do so."

John Paterson, recalling the years after Dean LaZerte's retirement from the University when he was a member and Chair of the Edmonton Public School Board, spoke of "the power which Dean LaZerte commanded through respect. He was respected for his ideas and for his consistent positions. You could predict on any issue what he would say and what stand he would take." In this regard, the Paterson view accords with those of his colleagues reported above, but on the matter of intimidation his recollection differed. He remembered Dean LaZerte as "intimidating to me, yes, because I knew that whatever topic we were talking about, he knew more than I did. He was intimidating that way, but certainly not in his manner."

One begins to form an image of Dean LaZerte as a distant, inflexible and authoritarian academic administrator. But this is not the complete picture, by any means. Wally Worth recalls several instances in which Dr. LaZerte showed a very different side.

"He was willing to bend the rules and regulations," Wally remembered.

"I was just out of the army and had decided that I wanted to be a teacher. The practice had been that any veteran who had attended normal school for one year would get credit for the first year of the B.Ed. LaZerte thought it was only fair that he would do that for anybody who was a veteran. Like many others, I got credit for one year of study for my military service."

Wally Worth also credits Dean LaZerte for initiating the faculty's practice of writing letters to students who had done well in their studies the previous year. "He went one step further and invited these students into his office to meet with him. I got lucky one year and received First Class standing, so I had an opportunity to meet him then."

Dean LaZerte stepped into the life of the young Wally Worth on a third occasion—this time to find him his first teaching position. "In those days, the Edmonton Public School Board was only hiring teachers with experience," Wally recalls. "There were a large number of students engaged in teacher education, and the school system was just starting to expand. Edmonton could pick and choose from a sizeable pool of beginning teachers. Similarly, in Calgary. LaZerte persuaded Ross Sheppard [Superintendent of Edmonton Public Schools] to hire three teachers who had not taught before. Beginners without experience. He further got him to agree that he would accept the nominations of the Faculty of Education to fill those positions. Fortunately, I was one of them. This story illustrates Dean LaZerte's clout in the field of education."

Dean LaZerte is remembered as an excellent teacher, but his methods also evoke some rueful recollections. Both Fred Enns and Wally Worth recall the LaZerte practice of administering a daily oral test based on the previous day's work. "That kept us on our toes," Wally says.

Fred Enns is more explicit. "He did a lot of lecturing. He spoke a good line and then his practice deviated from it. He emphasized to us on the first day of class that he did not expect us to memorize his lists of facts or to be prepared to give them back to him on the examination. He wanted us to read widely, to discover what the authorities in psychology were saying, and really become familiar with the field.

"The second morning he came in with a handful of file cards with a rubber band around them. As he walked in the door, he removed the rubber band, wound it around his forearm, and read off specific questions which we were required to answer. If you had not studied the notes from his lecture very carefully, you would not be able to answer the questions. We never challenged him on the discrepancy between what he had advocated and what he practised. You did not dare challenge him. Not as a student."

Fred Enns concludes his assessment of LaZerte as a teacher in this way: "His lectures were stimulating. He talked not only about psychology in a theoretical way, but he talked about his teaching experience as well. He talked about how a teacher could get on in a one-room school, and most of us knew a good deal about one-room schools at the time. He talked about developing a machine for teaching arithmetic. He was doing interesting things and he told us about them."

One gains the impression that Dean LaZerte exerted the great force of a dynamic personality. His was a big, bold and brash style of administrative leadership. One can understand that by 1950, when Dean LaZerte retired, the faculty was ready for a rest, or at least a change of pace.

The LaZerte years had been exciting. A great deal had been accomplished, and already the faculty's strong presence was recognized across the country. But these gains had been achieved at a cost. Instructors coming to the University from the provincial normal schools faced a very difficult adjustment. Many of them had not been prepared for careers as scholars. They weren't researchers; they were teachers, first, foremost and always.

Because their teaching skills and achievements were not always recognized by colleagues in other faculties, many of them understandably felt under-appreciated, even unwanted. Most were at an age when further study for advanced degrees and a new conception of their careers were not attractive prospects.

LaZerte, for all his strengths, would not have been particularly sympathetic or patient toward these concerns. His successor, Herbert Smith was.

"He had the right personality for that," Wally Worth recalls, "because he was not nearly as threatening a figure as LaZerte. He made people feel comfortable and at ease with him. He was a very sympathetic listener. He was a big man, smoked a pipe, spoke softly and moved slowly. He was a comfortable person to be around. Probably a little more reflective than LaZerte."

Herbert Smith served in the Dean's chair for the next five years. Worth calls him "the consolidator," in recognition of the skills he displayed in bringing the staff together and fostering an atmosphere of stability. When he left the position, the faculty was poised for a second stage of explosive, and often turbulent, growth.

HERBERT T. ("PETE") COUTTS: THE BUILDER (1955-1972)

Just as Yankee Stadium will always be known as "the house that Ruth built," the U of A's Faculty of Education is the house that Pete Coutts built.

The longest serving of all our Deans, Herbert T. (Pete) Coutts is the colossus in our mythology who stood astride the Education Centre for seventeen years. During his tenure as Dean, we built the south building of the Education Centre and planned Education North, which made it possible to consolidate the faculty in a single facility of exceptionally high quality.

Under Dean Coutts, we established our graduate programs, which defined the U of A as Canada's pre-eminent Faculty of Education, unchallenged for many years, and as a leader in the field of education worldwide. Dozens of outstanding educators eagerly joined our rapidly expanding academic staff. It was a time of unparalleled growth, energy and optimism.

Pete Coutts was the last Dean to be appointed without limit of term and without the selection committee and other participatory paraphernalia that now accompany the process. President Walter Johns simply got on the phone one day and said that he wanted him to become Dean of the Faculty.

Coutts was also perhaps the last of the Deans to feel obligated to present to the world a stern and gruff demeanor.

Fred Enns: "Pete tended to come across to students, especially students who were trying to manipulate the system, as being a very hard-nosed person to work with. That was not the case. I have seen him lean over backward, time after time, to help people get on the right road."

Myer Horowitz: "How did I first see Pete Coutts? A harsh touch, a cold touch, a sombre touch. But, oh my God, he was the world's biggest softy. There was so much concern, so much compassion, so much love, so much caring."

But could we imagine a Dean in the current era dealing with a young member of the academic staff in quite the way that Dean Coutts dealt with the young John Paterson?

Bob Patterson tells the story: "John received a gift from a student, a bottle of white rum which he placed in his office desk. Returning to his office after a weekend away from work, he found that the bottle was missing. John was enraged. He was really upset that somebody had pilfered the bottle from his desk. Off he went to the Dean's office, expecting to find Coutts eager to rout out the culprit. John told him what happened, whereupon Coutts looked up at him coldly and said, 'Dr. Paterson, are you familiar with the regulations of the University? You are not supposed to have alcohol on campus.' No sympathy at all!"

As John Paterson himself observes, however, "As I look back on this, it is interesting that while Dean Coutts had a reputation for being unapproachable, I would nonetheless feel that I could burst into his office to tell my story."

Gruff as he was, and sometimes abrupt in his relations with others, Coutts was nevertheless a civil and courteous leader of his faculty. Bob Patterson paints a vivid picture of the first few faculty meetings chaired by Dean Coutts, in the old Education Building (now Corbett Hall).

"There were a number of people on staff who had recently been hired from Great Britain, including people like Charles Anderson, John MacDonald and Brian Dockrell. Coutts really went out to find talented people and I think he succeeded in the main. Manoly Lupul was another new staff member who was inclined to engage in lively debate. Faculty meetings produced heated discussion, and Coutts was often the target of this small group of Young Turks. They could turn the most innocuous issue into something of worldwide significance. It was unbelievable! They would go after him as the Chair of Faculty Council and Dean of the Faculty. He had to take this whole crowd on almost single-handedly.

Herbert T. "Pete" Coutts

"He would get a little red and agitated. You knew there was something bothering him, but he would never lose control or composure. He would maintain a businesslike, serious manner. He was never critical or biased. He would absorb their abruptness and their confrontational tactics, and still show respect and regard for their work and accomplishments.

"And he held his own! That was very much a feature of him in these discussions. He could maintain the upper hand. In part, it was this ability that frustrated his adversaries."

Colleagues describe Pete Coutts as a dedicated and committed visionary with very high standards; as a hard worker, a superb organizer, a positive, and optimistic man; and as a practical, hands-on administrator. He was also a humanist, we're told, although he seldom laughed or even smiled.

Fred Enns: "Pete Coutts was a man of tremendous vision and commitment to that vision. He did more to give expression to the Alberta concept of teacher education than anybody else, and he did it well. He did it in our province and across the country through the Canadian Education Association. ...He promoted LaZerte's idea of teacher education as a university responsibility, with university standards, but also he promoted the importance of research in education."

Wally Worth: "There was no more determined or dedicated Dean than Herbert T. Coutts. He was determined that this Faculty of Education would become the premier faculty in Canada, and I think he achieved that. ...He also worked very hard to gain status within the University community for the Faculty of Education. He did it primarily by emphasizing what he used to refer to as the high-standards approach: high standards in terms of the kinds of students we turned out, high standards in terms of the staff that we appointed and high standards in terms of our demands on them for productivity and working with the field. He was the high-standards man."

Fred Enns: "Pete Coutts was a superb organizer and a very hard worker. Even though he was a great organizer, when he assigned a job to you, he stepped aside. He let you go ahead with it. ...He was first in the office and last to leave. ...He usually had a briefcase with him and it was full of work that he took home with him evenings and weekends. ...He had a portable dictation machine with him in the car and he would do dictation in spare moments."

Like M. E. LaZerte, Pete Coutts had firmly held and clearly articulated views of teacher education in the University. He once told us, "If all one wants to do in preparing teachers for schools is to give them methods for doing things, then the normal schools did a good job of that. ...But my idea of a teacher is something more than that. I want a teacher who has a background in the subjects he's teaching in both breadth and depth. If one is teaching English, one should have a rich program in English. ...And so for the other teaching areas. …All of this is not merely for the sake of the knowledge but to give [the teacher] more than a narrow blinker approach to teaching. …One can't justify … teacher education in a university unless one believes that the person who is to become the teacher is like a well—that when you dip one pail of water out of the well, there's a lot more water in it."

He continued, "I had certain fears that once colleges and faculties of education got themselves established in universities, they would tend to regard their professional studies as more and more important and academic studies as less and less important and they would move away from the things that made it possible for them to get started in the university setting."

Harvey Zingle tells two stories which illustrate Pete Coutts' complexity as a man and as a Dean. "Very early in my career," Harvey recalls, "I was appointed Coordinator of the Education Clinic. We reported directly to the Dean. It was intimidating—this person sitting on a pedestal and me going to see him. Yet I don't think I ever went in without getting what I asked for. Maybe I didn't ask for enough. I don't know. Sometimes I would get a lecture about you young guys expecting the world. In the old days, we had it tough. He would give me all the reasons why he couldn't do something and then he would do it!"

"It was really funny," Harvey continued. "I was sitting in the Dean's office one day and a junior Professor came in to ask for some money, and I was giving him this spiel about how we don't have the resources. 'You guys think I have pockets full.' Then it hit me: I am Coutts!"

Harvey's second story: "You've probably heard about Coutts' gruffness. His wife really made up for this. When new staff were hired, they were invited to his house, and she made you feel like she was your mother and that she cared. When Donna and I had our first child, Coutts and his wife came to our house with a little gift for the baby."

"There was this contrast—in his role sitting behind his desk in the Dean's office, and then here he is taking a personal interest in the family of a faculty member. The faculty was smaller, but it was no small thing for Mrs. Coutts to shop for a gift and then to take an evening to deliver the gift to our home. He had a faculty of seventy to eighty people, after all. They did that kind of gentle, warm, caring thing. I will never forget that. It was a very special thing for the Dean to come to the house with a gift for my baby."

Bob Patterson tells another story about seeking funds from Dean Coutts: "I had just come back from graduate school to rejoin the faculty, and I wanted to invite a historian to visit. I needed $50 to pay his travel. Calgary was paying the scholar to come there, and all we needed was the cost of ground transportation to bring him up to Edmonton for the talk. I asked Bernal Walker (his department Chair) and he said, 'No, I don't have it. We need to ask the Dean for it. You go over and ask him.' Off I went.

"Mrs. Cameron, his secretary, was a very generous and kind person. She and Dorothy Beckwith were in the outer office area when I arrived. They always made visitors welcome and were always kind to me. They said that I could just go in and see the Dean without an appointment.

"I knocked and entered. It was immediately obvious that I had interrupted him and that I had picked a poor time for this meeting. I hesitantly put forward my proposal and request for $50. No sooner had I completed my request than he began a very serious lecture on the shortage of funds and the failure of people like me to appreciate how tough conditions were in the faculty.

"I listened to this," Bob remembers, "and I found myself getting just a little upset. When he finished, I said, 'Look, all I want is $50. Is the answer yes or no?' I could not believe I had reacted to him in this manner. I was just a little perturbed that somehow I was getting dumped on with a lecture that was probably intended for someone else. Apparently I had crossed the threshold at the wrong time. He looked at me and said, 'Yes, you can have the $50.' I walked out. From that point on, our relationship was different."

Pete Coutts is remembered primarily for his leadership during a remarkable period of growth in the Faculty of Education. During his deanship, enrollments, faculty and facilities all expanded dramatically.

He played a key role in obtaining the multi-year grant from the Kellogg Foundation which led to the establishment of the Department of

Educational Administration. Its graduate programs won attention and acclaim from around the world. He led the faculty into the international arena with the Thailand Project. He was also an innovator, expanding our undergraduate program into the area of technical and vocational education.

In addition to all of these accomplishments, Coutts was a formidable scholar in his own right.

Myer Horowitz: "I didn't know what a dangling participle was until Pete Coutts circled a few in an early draft of my master's thesis for which he was one of the three examiners. His work on my thesis had a great impact on me, so much so that … . Well, let me put it this way. For my doctoral thesis, I have the bound final copy on my shelf. That is it. That is enough and I never thought of doing anything else. For my master's thesis, I have my penultimate draft, the draft that Pete Coutts went through, in just as prominent a position as my final bound copy."

Bob Patterson: "I spoke once to Bernal Walker [Bob's Department Head] about my nervousness and unease with Dean Coutts. During the first year of my appointment as a sessional instructor, I had another experience which increased my self-consciousness in his presence. Knowing that I might welcome the opportunity to earn a little extra money, Coutts arranged for me to prepare a summary statement of a collection of viewpoints reported at a major conference. I undertook the task and submitted a draft to him. It came back covered in red ink. It was probably the most embarrassing writing experience I have ever had."

"It had a profound effect on me, so much so that later, when I became a Department Chair, whenever I wrote anything to Dean Coutts, it was always in simple sentences. I made sure it was correct grammatically. I did not want him going through my correspondence with his little red pen. He might fault me for lack of style or eloquence, but I was determined to ensure he could not fault me for grammar, spelling or syntax."

"A lot of people did not know just how capable he was as an academic and scholar. He was so involved in his administrative assignments over such a prolonged period of time that he was not as appreciated as he deserved to be for his scholarly strengths."

Coutts could also be a man of action, who got things done. Many years ago, he told us a story which illustrates this side of his personality.

When Education South was first opened, the faculty shared the space with some other academic units. "One of the English Professors objected to the fact that all the lights on the floor were controlled from a master panel and that one couldn't turn the lights off in individual offices. I had communications by letter from him."

When the University's Building and Grounds Department could not find a practicable solution, Dean Coutts decided to take the matter into his own hands. "I had the bars from his fluorescent lights removed, installed a floor lamp which I borrowed from his department Head, and put a reading lamp on his desk 'courtesy of the Department of Industrial and Vocational Education.' I never heard anything more from him about lights."

In another conversation, Pete Coutts summed up his personal approach: "If I had to define my philosophical point of view, it would be a hybrid between pragmatism and idealism, if that is possible. On reflection, however, I seem to lean more toward a pragmatic point of view than any other. If a thing works, that's the direction to go."

Pete Coutts was a family man, and he saw the faculty and students as part of his extended family. Fred Enns, thinking back to his years as a graduate student, remarked, "Pete Coutts knew all of the graduate students and he looked upon us as colleagues, perhaps not as his equals, but certainly as colleagues and friends."

AN AFTERWORD

Leaders often give shape to the leadership positions they occupy. However, at a particular time, under specific circumstances, the leadership position may shape the leader.

Coutts and LaZerte led the faculty at a time when administrators were expected to be patriarchs. Each of them gathered together a community of men and women—the extended family—and led them in a manner which seems truly from another era. They could seem distant, aloof and authoritarian, yet at the same time they cared for their staff members in a highly personal way that we would now think of as quaint, and perhaps intrusive.

Because they were so defined by their positions, it's harder to know what they were like away from the job. Pete Coutts once made a very poignant admission to us, as he looked back on his deanship. Speaking almost as if to himself, he said, "There's a soft and gentle side to my nature that I had to hide for seventeen years."

What were these men like? At this distance, we must be satisfied with only a partial answer. However, thanks to this project, we have at least gotten to know them better.

THELMA DENNIS

Faculty Club Memories

THE FACULTY CLUB HAD ORIGINALLY been established as a male preserve, but by the time I arrived on campus in the fall of 1961, it was open to academic women. The Faculty Club on Saskatchewan Drive had yet to be built. Instead, members used a lounge in the old Students' Union Building (which later became University Hall).

For the next couple of years, my involvement in Faculty Club events was minimal. I occasionally visited the lounge or attended staff banquets, where we were entertained by Al Affleck, Al Forbes, Walt Gainer and Wilf Pilkington, to name a few, as they performed skits pertaining to University life. Because we had no suitable facilities, these events were held off campus at such places as the Windermere Golf Course or the Jubilee Auditorium (in the room which later became the Kaasa Theatre).

Somewhere during that time, some Faculty Club members decided to pursue the possibility of building a separate premises. They recorded their intent by signing a piece of brown cardboard (I have been told that it was torn out of a beer carton), which is still on display in the Club's lower bar lounge. Unfortunately, the document is undated.

In 1963, Club member Beth Empey invited me to become a member of the planning committee charged with the furnishing of a new building. The Club had successfully acquired the present Saskatchewan Drive site and hired the architectural firm of Rule, Wynn and Rule to design the building. The firm decided to use a scaled-down version of the Calgary Golf and Country Club, which it had designed a few years earlier. An undated photograph of the long-anticipated sod-turning ceremony can also be found in the lower bar lounge.

*In the spring of 1964, a sod-turning ceremony initiated the construction of the
Faculty Club Building on Saskatchewan Drive. Front, L to R: S. G. Davis, D. A. Baird,
J. Rule, J. Poole, J. G. Parr, R. S. Eaton, A. T. Elder, W. A. D. Burns, N. W. Howe.
Back, L to R: G. R. Davy, D. B. Scott, M. S. Cook, W. H. Angus, A. S. Knowler, R. C. W.
Hooper. (This identification is taken from Dr. Walter John's book, A History of the
University of Alberta 1908-1969.)*

Before long, I was regularly attending meetings of the Faculty Club's
planning committee. One of our key obstacles was financing, not only of
the building itself, but also the furnishings. At one particular meeting, we
were trying to figure out how to adequately furnish the building on our
limited funds. Murray Cook interrupted the discussion by saying, "We have
to go first class, or we won't be able to expand our membership."

A number of Edmontonians stepped forward to help with construction
costs. A plaque commemorating the official opening in November 1964,
gives recognition to them. For the furnishings, we decided to approach The
Bay, Eaton's, Woodwards and Sears for donations. Jim Parr, Richard Eaton,
Andy Elder, Lawrence Clegg and I met with store managers, and the result
was a hodge-podge of furnishings that had to be integrated with pieces

dating from the '50s from the Faculty Club Lounge in the Students' Union Building.

By the summer of 1964, the building was almost completed, and the furniture and fixtures were being delivered. As part of its contract, Rule, Wynn and Rule were to provide lighting fixtures. However, when Al Forbes and I opened the boxes containing the fixtures for the main dining room, we discovered that they were decorated with hideous metal flowers. I phoned Mr. Rule, the firm's senior partner, and told him that we simply could not accept them. There was dead silence on the other end of the line. Mr. Rule was not accustomed to having anyone question his judgement. Eventually, though, we did receive more suitable fixtures.

Back in the early '60s, liquor of any kind was still absolutely taboo on campus. However, by the time I became involved in the planning committee, the powers that be had already been convinced that this new facility should be allowed to serve alcohol.

We were still worried, however, about satisfying the Alberta Liquor Control Board, which had very strict regulations at that time. For instance, licensed clubs had to ensure that patrons consuming hard liquor were safely hidden from the view of innocent passers-by. Andy Elder, Club President in the summer of 1964, was very concerned that the donated draperies for the lower lounge were too sheer for ALCB standards. In the end, we chose to simply ignore the potential problem. Years later, the Club did add shrubbery and a low fence to make the building, including the patio, more private. These were desirable added features, whether part of ALCB regulations or not.

Once the Club opened, it took us awhile to find the right person to manage it. Our first manager couldn't understand why Faculty Club members were not in the club in the latter part of the morning drinking beer. After this false start, though, the executive hired Mrs. Dimple Barlow. Everyone thought she was irreplaceable until, of course, Mr. Peter Graf became the Club's manager.

By 1967, only three years after its opening, the Faculty Club was such a huge success that the executive decided to expand the building. Two extensions were added, one to the north and one to the south.

Upstairs, the north expansion doubled the main dining room, provided a serving area behind a wood-panelled wall and added the balcony. Downstairs, it allowed for an extended Saskatchewan Room. The south extension increased the bar area on the lower floor and created the Papaschase Room on the upper floor. Tony Fisher can be thanked for suggesting the name for the Papaschase Room, which honours the Cree Reserve that was located in what became southeast Edmonton, and the band's chief. The names Saskatchewan Room and Jasper Room were also chosen at this time to reflect Edmonton's history.

This major renovation also incorporated, among other things, a new office area for the manager, better cloakroom areas and, thanks to Don Scott, an elevator.

The Club's strong financial situation allowed us to redesign the interiors, adding new carpeting and new furniture (amazingly, the chairs we purchased for the main dining room are still used today). Shortly after, a sub-committee including Henry Kreisel and Al Forbes began selecting and purchasing paintings for the Club. The intent was to select works of artists associated with the University.

Under Peter Graf's management, the Club has continued to change and improve. Some of the original spaces remain, while others have disappeared to make way for improved facilities.

After serving on that early planning committee, I continued as a member of the house committee or executive until the early '70s. I have been able to contribute in a small way to the Club's success, and I have met many people from the larger university community, some of whom became personal friends.

Our Club is recognized as one of North America's most successful faculty clubs. We owe this reputation to the exceptional management of Mrs. Barlow and Mr. Graf, the input of the people who have served on executives and committees, and finally the support of members who have regarded it as "their" Club. Surely its success has far outstripped the expectation of those men who, over thirty-five years ago, signed that historic beer carton.

One person towers above all others for his contribution to the construction of the Faculty Club: Dr. Francis G. Winspear. Without his vision, generosity and hard work, the building likely would have remained a dream.

He backed up his vision with cash, donating $50 000 as a down payment and persuading George Steer and Gerald Heffernan to donate $15 000 each. He personally persuaded Mr. Alan Lambert, President and CEO of the Toronto Dominion Bank, to approve a loan of $200 000 for the project, even though it could not be secured by a mortgage (since the University owned the land). Finally (and this is no small matter), he almost single-handedly arranged the Club's liquor license, arguing the case before the Board of Governors, and then following through by meeting Premier Ernest Manning and Peter Elliott, Chairman of the Alberta Liquor Control Board.

The Club welcomes both the University's faculty and its professional non-teaching administrators, in contrast to the rigid separation that exists at most other Canadian universities. This policy, which wisely follows the lead of the Association of the Academic Staff of the University of Alberta (AASUA), has helped make the Faculty Club a resounding financial and social success over the years.

A. S. Knowler

ERIC GEDDES

The Foundation

IN 1978, DURING MY FINAL YEAR as Chairman of the Board of Governors, discussions commenced which would eventually lead to the formation of the Alberta Heritage Foundation for Medical Research ("The Foundation").

I originally agreed to serve on the Board of Governors at the request of Peter Lougheed, a close personal friend (and, like myself, an alumnus of the University). He maintained a close interest in the University, and we often discussed ways of enhancing its standing throughout North America.

Shortly after the Conservatives came to power in 1971, worldwide oil prices rose sharply as a result of the OPEC oil crisis. The province increased provincial oil royalties in order to claim a share of the windfall. The resulting revenues greatly exceeded the government's needs. Rather than placing the money into the operating budget, the government put a significant portion of it into the newly established Heritage Savings Trust Fund.

As the Trust Fund grew to unprecedented levels, the government was pressured to increase funding in many areas, including higher education.

At about the same time, leading Canadian academics were raising concerns about the erosion of medical research funding. Between 1970 and 1975, the number of researchers receiving support from Canada's Medical Research Council had actually dropped. In August 1974, the Canadian Society for Clinical Investigation, The Canadian Federation of Biological Societies and the Association of Canadian Medical Colleges issued a strongly worded joint statement entitled "Medical Research: The Immediate Need for Increased Funding."

Leaders in Alberta's medical research community brought the situation to Premier Lougheed's attention. Dr. Walter Mackenzie, former Dean of Medicine, was at the forefront of the consultation process which eventually led to "The Foundation."

Inflation was another immediate concern in those days, impacting on virtually every area of University expenditure. Price escalation in many areas outstripped the consumer price index, which was in double digits.

Premier Lougheed turned to a trusted and experienced senior bureaucrat, Dr. John E. Bradley, giving him the title of "Special Advisor–Medical Research." Jack Bradley, who, like myself, was a former Chairman of the U of A Board of Governors, played the leading role over the two years. Together with the Premier, he sought the advice of respected international scientists and consulted widely with Albertans in the government, academic and medical communities.

The Foundation adopted important guidelines that set the stage for its early success. It was decided that the Foundation would not provide operating funds for the Heritage scientists, but rather give them stipend support. This way, the scientists would be required to apply to national granting bodies and other sources for operating grants. This wise decision provided significant leverage to the funds provided by the Foundation.

After the Foundation's conceptual phase had been completed, the Premier exposed the proposal to wider discussions. On March 20, 1978, at a Government House dinner sponsored by the Premier, twelve prominent Albertans engaged in "a dialogue on a plan for medical research." In addition to Premier Lougheed and his special advisor, Jack Bradley, guests included Walter Mackenzie, Harry Gunning, Bill Cochrane, Lionel McLeod, Bernard Snell, Eric Geddes, Gordon Swann, Bert Hohol, Peter Macdonnell, Fred Mannix, Hoadley Mitchell and Tim Cameron.

Premier Lougheed opened the meeting by explaining that his government proposed to incorporate a Foundation through an Act of the Legislature, and to endow the Foundation with a grant from the Heritage Savings Trust Fund or from the General Revenue Fund. He then outlined the Foundation's proposed purpose:

- to establish and support a long-term program of medical research

- to provide research career opportunities
- to provide a long-term funding commitment
- to approve projects for funding
- to assist the development of a "Brain Industry"
- to provide a vehicle for public participation, by gift or otherwise, in the funding of medical research

Eric Geddes

He proposed that the Foundation be a non-profit public foundation, at arm's length from the government. It would approve all grants and awards, and account to the Legislature for its expenditures.

After a spirited discussion, the group warmly endorsed the concept and agreed that work should commence immediately to draft the Act of Incorporation and prepare legislation. The Premier asked me to provide input into the Foundation's implementation and planning.

When the Act establishing the Foundation was proclaimed, operations commenced on April 1, 1980. I was appointed as a Trustee of the Foundation for an initial term of five years and was re-appointed for a further term of five years ending in 1990. Throughout the entire decade, I had the privilege of serving as Chairman of the Board of Trustees. Dr. Lionel McLeod served as the Foundation's first President.

Looking back over twenty years, the Foundation has transformed medical research in Alberta:

- The AHFMR has granted more than $575 million to medical and health research since 1980.

- As of March 31, 1998, the original endowment of $300 million has grown to a market value of $975 million.
- AHFMR funding has helped Alberta's universities leverage federal funding, as well as non-government funding from charitable organizations and foundations.
- According to the last Annual Report, fifty-nine researchers in eleven different faculties at the three main universities have been offered awards in the form of salary support for three to five years, depending on the award category.
- The CERTAINTY of an endowment fund in perpetuity has relieved the research community from having to rely on annual budgetary allotments.
- A new emphasis is now placed on what is sometimes called "Wellness Research," which focusses on the detection and the prevention of diseases and the maintenance of healthy lifestyles.

Over twenty years ago, we dreamed of a province at the forefront of Canadian biomedical research. Thanks to the work of the AHFMR, those dreams have been substantially realized.

When I was teaching at the University of the West Indies (UWI) School of Education, I never seriously considered moving to Canada. In those days, individuals seeking academic positions overseas tended to apply to the United Kingdom or the United States, and if they thought about Canada at all, they would have considered McGill, the University of Toronto or Dalhousie. So when I received the first letter from the Department of Educational Foundations at the U of A asking whether I was interested in being considered for a position, I did not reply. After a few weeks, another letter arrived, so I replied, asking for some details.

As soon as my letter was received in Edmonton, I had a phone call inviting me to visit the University. An airline ticket was already at the Air Canada office in Kingston, Jamaica. When I came to Edmonton, I obviously wanted to find out more about the faculty and the University. But even more important to me was to assess

continued on next page

whether people at the U of A were as open as the Canadian educators I had dealt with over the years. Canadians had impressed me with their general willingness to work with others to solve problems.

I was not disappointed in my observations during the visit. I realized that with the internal support displayed by faculty members, the U of A would be an excellent place to develop a program in international education.

The first task was to introduce an international dimension to the faculty's existing programs. This was in 1969, when many young Canadians were interested in working with CUSO (Canadian Universities Services Overseas). We therefore developed a course for students who were planning to work overseas as teachers with CUSO. The course would introduce them to some of the realities they would face when teaching in developing countries.

The next step was to put together one of the best graduate programs in Education and Third World Development for students at the master's and Ph.D. levels. These became increasingly popular over the years. At one time, there were thirty-five full-time graduate students, about a third of whom were from Canada, with the rest mainly from developing countries.

In addition to their studies, the students formed their own club— the Club IDC (formerly Issues in Developing Countries)—which became a forum for stimulating interest in development issues among all students on campus. The Club has now been in existence for over fifteen years and continues to hold discussion sessions and presentations on human rights and other international issues.

In the early 1980s, the Faculty of Education established a Centre for International Education and Development (CIED). It aimed to attract funding for programs in international education, and at the same time to increase the number of international graduate students at the U of A. Between 1982 and 1992, the Centre received grants totalling about $6.25 million from the Canadian International Development Agency (CIDA), the International Development Research Centre (IDRC), the Canadian Commission for UNESCO,

continued on next page

the Canadian Department of External Affairs and the Alberta Department of Advanced Education.

In general, the U of A's involvement in International Education has been of great value not only to the developing countries in which projects were undertaken, but also to the Faculty of Education itself, in helping to broaden the outlook of the staff—an experience that becomes even more valuable with the development of multiculturalism in Canadian society.

M. Kazim Bacchus

NEIL B. MADSEN

Building a Department

I TOOK MY FIRST introductory course in biochemistry in 1948, during my third undergraduate year in Agriculture. After two more courses the following year, I decided to do an M.Sc. in the department.

My research on alkaline phosphatase, under the direction of Jules Tuba, was hardly earth-shaking. However, I did gain useful experience over two years and developed a taste for developing independent minor research projects. Further, Tuba was diligent in making his students write at least the first draft of all their papers and would work with the students on the revisions. Thus, he taught me how to write a scientific paper, a most important skill. I have seen too many Ph.D.s start their first job without ever having written a paper. They are in sad shape because writing a thesis is not an adequate preparation.

In 1950, the four staff members, seven M.Sc. students and five or six non-academic staff members regularly had tea and coffee together. Bruce Collier, Professor and Head of the Department, entertained us with his puns and Tuba with his anecdotes. Our social life revolved around the Department, with events at Professors' homes and picnics at Percy Beaumont's acreage. Percy was the senior technician responsible for the student laboratories, and he made a wicked punch with lab alcohol substituting for gin, measure for measure. Not surprisingly, this punch proved the undoing of more than one unsuspecting graduate student.

I went on to complete a Ph.D. with Carl Cori at Washington University in St. Louis, plus a post-doctoral year in the Oxford laboratory of Hans Krebs. Returning to Canada, I worked in the Microbiology Research Institute of Agriculture Canada, Ottawa, for five years.

In 1962, I learned that John Colter had been appointed the new Head of the Department in Alberta, with a mandate to expand. I applied at once and was interviewed during a trip home to see families. John and I hit it off and I was hired almost on the spot.

A year earlier, I had been interviewed for a position in Toronto. The incoming Head, Charles Hanes, named a figure for the salary, which was $200 less than my current salary in Ottawa even before an increment due that year, so I asked for the $200. His eyes glazed over and the subject was dropped, but I knew I would not be offered the job. A gentleman does not discuss money in Toronto, at least not at that time.

In contrast, I had the temerity to ask John Colter for $2000 more than my Ottawa salary, and he said he would try (and he did succeed). My friends in the East had warned me not to go to Edmonton because John had the reputation of being ruthless. Once I met him, I could see that this "ruthlessness" was really his dedication to building the best Biochemistry Department in Canada.

That same summer I had an employment interview with Dean Walter Mackenzie, who was doing much to turn a small backwoods medical school into a first-class health sciences centre. "Big Walt" as he was known, but certainly not to his face, was an impressive figure impeccably dressed in the most expensive suits in Edmonton, with the charismatic charm of a born leader. He told me that he was always glad to see Albertans return because he did not have to worry about them leaving after the first winter.

The Department had been in existence for forty years, but in 1962 Colter became only its fourth Head. Biochemistry was undergoing the kind of transition that seldom happens anymore, now that department Chairs usually serve only one or two five-year terms.

When I arrived, Jules Tuba had just transferred into Dentistry. Mary Spencer and Bruce Collier were still in the department but would leave shortly, Mary to Plant Science and Bruce to Clinical Pathology in the University Hospital. Both thrived in their new locations, with Mary, especially, continuing her distinguished career in plant biochemistry and training a number of outstanding graduate students.

In addition to Mary Spencer, Bruce had made two other excellent

H. Bruce Collier

appointments: Larry Smillie and Cyril Kay. They remained for the next thirty-some years and formed the core of our teaching and research program in protein structure and function, leading eventually to the renowned MRC Group in that area.

Of John's first four appointments, two failed to establish research programs at an acceptable level and were eventually required to resign after ample time and help had failed to rectify the situation. It is interesting that their inadequacies only became fully apparent long after they would normally have been granted tenure, but because they were on "soft" money, tenure was not an issue.

The third, Byron Lane, was an excellent scientist and lecturer in the field of nucleic acids. As a Torontonian, though, he never really felt at home in what he regarded as the raw West. For example, he once complained to me that he couldn't really drive in the countryside because the roads were all dirt. "What do you mean, dirt? They are all gravelled," I said in some puzzlement, for when I was a boy, even the main roads were really dirt with no gravel. When Byron got the opportunity, he returned to a position in the Biochemistry Department in Toronto (although he ended up complaining far more there than he ever did here).

I was the fourth appointment, but the Department failed to get rid of me until I reached the mandatory retirement age in 1993.

I have often been asked how John Colter managed to build the premier Biochemistry Department in Canada in the rather unlikely location of Edmonton. He strongly believed that excellent Canadian scientists would return to Canada if they felt they would find strong research support, good facilities and qualified colleagues. Fortunately, during the '60s, universities were expanding rapidly. There was plenty of money for Professors, facilities and extramural grants.

John took full advantage, constantly badgering Deans and Presidents for more positions, and then working hard to fill them with top people. If he felt he had a reasonable chance to gain one or two positions in the next budget, he would begin extensive recruiting a year ahead of time. He would bring candidates in for visits, allow the Department as a whole to identify the best and offer them jobs, conditional on budget success. Thus, we had first crack at the best candidates and seldom made mistakes. Departments who waited until the University budget was finalized had only a short time to fill new positions before the fall term and often found that the best recruits were no longer available.

Of course, we should also acknowledge the Government of Alberta's generous support in those years, which allowed us to make huge capital expenditures for buildings and equipment, and to expand the faculty.

Once you hire good people, you must help them get established. John, an excellent "grant swinger" himself, helped new staff members with their first grant applications. The resulting success rate was phenomenal. He tried to make sure that there were at least two people in each given area of research so that no one was isolated, even if this meant ignoring whole areas of traditional biochemical research. He kept teaching loads light, allowing ample time for research, and discouraged new specialized courses until at least two staff members demanded them.

This approach paid off in later years, as enrollments kept increasing while University funds became more scarce. By then, our research carried our teaching. Our excellent reputation enabled us to recruit high-calibre young scientists, who in turn were able to win grants to cover their own salaries. Thus, by the '90s, with only eleven University-funded positions (one less than in 1970) we had as many as thirty-one staff, the remainder on various forms of "soft money." These carried out their share of teaching so that the average load for all remained light.

To illustrate how much our research activity came to dominate in fiscal terms, for 1990-91 the Department received $1 995 000 from the University (0.97% of the total University budget), but attracted $9 486 000 in extramural research funding (11.8% of the total received by all departments). (From the 1990-91 Data Book, courtesy of Bill Bridger.)

During the 1960s, the Department developed a real esprit de corps for a number of reasons. We were all young, and we all faced the same perceived *enemies*. First, of course, there was the Eastern scientific establishment. Then there were the granting councils who, like figure-skating judges, made you serve your time and pay your dues before properly recognizing your merit. Finally, there was the University itself, especially the purchasing and personnel departments.

We were continually frustrated by the penny-pinching and obtuse procedures of the purchasing department. It seemed to take forever to obtain new equipment or even basic chemicals, even when (as was usually the case) it was "our" money, obtained through grants. Thankfully, the system has greatly improved since then.

The personnel department, then and forevermore, appeared to be headed by one dinosaur after another. This caused us endless trouble in hiring and managing non-academic staff, again, as in 1993, when seventeen were paid for from University funds, but seventy-six were paid for from extramural grants.

John always led the charge. A good hockey player in his youth, he behaved more like a coach than a Department Head. From his arrival in 1961 to his retirement in 1987, there was hardly a time when he was not embroiled in a fight with some President, Vice President, Dean or service department official. He used to come down to coffee and regale us with blow-by-blow accounts of the most recent contretemps.

Speaking of coffee, most staff decisions were made there, rather than in formal meetings. This was far more efficient; I have been on too many committees in my life, watching one person or other get on his hobby horse and ride it off at a tangent, to the intense irritation of everybody else. By constantly discussing departmental issues over coffee, John always had a pretty good idea of the departmental consensus.

It might be added that John was an efficient administrator who concentrated on larger matters, while letting others take care of the small details. Many of those details were left in the efficient hands of Laura Randall, the long-serving Administrative Professional Officer.

Laura took care of any vexatious problems with non-academic staff, right down to resolving personality conflicts between the department's two dishwashers. She administered an increasing number of larger and larger extramural grants, supervising a book-keeper, reconciling the accounts and making sure that the Professors did not overspend. She maintained many contacts within the network of administrative officers, assistants, secretaries and so on, who really ran the University, and always knew who to talk to if you wanted to circumvent official channels and actually get something done in a reasonable time.

She somehow also found time for other duties, serving as executive secretary for at least ten national and international scientific meetings hosted within the department, and designing and assembling departmental brochures and recruiting posters. She organized countless social events involving the graduate students and trainees, and enlivened them with her skits and cartoons, which spared no one. In all these tasks, Laura displayed charm, talent and tact. She deserves a large share of the credit for developing the department into a major academic and scientific force. At the same time, she made it a happier and more efficient place to work.

Life in an expanding department has its challenges, however. For instance, space was very scarce for new staff members. Bill Bridger ended up in a long, narrow, gloomy room in the Medical Building basement, with only one small, high window. When more appropriate space finally became available, we actually took Bill's old office and turned it into a dark room.

Fortunately, help was on the way in the form of the new Medical Sciences Building, for which planning began in the late 1960s. We managed to obtain two full floors, plus a reading room on the ground floor and a single staff lab on the fifth. Each staff member was assigned just over 1300 square feet, including an office. In general, offices were arranged on one side of the central corridor, with equipment and support labs opposite.

While the building exterior wins no architectural prizes, it is in fact a highly efficient research building. Our staff labs were all identical in size, with support labs sized according to need. We laughed at the Anatomy Department, which insisted on designating space in descending amounts for Full, Associate and Assistant Professors. What was supposed to happen on promotion through the ranks?

Initially, our space (approximately 55 000 square feet) was far more than we needed. Our empty staff labs, however, helped attract many talented new staff members over the years. Slowly, over the '70s and '80s, the labs all filled up, justifying what had seemed an overly generous allocation. Undoubtedly the new facilities constituted the greatest contribution the University made to our Department.

When we moved into the building in June 1972, our excitement was dampened by the knowledge that one of our best young staff members would not occupy his new lab. Chris Smith, a very talented scientist and excellent mountain climber, had been killed by an avalanche on Mount Edith Cavell the previous winter. We named our reading room in his honour.

After our move, it became obvious that we would no longer be able to rely on the University budget for expansion. We began to consider other possibilities. Larry Smillie and Cyril Kay, together with Michael James, began to plan for an MRC Group in protein structure and function. I was on sabbatical in Oxford at the time, and had an encounter with a future member of that group, although neither of us knew it then. At a lunch one day, I was introduced to a Harvard Professor named Brian Sykes, who was on sabattical at Bristol. He asked me where in Canada I was from, and I said "Edmonton." He instantly got a faraway look in his eyes, which I had by that time come to recognize as a sign of total non-comprehension. I tried to help him, "It's in Alberta; ah, that's north of Montana." "Yes, I know," he replied. "I grew up there and graduated in chemistry from the U of A."

A world-famous innovator in the field of Nuclear Magnetic Resonance, Brian was only one of the top people we were able to attract to the project. Another was Robert Fletterick, a protein crystallographer who became my chief collaborator for five years during the 1970s. When he left, his place was taken by Wayne Anderson. Bob Hodges, a native of Saskatchewan who had taken his Ph.D. under Larry Smillie, brought his energy and practical approach to the group. His work in peptide chemistry resulted in more than one commercial venture and several technological awards. Michael James, our other protein crystallographer, has established an enviable international reputation, and his laboratory has completed more protein structures at the atomic level than one can easily remember.

The six members of our MRC Group became the nucleus of our most conspicuous area of research. They also strengthened the department as a whole, generously sharing their equipment and taking part in valuable collaborations.

By 1980, we had reached another budgetary plateau, with a total staff of seventeen, twelve of whom were on the departmental budget. Our department was relatively well off, but the clinical departments in both Edmonton and Calgary had never been provided with sufficient staff to allow for adequate research, in addition to teaching and patient care. Alberta's two medical schools seemed doomed to remain second-rate compared to McGill and Toronto.

The Alberta Heritage Foundation for Medical Research changed that, possibly forever. The government decided to set aside a portion of petroleum revenues for medical research and designed, in collaboration with the medical community, an excellent system for administering the fund. Providing major equipment grants, salaries for outstanding scientists, training stipends for students and post-doctoral fellows, as well as special programs to help clinicians establish research programs, the AHFMR transformed Edmonton and Calgary's medical schools into world-class institutions. It may well prove to be the greatest legacy of the Lougheed government.

For our department alone, the AHFMR supported eight to ten new positions during the '80s and '90s. The Fund allowed us to work more closely with clinical departments, forming interdisciplinary research teams to address vital clinical problems at the most sophisticated level. The pioneering days are over. Alberta has taken its place among the leading research centres in the world.

Having taken part in this exciting, decades-long journey, I find this most gratifying indeed.

Neurology here in Alberta goes back to Dr. Egerton Pope, the University's first Professor of Medicine and first Director of Medicine of the University Hospital. In 1923, he was recruited from the University of Manitoba, where he had been an Assistant Professor. Dr. Pope gave the first formal lectures in neurology at the U of A.

The province's first neurosurgeon, Dr. H. H. Hepburn, came to Edmonton in 1932, and also became involved in teaching. One of the students in neurology in the early 1930s was Ken Thompson. After becoming the Department of Medicine's first resident, Ken went to London and spent some time attending sessions at the National Hospital, Queen Square and the Maudsley Psychiatric Hospital. In 1939, he joined the Navy, and for the duration of the war served as a specialist in neuro-psychiatry.

In the mid-1930s, Dr. Ken Hamilton had joined Dr. Pope in teaching neurology. Dr. Hamilton also enlisted in 1939, but returned to the University late in the war because of the great demand for clinical teachers. Universities were short on teachers, and the Forces needed more medical officers, so the Federal Government of the day arranged for teachers to be sent home.

After the war, Ken Thompson also came back to Edmonton. He took over teaching neurology and continued until I arrived on the scene in 1957.

In the late 1950s, the U of A's Department of Medicine graduated approximately fifty students per year, and the total University population was about 5000. Although the medical school was less than half the size of today's, the standards of teaching and patient care were as good as any I had seen in the U.K. There were only four full-time members in the Department: Don Wilson, Bob Fraser, Alan Gilbert and Lionel Mcleod. A large cadre of part-time staff formed the mainstay of the teaching.

George Monckton

Personal Reflections

Looking back,
looking within...

A. RICHARD MORGAN

Humanity in the Sciences

QUAECUMQUE VERA is a fine motto for a university, but even a U of A Vice President once told me that he tossed it off lightly at parties, to show academic brilliance, but had no idea of its meaning! Few people nowadays have a classical background, so it's time we translated the motto to "Whatsoever things are true" or "Whatsoever the truth."

It comes from the beautiful list that St. Paul writes to the Philippians (Chapter 4, verse 8), things we should think about to be civilized, truth being the first. If we could abide by this list, humanity would reach its apogee!

Now, what has this got to do with science? I would submit that science without humanity is a lost cause.

In 1969, I joined the Biochemistry Department as a rather nervous new Assistant Professor, having never taught (or attended) a course in biochemistry.

I had a Ph.D. in chemistry, under a great imaginative mentor at the U of A, Dr. Ray Lemieux. In the States at the University of Wisconsin, Madison, I had another great mentor, Dr. H. Gobind Khorana. He had made the metamorphosis from chemistry to molecular biology, really a branch of biochemistry. He obtained the Nobel Prize for his part in solving the genetic code: how DNA codes for protein (via RNA). Thus, I felt at times split between two worlds, and my first few years at the U of A were taken up completely by getting a research group going, teaching and avoiding administration.

Our Chairman, Dr. John Colter, took the weight of administration on his own broad shoulders, making sure it took none of our time. We were a small department, twelve and growing, and Dr. Colter was a father figure to the whole "family," constantly encouraging and humourous. We all spent New Year's Eve together, and about half the staff would go on hiking trips with visiting Professors. Dr. Colter called the newest members of the department "bright-eyed bushy-tailed young Turks." There was a great deal of collaboration amongst the staff.

However, inevitably with growth, you cannot know all your colleagues so well. As research became more sophisticated, it also became more expensive. Grant money hasn't grown at the same rate as the number of people hired to do research, and in the '90s, competition has become brutal.

I don't wish to sound as if it has all gone downhill. It has not. Smaller groups within the department, such as the protein and lipid and lipoprotein groups, have done very well. However, the expansion of knowledge has led to ever more specialization.

We are in some danger of becoming technocrats rather than scientists. By this, I mean a scientist should have a broad overview, extending beyond his specialty. When disciplines merge, they often give rise to really new advances in theory and concepts. Perhaps in the future, we will need renaissance people, put less politely, jacks of all trades and masters of none. Change is inevitable and we are challenged by it.

To get back to our motto, scientists have a habit of thinking they "know" the truth. I cannot enter into all the evidence against that, but most scientists who have thought about it enough agree we never know the "absolute truth." For example, Newton's laws, in their exactness, gave science almost the potency of a religion. Although Newton's law of gravitation is used by NASA to time satellites to fractions of a second in their orbits, it is an illusion to think the law is exact. Relativity, as well as quantum theory, quashed that.

So many things are unintuitive; that mass decreases velocity (that's why nothing can go faster than light, which is massless); that at speeds near the speed of light velocities are not additive. These are the sort of things students don't learn in class.

The situation is worse in the biological sciences because of the incredible complexity and chaotic nature of the subject. Laws are only found within restricted domains. However, great advances have been made and new techniques such as cloning, whether human or animals, will force us to consider entirely new ethical problems.

By telling one personal story, I hope to illustrate the science-human continuum. The event involved cultural differences and the nature of truth.

A Vietnamese student whom I supervised, *N*, came to see me, obviously miserable. His grades had dropped dramatically, and he said he could not study well. After twenty-five years of teaching, I knew that students often wanted to talk about their problems. *N* and I had got along well, and so I asked him if he had personal troubles he'd like to discuss.

He said "No" at first, but then came back into my office. His father had left his mother for a twenty-three year old, and according to their culture, the mother was at fault, or else why would her husband have run off? As a result, the local community had ostracized her and her two sons. The husband/father refused any contact with the family, apparently because his new wife was afraid he'd go back. *N* was in deep despair. He didn't even have a summer job.

Fortunately, I had some funds to do a summer research project. His first experiment failed, and I noticed he'd changed the protocol. *N* replied that he'd read in his textbook it should be done that way, to which I replied the textbook was wrong. I could see fear in his eyes as he insisted, "It is impossible for a textbook to be wrong."

This precipitated another crisis for *N*. He had the concept of absolute truth from his upbringing, and he needed this now—particularly with the disintegration of his family. My heart went out to him as he despairingly asked, "What then can I believe?"

I told *N* that this was the most important of questions, and there was no clear answer. However, he would understand better after four months of research in my lab. *N* never did ask again, but I had a wonderful supportive group, and I watched him grow in confidence and happiness during the summer. He discovered that research was a human endeavour; that a 100-year-old textbook would not be very useful now, nor would we recognize one 100 years from now.

N is now in the States, doing very well in a biotechnology company and recently visited Edmonton. He saw his father to say he'd forgiven him, and that he'd always be his father. It reminded me of Archbishop Tutu's visit, and his "truth and reconciliation" committee.

N and I are now firm friends, and I feel I learned more from him than he from me. The major lesson for me was to be more open and compassionate for students, especially those from different cultures. One also has to show one's own vulnerability. We need more humanity in everything we do. At universities, surely, we should be leaders in this. But are we, especially when the going gets tough?

One last point on science: Richard Feynman, the twentieth-century icon on Quantum Physics, wrote quite simply, "We must, incidentally, make it clear that if a thing is not science, it is not necessarily bad. For example, love is not science. So if something is said not to be science, it does not mean there is something wrong with it; it just means it is not science."

Quaecumque Vera!

In 1953, Alberta's reported polio cases skyrocketed to 1033, from a yearly average of eighty-one. The epidemic was handled at the Royal Alexandra Hospital by volunteer physicians from throughout the city, who responded without mention of payment or keeping track of the time involved. Likewise, nurses and orderlies freely put in extra hours without pay, sometimes working double shifts, deeming it a privilege to help.

Physicians should give a proportion of their efforts to help those in need, or to teach those who are learning, without expectation of payment. This was part of both the tradition and the responsibility of being a doctor. There was also a challenge and a venture about this epidemic. We still see this spirit in the medical volunteers who fly to Sudan, Bosnia and to the sites of earthquakes and other disasters.

Brian Sproule

ROBERT MACBETH

Reminiscences of an Alumnus

MY PERSONAL AND INTIMATE association with the University began in 1938 when I registered as a freshman in the pre-medical program. That was just twenty-five years after the first medical student enrolled at the University of Alberta, and only thirteen years after the first medical degree was granted.

My unofficial contact goes back even further because my father, a doctor in Edmonton, used to have the interns from the Royal Alexandra Hospital over for dinner on Sunday evening. On these occasions, I kept very quiet, while absorbing as much as I could of the impressive doctor table talk. Being in the presence of those learned interns was indeed a heady experience.

I spent seven years at the University as a student and intern, and twenty-three years on staff, including eighteen years as a full-time academic surgeon.

I am told that as one gets older, one forgets recent events, while events long past stand out in vivid relief. By that criterion, I am not yet old, since I have few clear memories of life as a medical student in the late 1930s and early 1940s. However, it was not the carefree student life about which one usually reads.

A devastating war was in progress. Although we were placed in the army for our last two undergraduate years, to ensure the continuation of our studies, we felt at best uncomfortable, and at worst somewhat cowardly, for being protected when our high school friends were serving overseas. In that atmosphere, the public did not look kindly on student highjinks, so we were careful to keep a low profile. When the top did blow off from time to time, we made sure that the setting was as far from public scrutiny as possible.

I recall medical school in wartime as a pretty serious adventure. However, the pressures on us as students were minimal compared to those placed on the faculty. Everyone who could pass the physical examination graduated from medical school into the armed services, and virtually all the physicians who would normally constitute the junior faculty joined up. Consequently, the medical education of those of my generation was dependent on very few not-all-that-young faculty. Some of them carried crushing teaching loads.

On behalf of those who attended university between 1939 and 1945, I should like to record our gratitude to these teachers: Ralph Shaner, "Bert" Rawlinson, "Johnny" Macgregor, John Scott, Fulton Gillespie, H. H. Hepburn and a handful of others. We were a class of only thirty-six and they became not only our teachers, but our role models and the object of our admiration.

My teachers and associates at the University of Alberta helped instill and reinforce some of the personal priorities that have shaped my life. I would like to focus on a few of these.

I was discharged from the army following an undistinguished period of service in Canada which consisted largely of an exciting sojourn in the Arctic as the medical officer to Exercise Musk-Ox. I found myself a civilian in Montreal eager to commence my surgical training.

In those days, there were only two surgical training programs in Canada, the Toronto "Gallie" course and the McGill Diploma Course in Surgery. I applied to both and was unceremoniously rejected. What to do?

I wrote to Dr. John Scott, my Professor of medicine, seeking advice. He was able to arrange for me to do research with Dr. J. B. "Bert" Collip. Research in endocrinology seemed very remote from my ambition to become a surgeon, but I reluctantly accepted.

Even though I had a superb eighteen months with Dr. Collip, my frustration continued the following year when both McGill and Toronto rejected my applications again.

Very depressed about my prospects of ever becoming a surgeon, I sent another letter to Dr. Scott. I will never forget his response. He wrote back,

"As long as you are happy and productive at what you are doing, don't worry about how long it takes. You will have lots of time in your life to practise surgery." How very right he was.

With considerably more resignation to my fate, I spent another year teaching anatomy at McGill with the memorable Professor C. P. Martin. Later still, when I was finally on the McGill surgery course, I remembered Dr. Scott's advice and "blew" another year with Professor Ian Aird at the British Post-Graduate Medical School in London.

When my wife and I went to London, I was the only person on the surgical program ever to do so. Everyone else who took "a year away" went to the United States. However, my surgical teachers from Alberta, Dr. Gillespie and Dr. Hepburn, supported my own contention that a year in England would be more generally broadening and that, in any case, one would likely be learning surgery all the rest of one's life from Americans.

I now look back on those three-and-a-half years, which were "wasted" in terms of fulfilling my training requirements, as among the most rewarding and pleasurable in my life. They were also remarkable examples of serendipity in that they opened so many doors to exciting and rewarding experiences and even second careers later in life.

We can so easily become too focussed on reaching our primary goals. In the years following the Second World War, the Department of Surgery frequently hosted distinguished clinical surgeons and surgical scientists from around the world. Often they would offer to take one of our trainees for a year. It never ceased to amaze and depress me to see trainees turn down such exciting opportunities simply because it would add a year to their training.

"As long as you are happy and productive at what you are doing, don't be afraid to accept exciting deviations from your primary career path and don't be unduly concerned about how long such deviations may take" is a bit of my medical school heritage which I have adopted and which has stayed with me all my life.

My second vignette is very different. It involves Dr. D. C. Ritchie, a friend and associate, an Alberta graduate, an Edmonton obstetrician and gynecologist on the faculty of the University of Alberta, and the holder of many offices associated with his Alma Mater. Doug eventually contracted cancer of the prostate with multiple metastases to bone. However, by virtue of aggressive medical care, including chemotherapy, he lived for something like three years after diagnosis of his disease.

I recall thinking how awful his situation must be, almost always in pain and forced to take treatments that made him terribly ill at intervals. That was surely no life at all.

However, the last time I visited him in hospital, not long before his death, he said, "You know, I am so very grateful for these last few years. For the first time, I have really sorted out my priorities and I am able to give more of myself and my time to Kathleen and the children than I was ever able to do before. These have been good years, very good years."

At the time, I could not really believe what I heard, but the years since then, eight spent as the Chief Executive Officer of the Canadian Cancer Society, have again and again reinforced what Doug was saying. I have now heard the same testimonial over and over from people of all ages, both sexes and from all walks of life. Not everyone reacts in this way. However, enough do that we would be well advised to listen.

Even though physicians must deal on a daily basis with the issue of mortality, they seem to be among the least prepared to face their own mortality. Further, I suspect that physicians who spend so much of their time and of themselves dealing with the ills of their patients are among the most negligent in putting their own house, and their own priorities, in order.

What a tragedy it is that this realization comes almost exclusively to the critically ill and those facing death. It is even more tragic that, in health, so many of us seem incapable of taking time to establish our priorities. Surely, we must establish our lifetime priorities now. To do so does not mean the adoption of a hedonistic and self-centred existence. Rather, this type of understanding leads us to do more with and for one's family and friends. It is to live one day at a time and to savour it to the fullest. Patients have told me that this attitude also gives them a heightened awareness and appreciation of little pleasures, the sensation of snow gently falling on one's face or the enjoyment of magnificent music.

Knowing and believing all this, I still find it hard to practise the philosophy on a daily basis when I am healthy, but I am trying. If we listen to what the seriously ill tell us about life, it will make our own lives much more worth living.

My third observation I first encountered during my time as a faculty member. I cannot now remember the exact source, and suspect that the colleague who passed it on to me was not the originator. In any event, this simple statement has stimulated a great deal of thought in me over many years: "Freedom is the availability of alternatives."

In the course of a lifetime, I have met countless students and physicians who feel trapped. Perhaps a physician may feel compelled to stay in a specialty when he or she would prefer family practice, or vice versa. Perhaps a student or physician feels it would be preferable to get out of medicine altogether. In most of these cases, individuals believe, for financial or other reasons, that there are no viable alternatives and that change is therefore impossible. Loss of freedom is a most incapacitating disease.

I have always had alternatives. Early in my career, as I have mentioned, I can take no credit for voluntarily planning for alternative career choices. However, those years of initially unwanted training qualified me for an exciting career in academic surgery.

Later, I decided to resign as Chairman of the Department of Surgery (after fifteen years). At age fifty-five, with tenure (although I have trouble with that concept), it would have been far easier for me to stay on in a full-time position. However, to me that would have meant forfeiting my freedom.

I was convinced that challenging alternatives would be available, and they were. First, I became a medical educator at Dalhousie University and then moved on to become an administrator with the Canadian Cancer Society and the National Cancer Institute of Canada.

When I reached the age of mandatory retirement, I looked forward to it with immense anticipation. Although I had not specifically prepared myself for it, I believed that many rewarding vocations and avocations still awaited me. A lifetime interest in medical history led to a wonderful four-year part-time administrative job with the Hannah Institute for the History of Medicine. In addition, an exciting opportunity presented itself to serve with the International Union Against Cancer as a volunteer in public education.

I have never been let down by my conviction that alternatives will always be available to those who prepare themselves for them and are willing to accept them. This principle has provided me with one of life's most precious gifts: freedom.

I will end by addressing a more general, even political priority. It, too, is deeply rooted in my time at the University of Alberta.

Early in my career, I sometimes wondered if those of us who attended medical school at the University of Alberta during the war were scientifically disadvantaged since the teaching staff was small, grossly overworked and contained the inevitable mixture of stimulating, informed teachers, and those who were considerably less so.

However, those years taught us two pearls of great value. One was humility. None of our teachers posed as being the foremost authority on a subject. Instead, they showed us that there was a great big exciting world of medical science out there for the taking and that we, through reading and study, could make it ours.

The second was an abhorrence of the parochial. At the University of Alberta, we were taught that medicine is a universal art and science and that to become good doctors, we should not look only to our Alma Mater, but observe widely and choose the best. In some medical schools, students are actually led to believe that their Professors have all the answers and that there is no need to search further afield.

If my abhorrence of parochialism was kindled as an undergraduate, it was fanned into an intense personal flame during my years as a faculty member under Walter Mackenzie, Canada's pre-eminent international surgical statesman.

Walter taught me that one best serves one's own department by assuring a strong medical school; that one best serves one's medical school by assuring a national consortium of strong medical schools; and finally, that one best serves Canadian medicine by fostering the advancement of medicine on a global level. He taught me that to try to develop a local centre of excellence at the expense of the national good was short-sighted and self-defeating.

I have had the great good fortune to live in four Canadian provinces and to visit the rest of this country. As well, my University of Alberta connections have led to extensive foreign travel and membership in international organizations. These experiences have instilled a deep love for this country as a whole, and faith in a world fellowship of nations. I am convinced that the common people, the world over, wish to live in harmony and to work together to create a better world. I may be dreaming, but I believe that these objectives are still attainable if we can overcome our present state of mind.

My years with my Alma Mater have left me a legacy of awesome proportions. On the personal side, my teachers and colleagues have taught me not to be too concerned with the speed of one's progress towards one's ultimate objective, as long as the task at hand is meaningful and fulfilling. They have shown me, sometimes by providing cruel examples, that now, and not tomorrow, is the time to sort out life's priorities. Finally, they have provided a window on an exciting world by demonstrating to me that freedom is nothing more than the availability of alternatives.

Even more important is the humility and abhorrence of the parochial which I have seen exemplified by teachers and colleagues at the University of Alberta. We can indeed rise above our institutional and provincial loyalties.

Our motto, *Quaecumque Vera*—Whatsoever things are true—goes on to exhort us to "think on these things." As alumni, we can do ourselves a great service by reflecting on our personal, organizational, national and global priorities and then putting our houses in order.

***Editor's note:** This article was adapted from a piece that appeared in IATROS: The University of Alberta Medical Journal, Vol. 10, pp. 24-28, 1995-96.*

WILLIAM ZIEGLER

Why?

FOREWORD

THIS IS A PROJECT I've had in mind for many, many years—so long that I've had lots of time to think about it. The plain fact is I'm grateful for being here and for being "me." Like all others, my life has had its ups and downs, but I wouldn't trade it for the life of anybody else.

I've had lots of time to think of the ancestors who bred me, directly or indirectly. I would love to have known them back over these 359 years. And, then, there is the wonder of what's ahead for the next 359 years—the year 2358. Ah well!

I want to thank my son, Rod, for his help in typing these sheets. He's been wonderful and so patient. His reward will be to have this story to think about when he reaches my age.

INTRODUCTION

"Who am I?"

"Where did I come from?"

"Why am I here?"

These questions have permeated much of my adult thinking. We know so very little of our world and even less of our universe. Yet, we are magnificent beings of exactitude. Otherwise we could not exist. Who created us? And for what purpose?

I'm neither a philosopher nor a theologian, but I have pondered these great questions for much of my adult life in an effort to obtain some understanding.

I have read Stephen Hawking's fine book, *A Brief History of Time*, but find my feeble mind cannot grasp the significance of our world or our universe. I believe that is for someone who can communicate with the mind of God!

I must be content in studying my past. I started this some fifty years ago when I was in Germany, the land of my forebears. More recently, I managed to trace my ancestry back to my great-great-grandfather, Georg Christoph Ziegler (born 1787) and thence back to his great-great-grandfather, Georg Wensel Ziegler (born 359 years ago in 1640).

For this article, though, I'll stick to presenting details of my own background—a privilege I take for posterity and which might be helpful to my son, Rodney.

MY LIFE

I am William Smith Ziegler, commonly known as Bill.

I was born in Calgary, Alberta, on April 5, 1911, and lived at 813-14 Avenue West. I attended Connaught Public School and CCI (Central Collegiate Institute) High School in Calgary, and was a member of Grace Presbyterian Church.

After my father died in 1925, my mother and I moved to Edmonton, to the home of my Uncle George, a CPR engineer who worked out of Field, B.C. We lived with his sister, my Aunt Maggie, a lovely lady who was most kind to us. In Edmonton, I attended Strathcona High School until 1928, when I was in Grade 11.

That autumn, I went harvesting along with two friends to the Claresholm area of Alberta. That was my first experience in "the school of hard knocks."

I returned to Edmonton as a man of means, with no less than $125 in my wallet! I found that I had a job waiting for me. My brother had been working with the Alberta Wheat Pool and had gotten me hired as the office boy at $60 a month.

The following spring, 1929, I found a job with the city assessor's office. I worked at the South Side office for three years. I quit in 1932 to become a lifeguard and swimming instructor for the summer.

With an invalid mother to support (although she was well looked after by Uncle George and Aunt Maggie), I needed to find another job for the winter. I figured that the boys who worked on the highway survey crews would be heading back to university and that there would be vacancies. So I applied, stressing the fact that I had experience—which I did not.

Within three years, I had saved the princely sum of $300 and decided to enroll in Engineering at the U of A. Because I did not have my Grade 12, it was a five-year course instead of the usual four.

I knew that $300 would not see me through the year, but thought that if I had to leave, I could at least say that I had been to university. I soon found that there were plenty of part-time jobs available, however. I took on all I could, starting as assistant in the chemistry lab.

Mathematics was my weak point since I had been out of school for seven years. I had to plug at it pretty hard, but soon became so good at it that I began tutoring at fifty cents per hour per student. This wouldn't have helped much, but before long my class had grown to nearly twenty, and at fifty cents each, it added up to a lot of money.

Since the age of fifteen, I had been in the Canadian militia with the Artillery. By 1939, I had achieved the rank of Captain. When war was declared, I had a frightful decision to make. I had four years of university under my belt, with just one more to go, and my marks were excellent. Should I turn my back on my education, or on my battery, which was going to war?

I made the decision and volunteered. I have never, ever regretted it!

I enlisted on September 4, and in January 1940, went to England as the Battery Captain of 61st Field Battery, which became part of the Eighth Army Field Regiment. I was promoted that September and became Brigade Major, Royal Artillery, Third Divisional Artillery of the 3 Canadian Division.

I had to go back to Canada to join the Division, which had just been formed. We served at Debert Camp in New Brunswick which had just been opened for us. I hear now, recently, that it has just been closed.

In England I had served under Colonel Brownfield, commander of the Eighth Army Field Regiment, and now I was to serve under him again as Brigadier Brownfield, the CRA (Commander Royal Artillery) of 3 Canadian Division. He is deceased now, but I cannot commend him enough. He was a wonderful gunner and a great man.

The 3 Canadian Division returned to England in 1941 for a great deal of training.

In 1942, I was assigned to attend the Camberley Staff College, which had the reputation of being the world's greatest staff college. Because of the war, their two-year course had been condensed into four months. It was tough. Real tough. We had to study, study, study.

A friend of mine told me, "Don't worry, Zig. There are two hundred people on the course but only ten Canadians. If you can just beat the other nine Canadians, you've got it made."

I didn't come out on top. I was second. Dan Spry led me. He was Royal Canadian Regiment and later became a Major-General commanding a division.

On graduating, I was promoted to Lieutenant-Colonel as GI-RA First Canadian Army. There, for the third time, I came under Brigadier Brownfield, who by then was BRA (Brigadier-Royal Artillery) of First Canadian Army.

At the end of May 1943, I was appointed to command 13 Canadian Field Regiment of 3 Canadian Division. I knew this regiment as I had earlier been Brigade Major RA of the formation. Unfortunately, I only enjoyed this command for seven months, during which time we were doing intensive assault training for the imminent invasion of Europe.

That December, I was promoted to Colonel and became general staff officer "training and staff duties" at Canadian Military Headquarters. There I worked under Brigadier Penhale, a gunner of the First World War and a great colleague of my idol, Brigadier Brownfield.

In February 1944, I was promoted to Brigadier, to be Commander Royal Artillery (CRA) First Canadian Division, which was by then fighting in Italy. I joined my division at San Vito on the Adriatic, south of Rome. They had been on the line in static positions for several months since the battle of Ortona.

By March 1944 we were told to leave our static positions and move to a central Italian area near Campobassa, where we would train for one month to once again become efficient in "fire and movement." I took on my new role with great gusto. After months of inactivity, the troops badly needed this training, and I was most happy to give it to them.

We then started the advance north, up Italy. We fought several battles, including the Gustav Line in the Liri Valley, near Casino. About May 19, we reached the Hitler Line. It was considered impregnable, on a high ridge with good command of the area to the south, where we were. As part of the British Eighth Army we, First Canadian Division (commonly called the Assault Division), were given the task of attacking the Hitler Line.

It was a tough project. The line stretched over four miles from the left, at Pontecorvo, to the Aquino airfield. The Germans had dismounted 105 MM guns from tanks and put them into the line. The place bristled with machine guns and anti-tank guns, all manned by crack German troops.

My staff and I took over a dugout, thirty feet underground, which had been left behind by the retreating Germans. My boss, General Chris Volks, GOC First Canadian Division, occupied a second dugout connected to ours by a passageway. For the next seventy-two hours, my staff and I drew up the assault plan, the most impressive plan that I envisaged in all my career. We had no sleep whatsoever. Finally, "H" hour was set for 0600 on the 23rd of May 1944.

We came from underground to watch it start. It was some sensation! Eight hundred ten guns of various types set up a barrage 3200 yards in width, moving at three minutes per hundred yards. All sorts of other targets were also embraced, including counter battery and counter mortar. The fire went on and on and on. The barrage moved from objective to objective, with a depth of 3000 yards.

Early in the afternoon, my General came in to see me and said, "Ziegler, we're being badly held up on the right on the Aquino airfield. The Princess Patricias and the Loyal Edmontons are taking a helluva beating from waves and waves of enemy tanks, twenty to thirty to a wave. On the left we're finding it easier going. What can you do to help us on the right?"

I said, "Sir, the best I can do is to bring down a William target" (firing all the guns available in the theatre of war). I plotted out the target on a six-figure map reference—about 500 yards in front of our infantry, right where they needed the support. I had to get special permission because it was the only William target by the Canadian Army in the entire Second World War.

Brigadier Johnny Plow, my gunner boss, gave me permission immediately. He said, "Bill, you'll do Scale One, won't you?"

I said, "No, sir. I've already called for Scale Five." That was five rounds per gun. In other words, we had 668 guns each firing five rounds on a single target!

It took just thirty-three minutes to calculate firing data and pass orders to the nineteen field, nine medium and two heavy regiments. When the last regiment reported "Ready," I gave the order to fire. There were no more tank attacks. I got compliments from the Edmontons and the Princess Patricias.

Later my General said, "Bill, I want you to pause your barrage. Can you do it?"

I said, "Sir, I can because I've got good communications."

"Why?"

"Because we're going to wheel and concentrate our attack on the left flank." So I paused our barrage for three solid hours, dropping from three rounds per gun per minute to half a round a minute. Then we started again.

At about five o'clock, my GOC came into my dugout again. He said "Ziegler, we've done it. Up above, the Germans are pouring through— hundreds of prisoners of war."

With the fire plan pretty well finished, we went into the GOC's dugout. Chris, my boss, placed a bottle of rye in front of me.

Now, Chris and I had not been getting on too well. The first day I arrived at San Vito, I had gone out on a fishing party. Chris took a dim view of that. I don't blame him.

"Ziegler," he said, "have a drink." So I poured myself one.

"Goddammit, Ziegler, I said Have A Drink!" I filled the glass half full.

"Ziegler, do you not understand plain English? I said HAVE A DRINK!" So I filled it to the top. Straight rye.

"Now," he said, "drink it!"

God, I did. I poured it down and promptly passed out. When I woke up, about six hours later, Chris was tending me. He said, "Ziegler, I wanted you to do that. You needed it. You were dead on your feet."

"You're a soldier," he said. From that point on, we got on famously.

We fought many more battles together, until the end of 1944 when we were ordered to rejoin the rest of the Canadian Army in Europe. Before leaving Italy, I took a quick trip to the Leaning Tower of Pisa. I climbed the stairs to the top, along with Ted Webb, our chief engineer. What a task. I don't know whether it's still leaning, but I hope to God it has fallen over by now.

The First Canadian Division moved over to Marseilles, and then up the Rhone. We were given the task of swinging left into Holland. After nearly five years of German occupation, the Dutch were destitute.

We fought one or two divisional battles on the way. Then, a period of quiet started and we learned that surrender was about to take place. My six regiments (about 6000 men) and I were given a segment of Holland to occupy—from Dordrecht, north, east, south and west. So we settled in around Dordrecht, a sizeable city of 200 000 people.

On the 4th and 5th of May, I took the surrender of two German Corps commanders. The first one was in the north. I rendezvoused with a German vehicle, which took me to Leiden, a little town in the middle of tulip country. I drove with my staff captain, interpreter and driver, in a Jeep flying a white flag. When we arrived at the town centre I was told, "The General is upstairs, sir."

I was a bit apprehensive because my captive outranked me. He was a Lieutenant-General and I was merely a Brigadier. At the top of the stairs, I took a deep breath, entered the room, gave him a sharp British salute, and said, "Brigadier Ziegler." In reply, he snapped his heels together and thrust his hand up: "Heil Hitler!"

I turned on my heel and stormed straight back down to my Jeep. The bugger wasn't going to "Heil Hitler" me. However, the whole street was packed with Dutch people, and we couldn't drive away.

The General's aide came running after us and said, 'The General would like to see you again, sir." I replied, "You go back and tell the General that I will see him when he learns how to salute properly." He said, "The General has already learned how to salute properly."

So I went back up, and this time I did not salute him. I just stood there and waited. Sure enough, he gave me a smart British salute. I felt that was a victory!

The next day, I took the surrender of Lieutenant-General Deistl south of Rotterdam. After we went through the formalities, he said, "I would like to have permission from you to transport my troops back to Germany on a Dutch barge. The barge belongs to Germany. I can prove that." I gave him permission.

The next morning, as we headed down to the barge, I could smell the stench from 400 yards. The general met me and told me that the men were ready to leave. I told him I would inspect them first.

I stepped up onto the causeway and looked into the barge. The men were packed in, standing shoulder to shoulder, about twenty in a row. There were no toilet facilities. Nothing. No wonder they were stinking.

"General," I said, "you will disembark all these men immediately and you will march them back to Germany, across the causeway from Den Helder to Leer in Germany." He argued, but they did it. It must have been a miserable march, but they were lucky. If I had permitted them to follow the orders of their own General, I believe few of them would have survived the three-day voyage.

In September 1945, I joined the troops heading back to Canada. I was only able to enjoy a brief reunion with my wife, Mildred, because I had already agreed to go back to Germany as an administrator. I had been invited by Sir Gerald Templar who was organizing the military government for Germany.

I returned to Europe in November 1945, and joined the British Control Commission in Hanover. The next five-and-a-half years were intensely interesting. Mildred came to Germany, and our son, Rod, was born in 1949.

I returned to Canada early in 1951, with no job. However, I was soon hired by the CNR, and from 1951 to 1956 worked as an administrator and a pseudorailroader under one of the most magnificent men I have ever known, Donald Gordon. I eventually ended up as Assistant Vice-President.

From 1956 to 1972, I served Inland Cement and Genstar Limited. I knew nothing about cement, but I did know something about administration. When I started, we had one plant in Edmonton, capitalized at about $10 million. When I left, we had four plants—Regina, Winnipeg, Vancouver and Edmonton—capitalized at about $350 million.

I greatly enjoyed my stay at Inland, first as executive Vice President, then President, then chairman of the board. I finally took retirement in 1972, at sixty-one years of age. I wanted to have some time to travel, to train dogs, to fish and to shoot over my dogs. I did have that time.

In 1980, I suffered a great tragedy. My darling wife Mildred passed away. She suffered greatly with cancer of the lungs and I suffered with her. I was with her when she died—it was right that she should go. She had suffered enough.

Now, I have been alone for over nineteen years. It's not good, but I thank God that I have Rod. He's a fine young man and a great guy. No father has ever been better blessed with a son. But we are more than father and son—we are close friends.

When he was a boy, I taught him to fish. In June of 1999, we went together to Langara to fish for the big tyee salmon. He outfished me and I'm proud that he did. Thank you, God, for giving me Rod.

Bill Ziegler lands a big one.

In 1996, I was greatly surprised by a phone call from Dr. George Ford, the Dean Emeritus of the U of A's Faculty of Engineering. "Bill," he said, "would you be able to accept your degree as B.Sc. in Civil Engineering at the fall convocation on November 15?"

I said, "George, I don't understand. I'm still short one year for my degree."

He replied, "We feel you've earned that fourth year many times over. The granting of the degree has been approved, and it's not an honourary degree either; it's an 'honest to God' degree."

I was flabbergasted, deeply honoured and, of course, I agreed with heartfelt thanks.

I attended the convocation with my son and two close friends. It was my firstever, and I heard Dr. David Lynch, the Dean of Engineering, say many nice things about me. Then that huge crowd gave me a standing ovation. I was thrilled and proud beyond words. That was a wonderful day for me—

perhaps the greatest of my life. I'm so proud that my university didn't forget me!

I've led a very rewarding and interesting life. I've done a lot of things, most of which I've loved doing. And yet, something seemed to be missing. For several months, leading up to my eighty-fifth birthday, I had been feeling quite melancholy. Then, I thought back to the introduction of this treatise—"Why?"—"Why am I here?"

Suddenly, I had it! Of course I'd done a lot of things—for my country, my family and for me. But I hadn't really done anything beneficial for Humanity.

Fortunately, it wasn't too late. There was still time and I had the resources. The day before my birthday, I arranged a small social gathering with Dean Lynch; Dr. George Ford, Dean Emeritus; Vince Duckworth, the Faculty Development Officer; and my son, Rod. From that meeting grew my desire to leave a legacy to the Faculty of Engineering. I have done so. I understand that the legacy will benefit deserving students for years to come.

That was just what I had been seeking. Now that I have found a way of accomplishing it, my happiness is complete.

Retirement does not mean loss of meaning in your life or a slow descent into vegetation. Like most retired faculty, I find myself busier than when I was working. There are plenty of ways to continue making useful contributions and to broaden your horizons as long as you are mentally and physically fit. Like many of my colleagues, I chose to retire to Victoria, the nearest thing Canada has to a banana belt. However, retirement could be as satisfying in any Canadian community. Retirement marks a new phase in your life, and to enjoy it you must let go of your former career. I can empathize with Browning's lines:

Grow old along with me!

The best is yet to be,

The last of life, for which the first was made.

Lloyd Stephens-Newsham

The
People

*Often, it's the people
you remember...*

AL MACKAY

Big Art

EACH OF US HAS A SET of standard stories about the people and places we've encountered over the years. Like many memories, they are partly fact and partly fiction. My set of stories includes many about the late Dr. Arthur W. Reeves, the founder and first Chair of the Department of Educational Administration. The three stories that follow are, I swear, mostly true, with only a few embellishments due to the passage of time, my failing memory and a desire to entertain my listeners.

First, I would like to put the stories into context. Art Reeves came to the U of A in 1957 to take over the new department. Reeves, who was noted for his intelligence and vision, quickly achieved success in recruiting staff and graduate students, maintaining financial support from within and outside the University, earning a positive national and international reputation and becoming one of the power-brokers on campus. My stories, then, refer to a respected and distinguished leader of a pre-eminent department of the University.

Big Art didn't have a lot of patience in dealing with either the pretentious or the emotionally needy. One of his favourite ploys was to forget their names, leaving the victims to wonder whether they were so unimportant that they didn't even merit a direct snub. This is not to suggest an absent-minded Professor, because he was anything but that.

Maybe my selection of stories tells more about me than about Big Art, because puncturing balloons of pretension has always been a favourite sport of mine, as both a spectator and participant. (By the way, while he was alive, I would have never dared to call him Art, much less Big Art. Now, at a safe distance, my courage abounds.)

One morning, back when we were housed in the General Services Building, a doctoral student named Jim A (who, for the sake of confidentiality, we will call Jim Angus) found himself alone in an elevator with Art. Now Jim had always been a nervous man; in fact, he often reminded me of the character in Leacock's *My Financial Career*. As the elevator door closed, Jim was paralyzed.

To Jim's surprise and delight, however, Art began a cheerful chat about the weather, sports and politics. For a few moments, Jim felt like a real grownup who, at last, had found his place in the sun. When they reached the top floor (Where else would a Reeves department be?), Jim smiled at his new best friend and said, "Have a good day, Dr. Reeves." With a grunt and a puff of his pipe, Reeves replied, "Okay, Bob."

For the rest of that day, that term and, for that matter, the rest of his career at the U of A, Jim never recovered. Who knows, but for that fateful elevator ride, he might have blossomed as a great leader in the field of education.

A few years later, I formed an audience of one in another classic Reeves psychodrama. I was nearing the end of my doctoral program in 1964 and, like most of my classmates, was looking for a job. Earlier that year, the first Alberta public college had been founded in Red Deer. The college started as a low-key operation, housed in a local high school, but the head person would be called a *Dean*.

I considered applying for the job and thought I would consult with Reeves in an effort to size up my chances. He gave me little in

"Big Art" Reeves

the way of advice, either positive or negative. Discouraged, I abandoned the idea and began to look elsewhere.

A few weeks later, I was walking past Reeves's office and heard him shout, "Come in for a minute, Al." I entered, my heart fluttering. Seated in front of Art's desk was Peter Raffa, a first year doctoral student best known to us for his classy suits, bow ties, expensive shoes and generally superior air. Art, without any preamble, said, "Al, you know that job at Red Deer that you turned down? Well, I just gave it to Pete Ratsoy here." I mumbled subserviently and backed out into the hall.

By the way, Pete Raffa did take the Dean's job at Red Deer, and served the College very well for a number of years.

One of Art's greatest characteristics was his interest in helping his graduates obtain significant jobs. So, it was not surprising that second-year doctoral students, especially during their final term of course work, waited and watched for signals from Big Art about possible jobs and other exciting matters.

One day, he sent word that he wanted to meet the second-year doctoral class that afternoon at one o'clock sharp. The students turned up well before the scheduled time, every one of them stiff with anticipation. They wondered, "Is there a big research project which needs all of us? Will it make or break our careers? Maybe he's got so many big jobs available that he needs to announce a selection process? What have we done wrong?"

Shortly after one o'clock, Art strode in, carrying an impressive looking file folder in one hand and his unlit pipe in the other. He sat at the head of the table, lit his pipe, took off his glasses, looked around the room, almost as if confused, and said, "What group is this?" Without pausing for an answer, he swept up the file folder, puffed a cloud of smoke and walked out.

To this day, no one knows what the meeting was about, although some veteran Reeves-watchers are certain that it was all staged to unsettle and deflate a pretentious band of scholars.

His personal manner may have been brusque, and his humour may have had a sharp edge, but those of us who knew Art Reeves admired and respected him. Throughout his time at the University, he offered remarkable moral and practical support to his staff and students. He'll be remembered for a long time.

My time as a medical student at the University of Alberta provided me with role models who would continue to inspire me for a lifetime.

I had many happy experiences with Professor William Rowan in the Department of Zoology, dating back to 1946-47 as I was studying pre-medicine. First as his student, then as his laboratory demonstrator and later still as his neighbour (with our houses across an alley from each other), I learned to admire him as a witty, self-deprecating person, a great teacher and scientist, and a warm friend. Evidence of his considerable artistry as a draftsman and sculptor remains in the halls of the Department of Zoology, but only personal experience can explain his lasting influence on me, which helped shape my approaches to academia.

Herbert Rawlinson taught me gross anatomy and also supervised me on a summer research project. He was a great teacher, a good scientist and above all, a true humanist. I particularly remember his remarkable ability to rapidly perceive the essence of any problem. Once, when he found me fretting about some problems and long-term decisions, he told me to focus first on the problems at hand and, after solving them, to consider the long term without undue anxiety or haste.

John W. Scott, my Professor of Medicine during my undergraduate years and shortly thereafter my Dean as well, left an indelible mark on my life. He was an extraordinarily lucid teacher both at the blackboard and at the bedside. I have consciously tried to emulate his hands-on approach and clinical emphasis. Among his many sound sayings was, "A good doctor is a perennial medical student."

Walter Mackenzie, my Professor of Surgery, was as dynamic and outgoing as John Scott was steady and reflective. He was another memorable teacher in the hands-on school, but in many other ways as well. His broad perspective on medicine and surgery, his warm interpersonal manners and his ability to get the best out of people remained a vivid memory throughout my twenty-three-year absence from the University. He once told me that to get ahead in resident training and beyond, it was important not merely to work

continued on next page

hard, but to make it evident that you **were** working hard. If the Chief of a service asked you to read up on a subject, you should do so promptly and submit a brief report to indicate that you had done so.

Howard H. Hepburn was my Professor of Neurosurgery, and I was his last intern before his clinical retirement. He was without doubt the best-organized human I have ever met. He showed me the value of good work habits. For instance, he gave each and every patient his complete attention during every encounter. When he left the operating room or a bedside, his conscience was at rest, knowing that everything that could or should be done for that patient had indeed been seen to. Among his many other admirable traits, I also remember his unostentatious persistence at sustaining his skills as a general surgeon, alongside his expertise in neurosurgery.

George Molnar

WILLIAM TAYLOR

Working with the Great Man

WHEN I BECAME ACTING CHAIRMAN of Pediatrics in 1968, I was well aware that I would have to deal with Dean Walter Mackenzie. Now, many wonderful eulogies have been written about the great man, and many of them are true, but when working with him every day from the insecure footing of an acting chairman, I found him to be a ruthless tyrant.

In my early medical training in Scotland and England, I had encountered many great men. All were forceful characters, some were eccentrics and some were petty tyrants, but I had never come up against anyone as awesome as Walter Mackenzie, especially when he was enraged.

He did have a gentle side. After performing a bowel resection on my seventy-two-year-old mother, he visited her twice a day for the next week, sometimes holding her hand and chatting with her for twenty minutes at a time. My mother worshipped him, and for his kindness to her, I held him in great respect.

But working with him on an academic or administrative basis was something entirely different. After one meeting I had with him, I recorded the events in detail. I quote them here in their entirety.

WEDNESDAY, 3 JULY 1968, 3 P.M.

Presented the preliminary budget estimates for 1969-70 to the Dean in his office. This experience was rather like having a conversation with an electronic computer. No friendly greeting and never a word of goodbye. Just straight to work and a ruthless elimination of any items in the budget directly relating to research.

Peter Bowen's $10 000 of equipment – Rejected.

Peter Bowen's $3000/annum salary for a dishwasher – Rejected.

Al Stewart's halftime technician – Rejected.

Yet all sorts of piddly little things, like teaching aids, teaching fellows' travel, travel for genetic patients, laboratory supplies and sundries were all approved. The Dean believes that any and ALL research activity must be supported by research funds and not by University money. A strange philosophy which has not been explained to me, when half the activity of the department has to do with research and half has to do with teaching or learning. I suspect a new half has been added, and that is administration, which keeps everyone above the rank of Assistant Professor very occupied indeed.

Never waste the Dean's time.

Never go to him without ascertaining all the facts.

Never expect him to help without a struggle.

I was out of the office ten minutes later, shaking with concealed rage.

On 7th January 1969, a fracas arose over a complaint lodged by the chief of the pediatric service at Hospital X. Because of the shortage of residents, we had been unable to supply Hospital X with a pediatric resident for the previous two years. At the end of 1968, in the rush of Christmas activities, I had forgotten to notify Dr. B. that the situation would continue for a third straight year. It so happened that Dr. B. was a fishing and hunting partner of the Dean, and he telephoned his friend Walter directly.

"Dean Mackenzie phoned me up in high dudgeon," I recorded in my notes, "demanding my presence in his office immediately." I headed up the thirteen flights of stairs to his office, in order to gain enough time to think up a possible excuse, and arrived all hot and sweaty.

He immediately launched into an indignant tirade, asking why I was so discourteous to a practising pediatrician. Without waiting for my breathless reply, he demanded that I immediately provide him with a written apology that he could send to Dr. B. As it was now 5:30 p.m., I asked if I could have it on his desk at 9 a.m. Reluctantly, he consented.

Like the good obedient chap I am, I drafted a letter—explanatory, apologetic, ingratiating—for the Dean to send to Dr. B. At the same time,

I sent Dr. Mackenzie another letter under separate cover, pointing out the complete lack of effort on the part of the pediatric teaching staff at Hospital X. I believe the Dean got the message, as there were no further difficulties with Hospital X.

Assisting and being associated with Dr. James Quarshie has been one of my satisfying highlights at the University of Alberta.

I registered two late-comers one year for an undergraduate course in educational administration. A pair of young CIDA scholars from Ghana, they ended up coming first and second in the class.

One of them, James Quarshie, obtained M.Ed. and M.A. degrees before returning to Ghana. Years later, he wished to return to the University of Alberta for sabbatical studies, but there appeared to be no financial assistance available for him. I invited him to apply to our doctoral program, for we could provide assistantships to graduate students.

After graduating with a Ph.D. in Educational Administration, he could not return to Ghana, as the poor country could not afford to pay his way home. After numerous unsuccessful applications, he finally got a position at the University of Gorka, Papua New Guinea.

Since then, he has presented papers at several international conferences and has been able to visit the University of Alberta. He rose to the position of Chair of his Department.

John Bergen

Don Bellow

The Man from Riga

B EING RETIRED has given me more time to do the things I enjoy without worrying that I'm neglecting more important things. Now that I'm retired, whatever I happen to be doing at the time is important.

When I was employed at the University, I rarely found time to read anything that was not germane to the work in hand. These days, I have been catching up on old spy mysteries and reading a gaggle of books about the Cambridge Apostles and all the havoc they wreaked back in the 1930s when they thought they were the only ones who could save the world. As distant as this seems in the 1990s, and as personally removed as I was from it, I'm fascinated by the intrigue of it all. Indeed (not to be too melodramatic), I, too, have been involved in some interesting encounters.

During my time as Chairman of the Department of Mechanical Engineering, I often played host to visiting academics, including many from behind the Iron Curtain. I was always delighted and proud to show them around our laboratories and the Mechanical Engineering Building, and to take them for a meal at the Faculty Club. If I wanted to impress them even more, I would prevail on my wife, Jean, to cook a typical Alberta roast beef dinner with mashed potatoes and garden fresh peas, plus rhubarb crisp for dessert.

On one such occasion, we entertained Professor Rumiatsiv, Head of the Department of Mathematics at the University of Moscow. He was a very fine gentleman who, by virtue of his position, enjoyed many perquisites denied to the average Soviet citizen. I recall our daughter, Denise, who was six or seven at the time, remonstrating him for smoking cigarettes, even though I still smoked cigars at that time.

My association with Communist visitors was not confined to Europeans. Over the years, many in our department entertained visiting scientists from Asia. Almost without exception, these were highly motivated individuals dedicated to their careers. One couple, however, stood out from the rest.

I received a letter from Beijing asking if two Professors could come and review my research on the corrosion fatigue of oil field sucker rods. I was flattered by the request and readily agreed. From that point on, however, negotiations became complicated. They wrote and asked me to find them a place to stay for no more than $30 US each for room and board. I wasn't used to acting as a travel agent, but I did manage to book them a room in Campus Towers for about $50/day, with two bedrooms, a kitchen and a magnificent view of the river valley.

When they arrived and were shown their "digs," the lady said that the room was too expensive. It was then that I realized that the two of them, although married, were not married to each other. I told them that they could stay at the YMCA/YWCA, but that the cost would be the same. After a private conference, they announced, with apparent reluctance, that they would stay one night only. "Tomorrow, we will look for something else."

When I picked them up the next morning, expecting to drive them all over town in a search for alternative accommodation, they said they would stay in Campus Towers. It seemed that twenty-four hours had softened their distaste for their decadent surroundings.

Throughout all of this, the lady Professor did all the talking. I assumed that the man could neither speak nor understand the language. Later, when we were alone together, he surprised me with his perfect English. This convinced me that the woman was the Party member, sent along to make sure her male traveller did not get out of line.

What surprised me most about this lady was how outspoken she was. At dinner in our home, and later at a Chinese restaurant in Parkallen, she wanted to know why and what and where and who. For example, she quizzed our daughter, Denise, about why she lived at home and why she rode in my car when I went to work. Her questions went beyond simple curiosity and became downright arrogant. I had never encountered such an attitude before, nor have I since.

After all was said and done, it turned out that we had very little in common on a technical level either. They were theoreticians and appeared not to have the slightest interest in what I was doing on the experimental side. I often wondered why they came over specifically to see me.

Our most memorable (and most bizarre) foreign visitor, however, involved a Professor at the university in Riga, Latvia. He wrote to us from an address at the University of Waterloo, asking if he could come and stay a few days with us in the department.

One morning a few days later, he arrived at my office door. He was tall and dressed like a westerner, but his most remarkable trait was that he spoke perfect English. I commented on his fluency and he said it came from watching NHL games on TV. When I asked him where and for how long he had been watching NHL hockey, he said it was during his three weeks at Waterloo!

He told me that his specialty was signature analysis, which examines a machine's vibrations in order to perform preventative maintenance and to predict machine failures. Since I knew very little about this subject, I introduced him to Tony Craggs in the department. Tony later confirmed that the "man from Riga" seemed to know his subject.

We took him to lunch, and then I offered to drive him around the city. Every so often he had me stop the car so he could take a few pictures. When it was time to head back to the campus from downtown, he asked to be dropped off at the Centennial Library. He said he would find his own way back to campus. When I offered to pick him up later from where he was staying, to take him to the dinner we were hosting for him, he told me he would meet us at the Faculty Club.

Sure enough, he arrived right on time. For the whole evening, he captivated the ladies in the party with his wit and charm. The next morning he arrived in my office to thank me and bid goodbye. He said he was heading to Calgary. I assumed he meant the University of Calgary. In any case, I never heard from him again. But I heard lots about him!

Within an hour of his departure, two burly men in dark coats arrived at our office and, with thick accents, asked our receptionist where the man was and where he had gone. I didn't know any more than the receptionist, so I didn't venture outside my office to confront these men. In any case, I didn't think it would be prudent to ask them what business it was of theirs!

I didn't have to wait long to find out what it was all about. That afternoon, the RCMP called and requested an interview in my office. They asked if a scientist from Riga, Latvia, had visited the department. When I said yes, they asked me to relate all that I knew and everything that had transpired. By the time I got to the part about the two burly foreigners, the officers were on the edge of their seats.

They said that our visitor was undoubtedly a KGB agent, and perhaps a "loose cannon," and that the two mysterious men on his trail might be KGB heavyweights trying to bring him in line. I asked them to speculate why the KGB would be interested in any of this, let alone being in Edmonton in the first place. They surmised that the "man from Riga" was interested in taking pictures of our city so that "escape routes" could be developed for future use by KGB agents.

It seemed so funny at the time, but the man's perfect English, his unwillingness to reveal where he was staying and his sudden departure made him look, in retrospect, very much like a secret agent.

Of course, during those years we received countless guests who were not spies, or even Communists! They came to the U of A seeking international fellowship, and the two-way exchange of knowledge and technology among scientists—with nary a cloak nor a dagger in sight. All the same, as I read my novels, I like to think that I once had my very own brush with international espionage.

In the early 1970s, I began to develop a set of lecture notes into a full-fledged book on craniofacial embryology. Finding a publisher was a daunting task. The University of Alberta Press showed only half-hearted interest, and when I wrote to John Wright and Sons (a British publisher of dental textbooks), they wanted me to subsidize the production costs. Fortunately James McCutcheon, Dean of Dentistry, was sympathetic to my request for financing. He "lent" me the money from an obscure faculty fund to launch my book, with royalties to be repaid to the fund.

Craniofacial embryology came out at a propitious time, right at the beginning of an explosive growth of research in the field, growth that continues unabated. The first edition sold out quickly, and a second edition in 1976 was translated into Japanese. This established an international reputation for the book, necessitating an updated third edition in 1981. That edition was not only translated into Japanese, but into German and Indonesian as well. I was able to rapidly repay the Dean's "loan."

My research enquiries into craniofacial embryology attracted the interest of fetal pathologist Dr. Geoff Machin. He moved to Edmonton from Victoria, and our collaborative studies resulted in numerous publications and to my entry into the field of fetal pathology. We employed summer students to prepare aborted fetal specimens for study, and subsequently for computer reconstruction analysis. My son, Steven, with youthful expertise in computer technology, became part of one of these teams. This sparked his interest in the field and led to his pursuing a Master of Science degree in developmental biology. The genes of my inquisitiveness have been passed on to the next generation!

Geoffrey Sperber

Academic Journeys

The surprising roads we travel...

Raymond Lemieux

The Boy from Lac La Biche

Dr. Lemieux was recently awarded the Wolf Prize in Chemistry, which informed people rank next to the Nobel Prize. This honour was conferred by the President of Israel, Dr. Ezer Weismann, to Dr. Lemieux at the Israeli Parliament in Jerusalem on May 5, 1999. The autobiography that follows was based on an interview.

THE EARLY YEARS

WHEN WE MOVED FROM LAC LA BICHE to Edmonton in 1927, my father bought a house in the Boyle Street–McCauley district. That community was not one you would want to brag about very much. Even in those days, it was the toughest part of the city. My main challenge was to avoid associations that could lead to reform school. A year later, when I was eight years old, my mother died. My older sisters looked after me until I was about twelve or thirteen. I had four sisters and three brothers (I was the seventh child). We were Catholic and all educated in Catholic schools. Everyone succeeded very well, each in their own way. At this writing, only my sister Yvette (Morin), a well-known local artist, and I survive.

In the summer, I played baseball nearly every day. In the winter, I went to the outdoor skating rink almost every day that it was warmer than –20°F. Mostly we played "shinny" hockey with several pucks on the ice at once. You had to learn to keep your head up.

My father brought us up to work hard and well. He was a finishing carpenter, and when I was a teenager, I would help him clean up after jobs.

I was careful to pick up every nail that he may have dropped. When he reached about sixty years of age, he found the winters too hard for carpentry and accepted the job of janitor at my high school, St. Joseph's. I would go in and wash floors on Saturdays. He had worked hard, long hours all his life and he was weakening. It was good that he still had me around to help.

My life provides a good example of how, given a caring family, a poor boy from "the sticks" can achieve worldwide recognition for his University, as the recipient of many world prizes such as the Wolf Prize in Chemistry, the Gairdner Prize of Canada, the King Faisal Prize of Saudi Arabia and the Albert Einstein World Prize in Science. I also received the first Canada Gold Medal for science and engineering. I am not trying to brag. I simply consider it important to recognize such achievements because these are the hallmarks of a free country. I worry that our freedoms are constantly eroding for the sake of achieving greater uniformity (equality in achievement rather than equality in opportunity).

Ray Lemieux accepting the 1999 Wolf Prize

I did well in school, but until the age of nineteen, my main ambition was to become a professional hockey player. In high school, I had absolutely no guidance towards a scientific career. My teachers in the Alberta of the 1930s didn't seem to know such opportunities existed. I met university students for the first time in the summer of 1939. I was unloading boxcars for a hardware company when I got a phone call from my oldest sister, Alice, who was working at the Jasper Park Lodge. She told me that the Lodge needed a busboy in a hurry, and that she had applied on my behalf.

At the Lodge, I found myself surrounded by university students. I decided that I would become one too, if I could find some way to meet the costs. When I was in Grade 12 at St. Joseph's High School, my sister Annette met a young man, John Convey, who was studying for a master's degree in physics at the U of A. John introduced me to the possibility of actually earning a living doing research. He told me that because the University had virtually no graduate students, second-year honours students in chemistry were often selected as teaching assistants in freshman courses. I therefore registered in honours chemistry. The $18 per month I could earn as a teaching assistant would prove crucial, especially for streetcar fare (I lived at home with my father). Fortunately, I won an appointment by leading my class in freshman chemistry.

I remember the summer after my first year at University. They had found a crack in the church basement and the priest roped me into digging a six-foot deep trench along the basement wall. I was down in this ditch the day my brother brought me a letter from the University announcing that I had won the McLeod Prize for a first-year organic chemistry course. If I remember correctly, the prize was $25 and this was a real Godsend. It seemed clear that there was a future for me in chemistry.

BIRTH OF A CHEMIST
Archie Gillies was my first organic chemistry instructor. The regular Professor, Dr. Reuben B. Sandin, was on sabbatical, and this master's student was hired as his replacement for the year. He was a very good teacher, and within a month or two I knew I wanted to be a chemist. I never looked back. I had no idea how exciting chemistry could be. I took to

organic chemistry as a duck takes to water.

At the start of my senior year, I asked my beloved Professor Sandin to allow me to prepare my B.Sc. thesis under his guidance. When he asked why, I replied that I wished to be an organic chemist. "Ray," he said, "you should first try to be a chemist. Go work with Jack Morrison (a physical chemist). He can use some help on a wartime project related to detonators." I worked with Dr. Morrison as a summer student, and I am still proud of the results we obtained on the activation of charcoal for use in gas masks.

Benjamin (Reuben) Sandin, or "Rube" as everybody called him, was a legend in his own time. He was a great teacher and a good person. I remember a comment he made after receiving a teaching award, "A pat on the back is worth much more than a kick in the seat." He had a lot of great sayings. He once said, "When you interview students who want to come into honours chemistry, you should always look at their shoes. If there is a little manure on their shoes, accept them." He was respected as a teacher throughout the world and, taking into account the circumstances and environment that then existed at the University, he made a truly remarkable contribution to the improvement of chemical knowledge. Thereby, he established a research atmosphere which is of vital importance to university teaching.

In my graduating year, the war was on. I volunteered for active service but was allowed to stay in graduate school to continue working toward a Ph.D. I was happy when the University of Toronto accepted me. My good Professor Sandin asked me, "What are you going to do there?" I told him the name of the Professor I would work for and he said, "If you go to work with that tyrant, I will never talk to you again." It was good advice. I later learned that this Professor was very difficult to get along with, and that many students left his laboratory after just a few months.

Professor Sandin suggested I work with Professor Clifford B. Purves at McGill University. I wrote to Purves and was accepted into McGill's graduate program in chemistry. In the fall of 1943, loaded with sandwiches for a three-day train ride, I left Edmonton to register for graduate studies at the McGill-based Pulp and Paper Research Institute of Canada.

Although I had volunteered for active service, it did not disappoint me that I was never called.

Purves proved to be a real inspiration. In his office (he never came to my laboratory), we had many private discussions and smoked many of his tailor-made cigarettes. Gradually, under his influence, I became completely entranced with stereochemistry. His most important lesson to me was to give students ample opportunity to read and think for themselves. I believe that I could have published twice as much work over the course of my career had I pressed students to do the experiments I wanted done. However, C. B. had taught me to give my students sufficient rope either to hang on or to climb higher. I felt that I was a rather easygoing and forgiving research Director, but Bert Fraser-Reid, now a world-leading chemist, loves to tell people that I was "both his mentor and tormentor."

I feel sure that students learn more if you let them work independently on the projects you outline, rather than guide them closely from the start. A student reads more and learns more after making a few mistakes on his or her own. Whatever I did could not have been so bad because most of my students developed brilliant careers, and we have retained a great level of mutual affection. I acknowledge with gratitude the contributions to my research programs by many who came, from virtually all parts of the world, to study in my laboratory.

By the time I finished my studies at McGill in the fall of 1946, the war had ended, and I had learned about the existence of postdoctoral studies. Prior to the war, organic chemistry students often went to Germany or Switzerland for postdoctoral studies. In 1946, this was no longer so attractive. Instead, I directed my attention towards laboratories in the United States.

At that time, a lot of research had been sparked by the discovery that the antibiotic streptomycin was a carbohydrate. I applied, with Dr. Purves' recommendation, to the laboratory of Professor Melville L. Wolfrom at Ohio State University, who was performing ongoing research on the structure of streptomycin. Purves must have recommended me warmly because I was invited by return mail to present myself in Columbus, Ohio, to be interviewed for a postdoctoral fellowship sponsored by Bristol Laboratories, Inc. in Syracuse, NY. I scraped together $60, earned from working in a bar in Montreal, and got on a train for Ohio. When I walked into Wolfrom's office for the interview, he simply glanced at me and muttered, "Oh! So you are Purves' student. When can you start?" That's all there was to it. I spent three whole days (and every cent I had) on a trip just to be confronted by this gruff man who had already made up his mind!

I was delighted to do research on the structure of an antibiotic. My younger brother Gerard had died of a streptococcal infection in 1936 at the

Ray Lemieux giving his acceptance speech for the 1999 Wolf Prize

age of fourteen, so the subject was near to my heart. His doctor had told us that his life might have been saved if Edmonton had had access to a new anti-infective drug called sulfanilimide. Later, when I learned more about anti-infective drugs in my introductory organic chemistry course, I began to drift toward that area of research.

More than any other incident, going to Wolfrom's laboratory set the pattern for my life (and my standard of living) as a research chemist. Not only did it give me a taste for "big league" research, it began my twenty-five-year association as a consultant with Bristol Laboratories, through its Director of Research and Vice President, Amel Menotti. Most importantly, however, it was at Ohio State University that I met my wife, Virginia, "Jeanne," née McConaghie, who was studying for her Ph.D. degree in high-resolution infrared spectroscopy. We were married in New York City in 1948. In a very real way, Jeanne provided all the necessary incentives, repairs and encouragement I needed to succeed in the highly challenging competitive business of basic chemical research. Despite my first impression of Wolfrom, we got along very well and became close friends. The only time I truly annoyed him was when I refused his offer of Research Associate in order to go to the University of Saskatchewan in the fall of 1947.

COMING TO ALBERTA

From 1947 to 1949, I was an Assistant Professor in the Department of Chemistry at the University of Saskatchewan. On my meagre salary, I could not afford even a used car, so I rode a bicycle in the summer and walked through the blizzards in the winter. We went shopping either pulling a little red wagon or a sled, depending on the season. It was hard on Jeanne, who was brought up in New York City. She contributed importantly to our welfare by accepting an appointment at the University of Alberta to replace Dr. Morrison who was on sabbatical for the 1948-49 academic year. She taught chemical thermodynamics to the fourth-year students of chemistry and chemical engineering. She also worked part time at the University of Saskatchewan, but with the arrival of our second child, Virginia, she dedicated her life to her children and home.

In those years, I desperately wanted to succeed and worked at least seventy hours per week. This was hard on Jeanne, but I could not see any other way to rise above poverty. Eventually, I thought of moving to the United States. Before making my decision, though, I talked to Dr. Alex Ledingham, the Director of the soon-to-open Prairie Regional Laboratory of the National Research Council. I told him that I could not possibly stay in Saskatoon unless I could earn at least $4000 a year. When the NRC finally said all right, I decided to stay. Why move? The NRC laboratory was new and the equipment was excellent. For example, I had the first commercial infrared spectrometer in Canada. This made me more competitive than I would have been at most Canadian universities.

After five years at the NRC, Dr. E. W. R. Steacie (President of the National Research Council) sort of "fired" me from the PRL. He wanted me to go to the University of Ottawa, where they were starting a Faculty of Pure and Applied Science. He thought I could help the newly appointed Dean, Pierre Gendron, build the faculty in which I would be Vice Dean and Head of the Department of Chemistry. I accepted his proposal and spent the period 1954 to 1961 at the University of Ottawa. I am exceedingly proud of what we were able to accomplish starting in an abandoned army barracks to build a faculty from the top down. I truly believe these were the most exciting years of my life. Along with building the department, my research led to two of the most important discoveries of my career: the use of nuclear magnetic resonance spectroscopy for the study of the stereochemistry of molecules and the applications that led to the establishment of stereoelectronic contributions to chemical bonding that I termed the "anomeric-effect."

In the spring of 1960, I presented an invited lecture to the American Chemical Society at a meeting in San Francisco. On my return trip to Ottawa, I decided to stop over in Edmonton to visit my father and brothers and sisters. When I arrived, I discovered that my father had died the previous day from pneumonia at the age of eighty-six. This unfortunate coincidence lengthened my stay in Edmonton. I decided to visit the Department of Chemistry at the University of Alberta to see my old Professor Rube Sandin—and perhaps meet Harry Gunning who was building a world-class department.

Harry, a physical chemist, asked me to help him find a top organic chemist to help him build that discipline. I returned the next day to say "How about me?" He immediately accepted and arranged a somewhat novel position for me, essentially equivalent to a research professorship. My main responsibility was to build a leading research group in an important area of chemistry. At the same time, Harry wanted me to use my experience to help him build a strong infrastructure for his department. It proved to be a great situation for me.

I was at the U of A full time from 1961 until I retired in 1985. My efforts were well recognized and rewarded. I was promoted to University Professor, was awarded the first U of A prize for research (now known as the Kaplan Prize) and the University has sponsored the annual Lemieux Lecture in Biotechnology since 1990. I was awarded an honourary Doctor of Science in 1991. I became Professor Emeritus in 1985 and continued to use the research facilities for ten years, until I was seventy-five years of age. I still come to the university to maintain correspondence, to prepare invited lectures and to write technical papers for publication on research we had accomplished before 1995. My secretary, Christine Elbrink, retired at the same time I did. Luckily, I can hire her to come to my office when needed; she is well acquainted with my secretarial needs and can read what I write without my seeing. I became legally blind from macular degeneration in 1995.

BUSINESS AND THE UNIVERSITY

Jeanne and I started to climb out of our highly budgeted lifestyle in late 1962, with the founding of R & L Molecular Research Ltd., in partnership with my brother Leo, a local businessman. At the time, R & L employed more Ph.D.s than any other private enterprise in western Canada. This situation arose when Amel Menotti asked whether I would accept a major contract to do research on the development of semisynthetic antibiotics, starting mainly from penicillin G and kanamycin A. Because I did not consider such a contract to be in the best interests of the University, I replied that I would only be interested if the work could be done in the private sector. Amel then suggested that my brother Leo and I establish a company to do so. We founded R & L Molecular Research Ltd. in late December 1962 to undertake a nine-year research contract paid in advance every three years.

Thus began an exceedingly interesting and exciting ten-year association between R & L and Bristol Laboratories. By 1966, I decided to establish a new company, Raylo Chemicals Ltd., because R & L's business was restricted to research for Bristol. Raylo eventually came to own R & L. Its main line of business was the sale of custom research and specialty chemicals. We established major research contracts with a number of companies, including Bristol-Myers Inc. in New York City, Atomic Energy of Canada Limited in Chalk River, Ontario, the Reynold's Tobacco Co. in North Carolina, and the Polymer Corporation in Sarnia, Ontario. In 1973, I decided to sell control of Raylo to the Canada Development Corporation (CDC). In 1976, I sold all my remaining shares of Raylo to individuals who had purchased the shares owned by CDC.

I assigned to the University of Alberta the developments in my academic research for which I had foreseen commercial application in the blood-banking business. On entering into the partnership with the CDC in 1973, I requested the University to license this technology to a subsidiary of the CDC, Connaught Laboratories in Toronto. When Connaught defaulted on the agreement, I requested the University of Alberta to repatriate the ownership of the patents, which it did.

The University owned the intellectual property but had no real notion of its potential worth or what to do with it. It occurred to me that it would best be exploited by a company originally to be owned by the University and ultimately to be sold to an Alberta private company. There was much talk on campus about how the University's investment in research would pay off in local industrial activity, particularly in pharmaceuticals. However, the main promoters didn't fully understand what was entailed in getting involved with high-tech industry.

I decided to use the technology I had in mind to "wet their feet." I prepared a business plan for a company that I named Chembiomed, in which I offered to be Chembiomed's President for at least two years. After the company was founded, I presented the plan to members of the Board of Governors, but I don't believe they fully tried to comprehend it. Nevertheless, U of A President Harry Gunning strongly supported my suggestion that we create a University-owned corporation. Thus, Chembiomed was founded in 1977. Taking this educational route to commercial enterprise, we encountered our share of difficulties. This was expected, as the effort was highly experimental. I knew from experience that the successful start-up of a high-tech company required an all-consuming effort. Somehow, Albertans in general and certainly the University in particular would have to learn by experience. By guiding a small, scientifically sophisticated enterprise, the University would learn a lot about how to serve a rapidly growing economy in need of industrial diversification. I felt that the experiment would take about ten years to achieve commercial success.

The three Ph.D.s that I hired to develop the company (all former students of mine) did wonders in bringing health-related products to market. It soon appeared as if Chembiomed would become a commercial success in as little as eight years, and at the same time bring a new maturity to the government's and University's attitudes towards high technology.

Unfortunately, the company was being undermined by a secret coalition instigated by ex-consultants to Chembiomed and supported by Government of Alberta officials and a venture capital company. Although I was quite closely associated as a consultant to Chembiomed throughout its existence (often as an honourary member of the Board of Directors), I was never advised of the planning and building of a $14 000 000 building financed by forgivable loans from the Government of Alberta. If the government decided not to write off these loans, Chembiomed would necessarily go bankrupt and a costly, highly specialized building would appear on the market at a bargain price.

The three Ph.D.s wanted, and I believe deserved, 60% equity in the company, but were not even appreciated for what they had accomplished. They resigned together and moved to Silicon Valley. The government-appointed Board members felt they could do better by advertising for a President in *The Globe and Mail*! As soon as the three officers resigned,

Chembiomed floundered. I recommended that Chembiomed be sold. Instead, the construction of a laboratory that the company could not afford began.

All three of my former students moved to the United States. Dr. Fred Daniel, MBA, is now a retired wealthy venture capitalist in Silicon Valley; Don Baker is now Vice President of a large Los Angeles pharmaceutical company, and after a brilliant five years as President of a start-up Boston company, Ives Fourons returned to France where he is now President and CEO of a new, well-financed start-up company in Paris. The hotshot that the board hired as the result of their head-hunting exercise left the company to accept a job in California where he lasted less than one year.

A lot of well-meaning people were in over their heads. They didn't stop to think about what they were getting into, preferring to think that they already knew everything they needed to know about business affairs. I remember overhearing a board member saying that Fred Daniel "had a strange French accent. I can't see him having breakfast with Peter Lougheed."

Chembiomed was suddenly and severely put into receivership in 1992. No effort was made to accommodate the customers (worldwide), and the technology was transferred to the Alberta Research Council. There, the mismanagement reached new heights.

The worst outcome is that politicians now seem to believe that universities have a role in developing the economy that includes being involved in commercial enterprise. It seems to have been forgotten that the role of universities is to produce graduates who are capable of properly identifying novel business opportunities for building companies that can develop profitable markets. These are rare Ph.D.s. Most of them will simply find jobs, rarely in Alberta.

I started these companies in order to establish a precedent. I wanted to show that new knowledge can be profitably applied in Alberta, thereby producing rewarding careers. As I look back, there were many disappointments, but the balance, in this best of all worlds, is not all bad but still not very encouraging.

LOOKING BACK

I accomplished important research at the University, right up to the time I closed my laboratory on March 31, 1995. In 1990, I was awarded the King Faisal International Prize in Riyadh, Saudi Arabia, the centre of the Muslim world. Now I have the Wolf Prize in Chemistry—the top prize of the Jewish World, presented to me in Jerusalem. These awards from two hostile countries are truly remarkable and a fine tribute to science.

However, despite the many prizes and honourary doctorates (eighteen) that have come my way, my most cherished compliment came from Dean Gendron, University of Ottawa. "Ray," he once told me, "you are easy to trust." I know that our mutual trust was the cornerstone for our success in building the Faculty of Pure and Applied Science at the University of Ottawa. Trust is what I cherish most in people.

Indeed, I owe my career to the trust placed in me by my family and employers. It is unfortunate that the element of trust in human affairs seems to have dissipated seriously in recent years. Trust and care are inseparable values, and it is difficult to believe that a society can persist in the absence of these most precious human qualities.

My years as a university Professor have allowed me to see much of the world and to have contact with many different cultures. I have been invited almost everywhere except Africa and South America. Most rewarding were study periods of a month or more in Denmark, Russia, France, New Zealand, Korea and Spain. My wife was able to accompany me on all these trips since she was self-employed as a homemaker. We also travelled extensively in Britain, Ireland, Mexico, the Caribbean, Indonesia, Thailand, Australia, Belgium, the Netherlands, India, Japan and just about everywhere in Canada and the United States. Jeanne had the best of it— mostly I worked.

Virtually none of our travel costs were met by the University of Alberta. The major portions of those expenses were defrayed by the host organizations. My trips to chemical conferences were paid for with research grants mainly from federal granting agencies and American research foundations and companies. Before I retired in 1985, most of my trips took a week or less. I took only one sabbatical leave. This was in 1983 for six months without pay.

THE MOST EXCITING EVENT IN MY CAREER

I am often asked, "What was the most exciting event in your career?" On a strictly scientific level, it was in 1967 when I was elected Fellow of the Royal Society. I was still young, at forty-seven years of age, and this brought me into contact with a world I had not imagined. At the ceremony in London, I wrote my name with the same quill pen and in the same book that was signed by King Charles II and the founding members. The signatures of such illustrious people as Isaac Newton, Christopher Wren, Michael Faraday and Charles Darwin were there. That was a high point I will always remember. It gave me the feeling that "I had made it."

I was subsequently appointed an Officer of the Order of Canada in 1968 and elevated to Companion in 1994, Canada's highest civilian award.

Certainly, I was able to make several fundamental contributions to science that will last as long as science is practised and for which I will be remembered. Best of all would be that my children and grandchildren remember me as a good father and a good grandfather. My children are my proudest achievement. They are six remarkable kids. Between them they have thirteen university degrees. Laura is a very famous Professor in Molecular Microbiology at the University of Alberta. This year she is a visiting Professor at Edinburgh. She and two other children live in Edmonton. Virginia has her own company in graphic design and is well known at the University. Most every time I went to the campus Photo Services, someone would say, "There's Virginia's father." A great compliment. Four of our children came to Jerusalem for the Wolf ceremonies. Laura and Virginia from Edmonton; Michèle from Los Altos, California; and Andrée from Spirit River, Alberta. My son Raymond could not get away from his job, and my youngest daughter, Janet, gave birth to her second son, Gavin, on April 23, a week before we were expected in Jerusalem.

I learned of my first prize at a church and accepted my last prize in Jerusalem! The Wolf Prize in Chemistry is one of the world's greatest honours, but that $25 McLeod Prize had a bigger impact on my life as a whole. I believe the Wolf Prize will be most felt in the lives of my children and grandchildren. Raymond and his wife, Patricia, came to Riyadh for the

King Faisal Prize ceremonies. Janet has travelled extensively on her own, especially as a member of the first Canadian Women's National Soccer Team.

BRIDGING THE GAP

The Wolf Prize was very important to me because it is awarded in both Art and Science. Both disciplines are dedicated to the betterment of the welfare of mankind. Art and Science are a continuum of the human experience. People appreciate beauty and music at a very early age. It comes naturally, as it does for lower animals, for example, the plumage and song of birds. At my summer home on Lake Edith in Jasper, a large female elk comes each year to a prominent region of our front lawn to chew her cud. I have no doubt that it is to appreciate the beauty of the lake and the mountains of the Maligne valley. For these reasons, it is not surprising that forms of Art were developed by mankind as long ago as the Stone Age. Certainly, Science has contributed importantly to the development of many art forms. Many modern artistic accomplishments are dependent on materials and instruments made possible through applied sciences. Contributions to scientific knowledge are no less demanding in creativity, effort and reward than are important contributions to writing, painting, sculpture and other arts.

One finds humanists in both groups. People in the arts should not try to downgrade something that they know little about. The average scientist knows a good deal more about artistic endeavours than the arts people know about science. I can't possibly believe that these two cultures will ever come together if they don't start doing it in grade school. We can't continue to treat science simply as a tool for engineers. Science embodies habits of thought that are based in reproducible observations. It develops a frame of mind that is not popular among mystics, and this has had a deleterious effect on science education and the promotion of science.

I hope that this brief and cursory autobiography documents clearly that I enjoyed a good and meaningful life as an academic and that it will echo well in the halls of time.

I have fond memories of my early association with Bob Cormack, who was not only a very fine researcher and teacher but a wonderfully generous mentor and human being.

As Bob and I occupied offices on the same floor, we saw a lot of each other and rapidly developed a close friendship. At staff meetings, Bob could be relied on to make good suggestions and also maintain his good humour even during heated debates. At one meeting, we were discussing possible display material for the foyer of the new Biological Sciences Building. One member thought petrified tree stumps would make a strong botanical statement. With a twinkle in his eye, Bob whispered to me that bringing in dead wood was not a good idea!

To the general public, Bob is best known for his beautifully illustrated books—*Wild Flowers of Alberta* (first published in 1967), and *Wild Flowers—Banff, Jasper, Kootenay, Yoho National Parks* (published in 1972). Both received wide acclaim and continue to be used by amateur and professional botanists alike.

Edwin Cossins

Bob Cormack

MALCOLM McPHEE

Reflections on Edmonton Urology Through a Personal Retrospectoscope

PROLOGUE

I FEEL VERY GRATEFUL and proud of the life my family and I have had in Edmonton, both personally and professionally. This article looks back at our move west from Ontario, my urological practice and some memorable relationships with residents, students—and non-urological friends. The vast majority of this story is wonderfully exciting and fondly remembered, but I have also included some recent "bumps along the road" in the hope that they may be avoided, or at least modified, by others in the new millennium.

It is important to me that you appreciate the pivotal role my wife, Barbara, played in my life, and understand my passions for aviation and art as well as my rewarding career in urological oncology. In preparing this article, I am indebted to my good neighbour, Mrs. Lynda Somerville, a retired English teacher, for proofreading and giving me a lot of very sound advice. Shirley and Bill Lakey also greatly helped with the article, as they have on numerous other occasions over the past thirty-five years. Susi Reinink, my best friend and confidante, has also been of tremendous assistance and has developed a remarkable tolerance for my idiosyncrasies.

THE EARLY YEARS

At age sixteen, I dreamed of becoming a fighter pilot in the RCAF. My world crashed in 1956, however, when tests revealed my red-green colour deficit (present in 8% of males). Since I could never be a professional aviator, I made the default decision to enter Queens University Medical School.

My family moved to Kingston from Napanee in 1958. Life was sure different in the big city. I had to do nine papers during Grade 13, including Latin, my worst subject.

The good news that year (in addition to passing the nine papers) was that I fell in love with Barbara Hogg. No one else knew "for sure" for a very long time, but Barb secretly wore my med school pin on her bra strap until our marriage in 1963.

Barb knew that she would have to contend with her lover's lifelong passion for flying small planes. It was rumoured that I proposed while we were flying upside down in a Fleet Canuck, in order to force her to say yes, but it wasn't really necessary.

Our time at Queens was wonderful. After graduating in Arts, Barb supported us by running the research electron microscopes in the Pathology Department of the Kingston General Hospital (although my mother was horrified that I couldn't provide for Barb). In fact, Barb handled the finances throughout our marriage. All I really needed was money in my wallet and, somehow, whenever I took my pants down from the bedroom hat rack, the money was there.

In 1962, I had a wonderful externship with cardiologist Dr. Jack Parker, doing experimental cardiac catheterizations just two years after the process had first been attempted on humans. This experience came back to me very dramatically in 1992, after my own cardiac arrest.

Following graduation in 1965 and a rotating internship at the KGH, Barb and I headed west to Edmonton. I planned to study general surgery under the renowned Dr. Walter Mackenzie, and then do my residency in obstetrics and gynecology. After spending our first night in Alberta camped in Elk Island Park, we arrived at the University of Alberta Hospital (UAH) in June 1966.

BECOMING A WESTERNER, 1966-1976

At the time, Dr. Peter Beck, Chairman of Obstetrics and Gynecology, maintained that every gynecologist first needed a strong exposure to urology. I therefore presented myself to Dr. James O. Metcalf, the UAH Head of Urology.

The surgical endoscopy suite and "cysto" were affectionately known by medical students and interns as "the swamp," because of the numerous bottles of irrigating fluid (water at that time!) hanging on IV poles and the copious blood-tinged water often adorning the surgical drapes, gowns, pants and shoes of the surgeons, as well as the floor.

Mrs. Jennie Flowers, the Head Nurse, led me into the swamp for the first time to meet "J. O." At first, all I could see were a patient's legs thrust skywards, a huddled figure between them and two residents (Nick Rety and Ian Wright) looking on. I crept in quietly and said in my most reassuring voice, "My name is. . . er. . . McPhee." This was met by a very gruff and very loud, "What's that, you say?" I reeled back, struggling to regain my composure.

I soon learned that J. O.'s bark was due more to his hearing than his personality. He headed a very dynamic division based on excellence in the operating room, the bedside, the lecture hall and the laboratory. He was also a fanatic about getting up early in the morning, often starting work before 7:00 a.m. after playing eighteen holes of golf. I tried very hard to beat him to the wards, but when I arrived, I could often hear his voice booming down the hallway, asking a patient such things as, "Can you pee over a fence?"

His most admirable trait, however, was his ability to get urologists and residents to work together in a constructive and wonderfully friendly manner. He established city-wide rounds (8:00 a.m. Saturday morning!), journal club at a urologist's house every month and the Prairie Urological Association (PUA) each February or March. The PUA gave residents a forum to practise delivering scientific papers and delightfully bonded the urological community together on the ski slopes of Lake Louise or Banff.

By the time I completed my brief stint in the department, I had decided to switch from the O/G program to urology.

I spent the rest of the year working with Drs. Les Willox, H. T. G. Williams, Robert J. Johnston, T. S. Wilson, Alan B. McCarten, Micky Michalyshyn, Peter Salmon, Olin Thurston and Ken Bowes, in addition to

Dr. Mackenzie. It was hard work with long hours, but it exposed us to a vast number of very interesting surgical problems.

To me, Les Willox was a "no-nonsense-get-the-job-done" type of surgeon who, in spite of being a very large ex-boxer, was very facile in the operating room. I will never forget seeing him stand in his polka-dot shorts in front of the O.R. desk late one night saying, "Why hasn't this (bleeping) hospital got O.R. greens for normal-sized people?"

On another occasion, Les was making his weekly rounds with a whole host of residents when a very officious fire marshal came along and placed a "fire" in the hall near the nursing station. The very competent and efficient Head Nurse told him, "I don't have time for a fire!" and continued making rounds with us. When the hospital administration subsequently pounced on the nurse, Les stood up at a staff meeting and declared defiantly, "She really didn't have time for a fire!" before embarking on a colourful description of the fire marshal.

Walter Mackenzie was President of the American College of Surgeons that year, so he was away for much of 1966. I did get to know him, though, and considered him a friend. I marveled at his organizational skills and ever-present charisma, as well as his ability to remember names and "work the room" at any function he attended. He was, however, genuinely interested in your life, your spouse's life and the welfare of your children. He influenced my career on several occasions.

Al McCarten was the UAH's finest technical surgeon at that time, often using the scalpel for even the most delicate procedures. I think my fortuitous exposure to Al first sparked my interest in surgical oncology.

Tom Williams was laid back, logical, and always the master teacher. T. S. (Tom) Wilson, however, was the man who taught me the most technical surgery that year—even a gastrectomy and splenectomy. That was really neat for a Junior Assistant Resident more familiar with holding retractors for gall bladder operations performed by chief residents Sam Cox or Gordon Olsen.

We had fun, too. I particularly remember one party for the house staff. Olin Thurston had volunteered to be on call for emergency. During the party, we decided to play a practical joke on him. We pretended to be part of the air ambulance team. I, playing the patient, was whisked into the E.R. on a stretcher, swathed head to foot with impressive bandages, complete with a fake endotracheal tube and I.V. running. We really thought we had him.

Olin took one look at me and said, "Nurse, would you please get me a #34F (really, really big!) Foley urethral catheter, STAT?" I sat bolt upright on the stretcher. He had outfoxed us again.

Duncan Brown, a resident in plastic surgery, was well known for his sense of humour. Once, while dictating a patient's discharge summary, he got giddy doing the skut work and submitted something like this:

Name:	John Smith
Chief Complaint:	piles
History of the Present Illness:	piles
Physical Examination:	piles
Final Diagnosis:	This man has piles and piles of piles.

The man happened to be a veteran. When Veterans Affairs noticed the report, Dr. Peter Salmon, acting Head of Surgery at the time, was forced to formally reprimand Duncan for his "shameful behaviour towards our veterans!"

In 1967, I began my year of research at the Surgical Medical Research Institute (SMRI) under Dr. William H. Lakey, marking the beginning of a lifelong friendship.

That year, Bill Lakey performed Alberta's first kidney transplant, with Dr. John Dossetor's pre- and postoperative help. My senior residents (Shaun Robinson and Nick Rety) and I had the honour of assisting. Rex Boake soon joined Bill to build a truly superb transplant team. That program has flourished for well over thirty years because of their incredible devotion.

Bill has also had a great love of growing orchids and of fine art. He and his wife, Shirley, still pursue these activities passionately.

My life in the SMRI had its share of difficulties, but with the generous help and advice of Ray Rajotte, a radiology technician at the time, and Dr. Jim Russell, Head of the Biochemistry Lab, I was able to obtain my M.Sc. in experimental surgery. Both Ray and Jim have continued to influence surgical research and residents for the thirty years since then.

I was also very much indebted to Malcolm Wharton, my assigned O.R. technician, and Ted Germaine, his supervisor, for teaching me about experimental surgery on dogs and pigs for the physiological part of my research project. Both of these friends have been real assets to the SMRI over the years as well.

Most of all, I remember this year vividly because our first daughter, Tracey, was born October 17. I spent many very late nights in the main operating room measuring angiotension in my rats, with Tracey on the bench in a sleeper and Barb knitting beside me. It may have been an unorthodox domestic arrangement, but it was truly quality family time.

With Tracey's arrival, Barb decided to forego a biology career. Instead, she assumed almost sole responsibility for the care of our kids and took charge of the fiscal management of our home and practice. From that point on, I didn't even know where our bank was! This division of responsibility worked well for the thirty-three years of our marriage, but required a huge amount of effort on Barb's part.

During this time, Dr. K. K. Kowaleski was in charge of the SMRI, developing surgical research projects and assisting divisional projects. At eighty-seven years of age, he still has a passion for research. I feel honoured to have known him.

Livingstone "Wave Cloud" over Cowley

THE CLINICAL UROLOGY YEARS

I spent the next years in clinical urological surgery, dividing my time between the Royal Alexandra and University Hospitals. The Alex urology unit was headed by Dr. Robert Francis, a man of remarkable patience and profound "horse-sense."

Always a gentleman and father figure, Bob was also a master at handling emergencies during operations. I will never forget him removing a huge and very vascular renal cell cancer at the Charles Camsell Hospital, when he suddenly encountered massive bleeding. Blood began welling out of the incision, making it absolutely impossible for Bob to see what he was doing. By feel alone, he managed to control the aorta and remove the tumour. I clearly remember how frightening this was and thinking "I sure hope I can learn to do that!"

In 1969, Joanne, our second daughter, was born. Barb shared a hospital room with Patience McCarten (Al McCarten's wife) who had just had her eleventh child. Barb often mentioned their wonderful discussions about raising kids, and how much she had learned from Patience the Pro.

J. O. successfully supported my application for a fellowship in urological oncology at Memorial Sloan Kettering Cancer Hospital in New York City under Dr. Willet F. Whitmore. And so, Barb and I moved our young family to Manhattan in 1969.

I felt intimidated at first, but soon appreciated the quality of my training in Edmonton. On arriving, each of the four urological fellows scrubbed with "Whit," to allow a personal preliminary assessment of surgical skills. I took out a kidney tumour, with Whit as my first assistant. During the dissection, Whit inadvertently pulled the renal vein off and I had to scramble to control the bleeding, in much the same way Bob Francis had taught me. After the vessel was secured, Whit said, "I am sure glad you didn't do that, Malcolm!"

After that experience, Whit allowed me to operate without a staffman present, and asked me to routinely assist one of the other fellows "until he had more operative experience." I had, in fact, been exposed to more open surgery and transurethral operations than had any of the three American-trained fellows.

J. O. had dictated that I write my certification exam one year and the fellowship exam the next year. This meant that I had to study for my fellowship exam in New York.

The exam was foreign to the Americans because American Board exams usually took place at least two years after starting practice. I felt a bit isolated from the Canadian training system and really appreciated Tom Williams sending me exam questions and marking my answers by mail as if I were still in Edmonton.

Sadly, my father died in 1970, two days before my written exams in Kingston. This meant that I spent the three days of the exams moving between the funeral home and the examination hall.

Around the same time, Andrew Bruce asked me to join him at Queens. However, Barb and I were so thrilled with our Edmonton life that we made the decision to return to the west permanently. We loved Alberta for its weather and extraordinarily friendly people—particularly the urological community. The mountains were fantastic and the flying opportunities—especially gliding and soaring in sailplanes—superb. We never regretted our decision.

ESTABLISHING A UROLOGICAL PRACTICE

In 1971, I set up a practice at the Royal Alex with Bob Francis, Fred Marshall and Les Dushinski. This extremely congenial relationship allowed for cross-coverage for emergency calls and cross-consultation for our patients.

My practice and interests gradually became progressively more focussed on cancer, especially cancer of the testis, adrenal, bladder and kidney. The era of chemotherapy and radical surgery for testis cancer was upon us, and I was pleased to be very much involved with this period of uro-oncology at Sloan Kettering in New York and the Cross Cancer Institute (CCI) in Edmonton. I was particularly thrilled to be closely associated with Dr. Neil Macdonald early on for the new testis cancer patient protocols. Initially, there were significant turf wars among chemotherapists, urologists and radiation oncologists, but when we finally joined forces, the cure rates skyrocketed.

In 1972, my passion for aviation resurfaced. I joined the Edmonton Soaring Club (ESC) and began to fly sailplanes. In October 1974, I had the glider ride of my life, soaring to over 29 000 feet on the "Livingstone mountain wave," a legendary rising air mass near Pincher Creek.

The really big event of 1974, however, was the birth of our son, Christopher, on August the 12th.

DIRECTOR OF SURGERY—CROSS CANCER INSTITUTE

In 1975, Dr. Walter Mackenzie summoned me to his office at the Alberta Cancer Board (ACB), where he was Executive Director. Al McCarten was also in the office when I arrived, and they both informed me that they wanted me to replace Al as Director of the Department of Surgery at the Cross Cancer Institute.

My new position at the CCI, which I began in January 1976, brought me into close contact with basic scientists, clinical oncologists and researchers in many disciplines, and allowed me to perform clinical research with Neil Macdonald on the testis tumour protocols.

Both Neil and I soon developed a profound interest in the hospice/palliative care movement as championed by Dr. Cicely Saunders in England and Dr. Balfour Mount in North America. Balfour Mount and I had been good friends at Queens (where he graduated two years before me), and we had continued to stay in touch.

Ms. Rhea Arcand, the CCI's Director of Nursing, had taken a master's degree in palliative care and became enthusiastically involved in our new Supportive Care Committee, as did Dr. Garner King. Neil became so immersed in these principles that he eventually resigned as Executive Director of the ACB to study under Cicely Saunders and Balfour Mount. Ultimately, he became a renowned authority in palliative care.

DEVELOPING A BASIC RESEARCH LASER PROGRAM

As early as 1970, I had been thinking that we should try to use lasers with our urological endoscopes, but it hadn't been feasible at the time.

The American army had in fact been suppressing the development of Neodymium-YAG (Nd:YAG) lasers because they wanted to use them in their tanks as gun sights. In the mid-70s the technology was finally revealed.

Dr. Alfons Hofstetter and Dr. Gerd Staehler of Munich began urological studies using Nd:YAG lasers for the treatment of superficial bladder cancers. I visited them in 1979 and came home to raise funds to buy a laser of our own. Prominent Edmonton businessman Dan Roper solicited patient donations, and we received an electrical engineering grant and a large contribution from the South Edmonton Lions Club. That same year, Dr. John Tulip (Ph.D. electrical/laser engineering) and I bought a $120 000 Nd:YAG laser, and we began basic laboratory research at the SMRI and CCI.

By 1981, we had constructed a laser resectoscope and had developed a means to destroy a segment of the bladder (full thickness) without perforation, in experiments on thirty dogs.

Bob Francis had a patient with an infiltrating bladder cancer who was considered to be a very poor risk for open surgery. He wondered if she might benefit from Nd:YAG laser irradiation to the tumour base. Complicated legal discussions ensued, as well as ethical discussions with the ethics committee, the administration of the CCI and the patient.

Mrs. Alice C. Sutherland, in a very brave decision, finally agreed to be one of the first (possibly **the first**) bladder cancer patients in North America to be treated by laser irradiation. We performed her operation at the CCI on July 6, 1981. Thankfully, her postoperative course was completely uneventful, and she lived for another twelve years.

I joined Drs. Barry Stein and Richard Kendal to give the first urological laser course at Temple University in Philadelphia in October of 1983 based on our laboratory and subsequent clinical experience. Soon after, Dr. Ralph Benson from the Mayo Clinic and Dr. Joseph (Jay) Smith, Jr. from Salt Lake City also joined us. We presented many subsequent courses at the Mayo Clinic, annual meetings of the American Urological Association and the University of Utah in Salt Lake City.

Our crowded lecture schedule often interfered with our clinical urology, laboratory work, teaching and family life. It was exciting, though, and we made many good friends with colleagues from around the world.

We continued our research on hyperthermic (heat generating) lasers throughout the '80s. We had the good fortune to have Dr. Donald Chapman, a world-renowned radiobiologist at the CCI, join our lab activities. With his

Malcom McPhee and John Tulip stand beside the laser at the Surgical Medical Research Institute. (photo courtesy of Dean Bicknell, Edmonton Journal)

support, we were now ideally situated to do basic research, even at the cellular level. His presence also enabled us to pursue large grants from a number of sources.

On the clinical side, we now frequently used the laser resectoscope for high-risk bladder cancer patients. I had also begun to treat other cancers palliatively, particularly metastatic cancers. Although this was a very long way from urology, I had Canada's only surgical laser and felt we had to help these patients if at all possible, even if the technology was untried. I was able to very significantly relieve pain in some patients and none, thankfully, required skin grafts.

Gamer King, now Chairman of the Department of Medicine, also became interested in the YAG laser and was able to use it to open obstructed bronchi from lung cancers. This allowed palliative care patients to breathe much more easily, even before leaving the operating room.

Dr. Sid Usiskin, Head of the Department of Physics at the CCI, played a pivotal role in our laser maintenance and experiments. We developed a wonderful friendship, and he got to know my sister Viki Bjekelund as well (so well, in fact, that they were married in March 1988!).

In 1980, I met Ronald Moore, a chemistry student, at his parents' cottage west of Edmonton. After water skiing with him for a week, I casually remarked that if he didn't have a job next summer, we might be able to use his chemistry background in the laser laboratory. Much to my delight, he spent the next two summers engrossed in laboratory work at the CCI. This experience made him decide to apply to the Faculty of Medicine. He would be heard from later.

ASSUMING THE REINS, 1986-1996

Dr. Bryce Weir replaced Tom Williams as Chairman of the Department of Surgery in 1986 and appointed Dr. Ken Petruk Director of the Division of Neurosurgery. I was made Head of Urology succeeding Bill Lakey. These moves were designed to promote cooperation among all of Edmonton's teaching hospitals.

As a first step, Ken and I were moved to the Royal Alex Hospital to run our divisions jointly between the U of A Hospital and the RAH. The move was controversial at times because of years of rivalry between the two hospitals. Ken and I thoroughly enjoyed the new arrangement, however, because of our common interests and problems. We also shared a talented secretary/office manager, Ms. Jane Kornelsen, who created a friendly, efficient work environment and really kept us hopping. She was my right arm, and a surrogate mother to our residents, students and patients.

Nineteen eighty-six was also the year that Barb and I took our son, Christopher, age 12, to the remote African mountains of Banso, Cameroon, to assist general surgeons with endoscopic therapy and stricture therapy, as well as fistulae repairs and prostate treatment. I had been invited by

Dr. Dieter Lemke, a Baptist missionary and an emergency physician at the RAH, and he and his wife, Marlis, welcomed us and introduced us to the local people and customs.

For one very memorable month, we converted both the Baptist and Catholic missionary hospitals into temporary urological units. I performed up to fifteen operations a day alongside the keenly motivated missionaries, and despite the workload, enjoyed the month immensely. We were thankful that we could bring and leave $30 000.00 worth of brand new electrosurgical and endoscopic equipment donated by Ray Laborie Surgical Ltd. and Valley Lab.

We also brought along a "Mr. Fix-it," Henry Schroeder, a close friend and flying buddy. His brother, Gary Schroeder, had been killed in an automobile accident after serving as a missionary in Banso for many years. A chapel had been built in his memory, and we felt privileged to visit it with Henry.

Henry was well known for being able to solve mechanical problems under any conditions, so he was perfectly suited for the task at hand. He and Christopher spent their days repairing incubators, cars, a methane-generating latrine, x-ray units and dental cavitrons. Shortly after our return to Edmonton, Christopher and his friends fixed up some of their old bikes and sent them to Colonel Valentine's Boys Club, a shelter for orphaned boys in Banso.

Barb spent much time in the Baptist Hospital nursery and set up weaving facilities for leprosy patients at a nearby leper facility. The whole African experience made a lasting impression on all of us.

In the fall of 1986, we began our Photodynamic Therapy (PDT) studies. PDT uses a chemical reaction to destroy cancer. Patients are injected with photosensitizers, chemicals that kill cells when exposed to light. Normal cells typically clear the drugs in forty-eight to seventy-two hours, but for some reason, cancer cells take longer. Therefore, if you can apply the right wavelength of light at the right time, you will selectively kill the cancer cells.

We wanted to improve the systems for delivering light and to find ways to measure the light distribution in order to use PDT to treat solid tumours, such as prostate and breast cancer. We were fortunate indeed to have very competent laser engineers and radiobiologists on our multidisciplinary team.

Don Chapman left in 1992 for the Fox Chase Cancer Center in the U.S., putting our laser project in some jeopardy. However, we had accepted Ron Moore into the urology training program, and he had continued his work in the lab. He had also requested two years of urological research to earn his Ph.D. He received the Surgical Resident Research Award in 1989 from the Royal College of Physicians and Surgeons of Canada for this work in our laser lab.

Next, Dr. Gerry Miller from radiobiology and Dr. William Lown, a widely respected organic chemist, joined our group. And so the laboratory flourished again, despite Don Chapman's departure.

We continued to have urology residents intimately involved with all of this work. We were not trying to transform them into future researchers, but we felt that even clinical urologists should understand what goes on in basic research labs. Many of our surgical colleagues nationwide envied this aspect of our training program.

In August 1990, I talked Barb into flying with me to Slave Lake in the Grob109 motorglider to visit good friends for the weekend. Barb was never very keen on flying in small airplanes, claiming that "she only did it for me."

We took off and were heading west on a beautiful sunny day, when suddenly our bubble canopy blew off at about 800 feet. Fortunately it missed the tail, and the controls seemed to be still functioning normally.

I could barely breathe because of the propwash. As I tried to twist and turn to escape its full force, my sunglasses blew off. Now I couldn't see very well either! To make matters even worse, I couldn't communicate with the tower because of the air rushing loudly over the microphone. I solved the problem by putting my Tilley hat over my face, and managed to land the "convertible" motorglider by the seat of my pants.

As we taxied in, I said to Barb, "That sure was a postgraduate landing!" She was remarkably cool during the entire incident, and actually did get into the aircraft again. However, this tale has hung over my head ever since.

The only story my kids repeat so often is the time I was caught in an automatic car wash, which wouldn't stop washing me for over thirty minutes. Unable to get out of the car or attract attention with the horn, I eventually dialled 911 on my cell phone. I think the fireman who ultimately dealt with the call is still laughing.

THE ERA OF THE CAPITAL HEALTH AUTHORITY

In the fall of 1992, a cardiac arrest, emergency angioplasty and triple bypass tempered somewhat my contributions to the Division of Urology. Thanks to the skills of my cardiology and cardiovascular surgical friends and colleagues, Drs. Bill Black, Bill Hui and Arvind Koshel, I was able to return to the fray in 1993. This was just in time to meet the challenge of the Klein government's new fiscal restraints, as implemented by Capital Health managers.

The first noticeable change was a gradual loss of specialized nurses. We had built highly efficient urological nursing units at the RAH and the UAH, ready to deal with emergencies, provide excellent post-operative care and deliver compassionate palliative care. Our operating room nurses were also highly trained in urological surgery. Following the cutbacks, nurses were laid off strictly according to seniority, regardless of their specialized skills. We now had entered the era of the "generic nurse," which freely translated into "you get whoever's left over from the cutbacks." We were left with some excellent "golden oldies," but not nearly enough to go around.

Specialty nurses and specialized caregivers were almost extinct. Gone were the days when we could depend on nurses like Jennie Flowers in the UAH "swamp," Karen Wyllie in the RAH "swamp" and Gina Halliwell and Anne Radke on Station 31 at the RAH.

Next, the Capital Health Authority abolished the boards and chief executive officers of the RAH and UAH. Dr. Tom W. Noseworthy, a brilliant academic intensivist with a master's degree in Public Health from Harvard, left Edmonton to chair the National Forum on Health in Ottawa, after being terminated by Capital Health. Beyond mere political expediency, I could not identify the wisdom of such rash and very rapid decisions.

Caritas hospital boards were somewhat immune to the new restructuring at this time. As a result, urologists could be unilaterally assigned by Capital Health to Caritas hospitals, only to find themselves threatened by Caritas with loss of admission and/or surgical privileges if they performed sterilization procedures in their practice. We nearly lost two of our most respected and productive academic urologists over this mixture of church and state.

Our main concerns in urology, however, were the unacceptable delays in getting urgent cases into operating rooms or treatment facilities. Patients with aggressive bladder cancer faced waits of eight weeks or longer, and some prostate cancer patients had to wait over twelve weeks. Emergency beds, ICU beds, operative beds and the specialized nurses to support them were either scarce or completely unavailable.

You would expect such conditions in third world countries, and yet right here in Alberta, we heard our fiscal managers and politicians actually defending and rationalizing this deplorable situation.

Another particularly demoralizing setback was the loss of funding for a possible research year in the surgical training programs, which had become such a prominent and valuable part of our system. Due to the fiscal cutbacks, not a single urological resident has been directly exposed to laboratory research since 1997. A glance through some of the names that passed through our lab between 1979 and 1997 will clearly illustrate what a serious loss this represents.

With residents and urologists decentralized to four hospitals, we now had to spend much of our day travelling between our offices and the hospital to see our patients and teach our students, interns and residents. It also meant that we could no longer provide graded responsibility and adequate supervision for our residents, as dictated by the Royal College of Physicians and Surgeons. When I brought this concern to the Capital Health Authority, I was told, "Maybe it is time for the Royal College to change their standards!"

At the time, I was chairman of the Royal College's Committee on Post-Graduate Medical Education (CPGME), the body responsible for monitoring those standards. I could not believe that such intelligent people could be so insensitive to these very significant issues. For the first time, I realized that in practice, my immediate superior was neither my

University Departmental Chairman nor my Dean, but a politically appointed fiscal manager. A major power shift had already occurred.

YEAR 2000—THE NEW MILLENNIUM

As we enter the new millennium, we must remember the wisdom of Walter Mackenzie, Tom Williams, Bryce Weir, Stew Hamilton, Jim Metcalfe, Bill Lakey and Lorne Tyrrell, and support excellence in our surgical training programs.

The fiscal managers have indeed succeeded in balancing the books, but at great cost. Since 1995, patient care has declined dramatically, and our surgical training programs have faced profound threats. For four years the government has excluded significant input from nurses and physicians, deeming them "vested interest groups." Hopefully, these unfortunate policies will end as we enter the damage control phase and begin to restructure and rebuild our heath care system. Teaching and research, as well as patient care, must be given adequate budgetary support.

A Dean or Departmental Chairman must have the power to build and promote university programs. Since the mid-60s, this has allowed the U of A to compete with programs in Montreal, Toronto and Vancouver, helping us attract the very best students, residents and faculty in spite of our more limited population base. Excellence in training and research interrelate; this in turn translates into superior patient care and attracts superlative nursing personnel.

We must continue to bring these interrelationships forward to future fiscal managers and politicians. Our program has given Alberta some wonderful academic surgeons—people like Ted Elliott, David Mador, Eric Estey, Gerry Todd, Ron Moore, Tim Wollin and Mike Chetner. I certainly was attracted to urology and oncology because of my year at SMRI under Bill Lakey, and because of J. O.'s wisdom that research should form an integral part of surgical training.

Katherine Moore, an extremely competent and caring nurse, obtained her Ph.D. (Nursing) after exposure to our urological research. I thoroughly enjoyed cooperating with the Department of Nursing on her project, which studied the quality of life after radical surgery for cancer of the prostate.

Fiscal managers and government officials must learn that research should form an integral part of at least some of our surgical programs.

I remain cautiously optimistic regarding urology, thanks to the high-calibre people currently in place. Mike Chetner is the Director of the division and Gerry Todd is in charge of the transplant program. Ron Moore is running the laser project (without resident participation) and was made an Alberta Heritage Scholar in March 1999. There are superb urological surgeons at all our hospitals, and we even have an excellent urologist prominently situated in Capital Health. What more can I ask?

ESTABLISHING A SECOND CAREER

Alter thirty-three years of glorious marriage, Barb died very suddenly on January 1, 1995. A month later, my ninety-year-old mother, Jean Rebecca McPhee, died. My cardiac problems also recurred in the fall of that year. Drs. Vlad Dzavik and Max Finlay were able to skillfully stabilize my heart, repair a carotid artery and clip a brain aneurysm. Although I had to retire from medicine, I have been able to enjoy a remarkably good quality of life since then, including being a proud grandfather.

Tracey graduated from Queens University in Physical Education and is currently pursuing a Ph.D. degree, and has a beautiful two-year-old daughter, Meghan. Joanne, with a degree in French from McGill University, teaches French in Lac La Biche, and has two wonderful boys, Connor and Brennan. Christopher obtained a master's degree in Botany from Queens in 1998 and is beginning a career in science.

My sister Viki moved from Ontario to Edmonton in the mid-80s with her three daughters, Leslie, Kirstin and Caroline. She soon developed a very successful career as a medical secretary, office manager and "den mother" for the research fellows in the Departments of Radiology, Radiobiology and Molecular Genetics at the CCI. I am extremely grateful for the loving care she provided to our ailing mother during the last years of her life.

I have always been doodling and drawing. When I started my practice, I took two drawing courses, but it was not until I retired that I had the time to take formal instruction in painting techniques, composition, colour theory, life drawing and abstracts. I have now completed over three years of such schooling and very much enjoy my life as a struggling art student and retired "old fart."

Adding to my happiness is the close relationship that I have developed with Barb's longtime best friend, Susi Reinink, a master weaver from Desmond, Ontario. We have known Susi since 1961. She was at our wedding in 1963 and my graduation from Queens in 1965, and has been a part of our family ever since. Our common interests in art, music, travel and flying fill our lives with excitement, while still allowing each of us to pursue our artistic creativity in painting and weaving. This new relationship is wonderfully fulfilling and gives both of us happiness again in spite of our past hardships. I suspect Barb somehow arranged this as well.

Life is truly great!

Elk Island Sunset 1966

NICOLE MALLET

Dancing with Time

*J'ai plus de souvenirs que **si** j'avais mille ans.*
Baudelaire, *Les fleurs du mal*

I S IT POSSIBLE, is it feasible, to appraise time in order to appreciate it? Millennium, Centennial, three decades in Edmonton, half of my life spent in Canada: all these words dance in my head and conjure up a myriad of vignettes, some funny, even hilarious; others full of nostalgic, not to say very sad undertones; all of them part of my own history, which oddly enough coincides with a fascinating slice of the history of the U of A.

I came to Canada in 1967, the Centennial Year, supposedly for one year. Over thirty years later, I am still around, happy and proud to be so. In the meantime, the Department of Romance Languages, then freshly issued from that of Modern Languages, has been paradoxically, recently "downsized" into its own original babelic form.

At times, I feel I have jumped from the status of a "junior instructor" into the dignified position of a "senior Professor" in no time. At others, parodying Baudelaire, I could boast that "I have more memories than if I were a thousand years old!" I am overwhelmed by a whirling host of dancing memories.

FLASHBACK 1, SEPTEMBER 1967

I arrive in Canada as a young bride, holding in one hand a contract as a sessional lecturer, duly signed by Dr. E. J. H. Greene, the last person ever to be "Head" of the Department of Romance Languages. In my other hand,

I grasp a stack of precious papers amassed over the past six months, in order to get the landed immigrant status I need to teach in Canada.

I hold out the bundle of documents to the immigration officer, a tall, impressive fellow who looks down on my diminutive figure and bashful countenance, and half puzzled, half suspicious, inquires, "Romance languages ?. . .You mean you are going to teach romance?"

I am flabbergasted; my feelings are hurt, my dignity ruffled; is there no avoiding the French girls' reputation of frivolity? Prompted by a pompous sense of my intellectual importance, I am about to try and explain to him priggishly the linguistic nuances between *romance, roman, romanesque, romantic/romantique*, all these pitfalls of the French and English languages known as *Faux Amis/Treacherous Friends* by bilingual instructors. Then I stop short, burst out laughing, look at him right in the eyes and remark flippantly, "Maybe!"

He appears embarrassed, yet slightly amused or ... envious?...!

Thus I start my romantic love affair with the University of Alberta.

FLASHBACK 2 , THE OLD ARTS BUILDING

It is the mid '60s, and the charming, quaint building is not in the shape it is now (after the great renovation of the mid-80s). It still houses various offices, since moved to the Humanities Centre, among them the Dean's office on the second floor. During my first years, it is Dean Smith. I can still see his benevolent eyes, behind round spectacles that give him the look of some of Watteau's playful, naive characters!

In those days, there are still Toilets for Staff and Toilets for Students in the Old Arts Building—let's keep our privileges! One morning, I push open the door of the former with shy and discreet solemnity, to find myself in the company of two middle-aged ladies, undoubtedly clerks from the Dean's office. They are absorbed in the painstaking task of arranging their intricate hairdos—remember, we are in the '60s.

At the sight of me, they interrupt their activity, look down on me (again! —only Ted Blodgett has the elegant kindness of making me feel I am on a level with him, whenever I meet him in an elevator!), size me up with some disdain and inform me in loud, condescending voices, "You know, this is reserved for staff, dear!" "But I am a faculty member," I venture timidly, feeling guilty and stiff, rather than staff.

Oh! what would I give now to be taken for a student! When I ask for a senior's discount, people do not even ask me for I.D. Time, time, what do you do to us?

FLASHBACK 3, TWENTY YEARS LATER

The Old Arts Building is being renovated. We have all been temporarily relocated to big trailers next to the greenhouses. I am now Associate Chair of the Department and busy with the very successful M.A. program in Literary Translation we—a wonderful team of committed colleagues— have created, the only one of its kind in the whole of Canada at the time. It is a program which, sadly, has been made dormant by the downsizing of the past few years. I sometimes wonder if it was not rather put to sleep? Wait and see, anyway!

I receive a phone call from the French Consulate in Edmonton. This one was eliminated for good, three years ago! The French Ambassador is coming to Edmonton, eager to visit the avant-garde installation of our wonderful language lab.

I clumsily try to explain the present situation. Would His Excellency consider, in His clemency, postponing His visit for a few weeks, until we have comfortably resumed our graciously restored professional mansion? No, His Excellency cannot in any way change plans that originate from Paris. It is now or never! And He is looking forward to being given the grand tour of the famous Language Laboratory ... by guess whom?

So, I quickly gather all the French graduate students under my supervision in our trailer "common room," and order some "refreshments." These turn out to be plain coffee that has to be served in styrofoam cups! Ah! Versailles: you are so far away, indeed! At the last minute, I inspect the premises and discover, with horror, a huge dirty spot in the midst of the cheap carpet of our "reception room!" What to do?

In my own tiny office, I have a pseudo Persian rug that I got for ten dollars in a junk store on Whyte Avenue. In an act of grandiose generosity, on account of this exceptional function, I offer to lend it to the Department for the duration of the august visit.

Then, hurriedly, and laughing our hearts out, Richard Young, the Chair, and I transport the rug through the narrow corridor. We laugh so much that the rug seems to weigh tons! We dump it on the dreadful spot at the very moment the official consular limousine stops in front of our trailer.

On that memorable day, we felt as though we were re-enacting a scene from *Fawlty Towers*! But our honour was safe, and so was the other official language of Canada.

I could undoubtedly narrate many more comical episodes of the epic of our Department over the past thirty years. I could also choose to evoke the figures of so many talented colleagues, dear to my heart in various ways, who have left us prematurely, but who, for people of my generation, still haunt the corridors of the Old Arts Building: Eugene Dorfman, Roland Bonvalet, Carla Colter, Manoel Faucher, Henry Kreisel, Ed Greene, Colette Dimic and, more recently, Jim Algeo, Gerwin Marahrens and José Varela. I am sure that wherever they are, they watch over the destinies of all those who still care for the great university family.

When I think of it, it is sad that in the renovating process, two memorial rooms, originally dedicated respectively to Eugene Dorfman and Roland Bonvalet have disappeared. At least I take comfort in the charming thought of little Florian Bonvalet, Roland's very recently born grandchild, our grandson. This is the best way to be remembered.

When I arrived in 1967, Alberta was not the booming city it became in the '70s and '80s. Ernest Manning was premier and had imposed a strange kind of puritan discipline on the province—strange at least for a French girl who was looking forward to celebrating her first Sunday in the wild West, a well-deserved Sunday's rest with a nice dinner in a fancy restaurant and a glass of wine, followed by a good movie in the nearby cinema, and who discovered that none of these simple epicurean pleasures were available on a Sunday in this corner of the world.

Time has passed; times have changed. Nicole Bonvalet is now Nicole Mallet. *Plus ça change, plus c'est la même chose!* Shall we know better in the next millennium?

Complete List of Submissions

The articles submitted for this project have all been preserved in their original forms and are available through the University of Alberta Archives. If a quote or an excerpt has piqued your interest, please find the author in the list below and go to the Archives to enjoy the complete article.

The Association of Professors Emeriti also received a number of other submissions (photos, brochures, books, etc.) and has filed them in the Archives as well. For a list of these contributions, please contact the Association.

Dr. W. A. (Bill) Ayer
41 Years at the U of A   3p.*,d.s.

Dr. M. K. (Kazim) Bacchus
Some Observations of the Early Development of   12p.,d.s.
    International Education at the U of A

Dr. D. R. (Doris) Badir
A Recollection from 30 Years in Human Ecology   3p., s.s.

Dr. R. G. (George) Baldwin
Untitled   5p., s.s.

Dr. D. G. (Don) Bellow
Patriot Games and All That   13p., s.s.

Dr. C. F. (Fred) Bentley
Free-Wheeling Ramblings by C. Fred Bentley   7p., s.s.

* p.=number of pages; s.s.=single spaced; d.s.=double spaced

Dr. J. J. (John) Bergen
Providential Choice   1p., s.s

Rev. Charles Bidwell
Out of the Closets and into a Locker Room: the History of   3p., s.s
  the Health Sciences Media Library

Mrs. Einer Boberg (Julia)
A Dream, a Hot Tub, and an Institute   3p., s.s.

Dr. J. P. (John) Bowland
Memories of the University of Alberta—John Bowland   3p., s.s.

Dr. R. E. (Robert) Brundin
The Founding of the School of Library Science 1964-1970   21p., s.s.

Prof. F. (Frank) Bueckert
Millennium Submission   4p., s.s.

Dr. A. (Art) Burgess
1. An Old Time Skating Party   1. 5p., d.s.
2. 1977—The Fitness Movement Gets Moving   2. 6p., d.s.
3. Canada's Fitweek ("Don't Point that Gun")   3. 1.5p., s s.

Dr. J. N. (Jim) Campbell
1. The Christmas Party   1. 1.5p., s.s.
2. The Canteloupe War   2. 2p., s.s.
3. The Path to Paranchych (journal)

Dr. W. G. (Bill) Corns
1. Career Resume   1. 1p., s.s.
2. Department of Plant Science, Agriculture Bulletin 1965   2. 3p., s.s.

Dr. E. A. (Edwin) Cossins
Professor Robert G. H. Cormack, FRSC: scholar, gentleman,   2p., s.s.
  and good friend

Prof. T. B. (Thelma) Dennis
Memories of the Faculty Club   3p., s.s.

Dr. L. (Louis) Desrochers
Untitled   1p., s.s.

Prof. K. A. (Kay) Dier
The Northern Nurse Practitioner Program   5p., s.s.,

Dr. E. A. (Betty) Donald
Millennium Project-Elizabeth Donald 1946-1949   2p., s.s.

Dr. E. L. (Elizabeth) Empey
My Experiences at the University of Alberta   2p., s.s.

Dr. D. J. (Doug) Engel
Dangers of Getting Too Close to Your Graduate Students   1p., s.s.

Dr. F. C. (Fred) Engelmann
My Millennium Contribution   2p., d.s.

Dr. R. S. (Bob) Fraser
Simpler Times   2p., s.s.

Dr. R. E. (Bob) Folinsbee
A Brush with Billions in the Barrens   8p., d.s.

Dr. G. (George) Ford
Sons of Martha and Lantern Slides (3 boxes)

The Hon. Dr. Jean Forest
Recollections of a Decade at the University of Alberta   8p., s.s.

Dr. E. A. (Eric) Geddes
The Formation of the Alberta Heritage Foundation for   5p., s.s.
  Medical Research

Dr. P. R. (Paul) Gorham
My First Weeks at the University of Alberta   9 p., s.s.

Dr. H. R. (Harry) Gunning
The Way It Was   6 p., d.s.

Dr. W. E. (Walter) Harris
1. Aspects of the Life of an Analytical Chemist   1. 20p., s.s.
2. President's Advisory Committee on Campus Reviews   2. 12p.,s.s.
  (draft)
3. The Tenth Annual Report of PACCR   3. 58p., s.s.

Dr. A. K. (Kåre) Hellum
1. Reflections on Teaching   1. 2p., s.s.,
2. Submission Two: Consulting   2. 3p., s.s.

Mrs. M. (Margaret) Henderson
Untitled   3p., s.s.

Dr. S. M. (Steve) Hunka
The IBM 1500 Computer-Assisted Instructional System: 7p., s.s.
  1968-1980

Mr. E. J. (Ernest) Ingram
Teaching, Scholarship, and Service: Fussing the Pillars   15p., s.s.

Dr. R. Norman Jones
1. Analytical Application of Vibrational Spectroscopy—A Historical Review Quantitative Infrared Spectroscopy— Publications from the National Research Council of Canada
  1. 21p., s.s.
  2. 35p., d.s.

Dr. A. N. (Abdul) Kamal
Remembrance of My Arrival in Edmonton
4p., d.s.

Dr. A. P. (Anne) Kernaleguen
Clothing for the Physically Challenged 1970-80
2p., s.s.

Dr. D. K. (Dianne) Kieren
Remembrances of The Staff Development Seminar of the Faculty of Home Economics
3p., s.s

Mr. A. S. (Bert) Knowler
1. The Great Heist at the University of Alberta (or The Anatomy of a Holdup)
  1. 11p., d.s.
2. The Greening of the Association of the Academic Staff at the University of Alberta
  2. 4p., d.s.
3. The Genesis of the Faculty Club, University of Alberta— A Personal Recollection
  3. 10p., d.s.

Prof. R. H. (Hugh) Knowles
Submissions to the Millennium Project:
1. Life and Times in Rabbit Row
  1. 2p. s.s.
2. Campus Life of the Fifties and Sixties
  2. 1p. s.s.
3. Some Botanists I Have Known
  3. 1p., s.s.

Ms. P. N. (Pauline) Kot
1. Footprints in the Hall of Learning;
  1. 2p., s.s.
2. Launching a Computer Course in Nursing
  2. 4p., s.s.

Dr. W. H. Lakey, et al.
Urology at the University of Alberta—The Early Years 1900   19p., d.s.
   to 1958

Dr. R. U. (Ray) Lemieux
Interview With Raymond Lemieux (McIntosh/Spencer)

Professor C. M. (Charlie Lockwood)
Reminiscences: Thoughts from my 23 Years at Extension   8p., d.s.

Dr. R. A. (Bob) Macbeth
1. Deviation into the Right Direction   1. 3p., s.s.
2. Reminiscences of an Emeritus Professor of Surgery   2. 21p., d.s.

Dr. D. A. (Al) MacKay
Untitled   3p., d.s.

Dr. N. B. (Neil) Madsen
The Biochemistry Department: Personal Reminiscences by   20p., s.s.
   Neil B. Madsen

Prof. N. E. (Nicole) Mallet
Dancing with Time   5p., d.s.

Mrs. T. W. (Travis) Manning
Travis Warren Manning: Memoir and Photo   1p., s.s.

Dr. G. S. (Gerald) McCaughey
1. How I met "The President"   1. 3p., s.s.
2. University Life - Upside- Downside   2. 2p., s.s.

Dr. R. (Richard) McClelland
Untitled   1p., s.s.

Ms. R. (Ruth) McClure
Untitled   1p., s.s.

Dr. R. G. (Gordon) McIntosh and
Dr. H. W. (Henry) Hodysh
Portraits of Change   41p., s.s.

Dr. M. (Malcolm) McPhee
1. Reflections on Edmonton Urology Through a Personal   1. 20p., s.s.
   Retrospectoscope
2. Urology at the U of A   2. 19p., d.s.

Mjr. R. (Robert) Middleditch
Millennium Project Arts Anecdotes   3p., s.s.

Dr. G. D. (George) Molnar
Deptartment of Medicine 1975-86   41p., d.s.

Dr. G. (George) Monckton
Neurology in Alberta, 1957-1985: A Personal Review   14p., s.s.

Mr. Kevin Moodie
Building Services   37p., s.s.

Dr. G. (Gamila) Morcos
From the Sublime to the Absurd and Everything in Between   2p., d.s.

Dr. A. R. (Richard) Morgan
Humanity in the Sciences   2p., s.s.

Rev. Dr. G. (Garth) Mundle
"Principal is no Stereotype (from the *Edmonton Journal*,   2p., s.s.
   1979); letter descriptive of the times

Dr. J. (Joan) Munro
University of Alberta, 1953: A Student's Recollection   5p., d.s.

Dr. J. R. (Ralph) Nursall
1. Early Days   1. 6p., s.s.
2. Adventures in the Tongue Trade   2. 4p., s.s.

Dr. V. R. (Verne) Nyberg
A Not-So-Nostalgic Look at University Life   6p., s.s.

Dr. J. E. (John) Oster
Earl Buxton: Exemplary Teacher   4p., s.s.

Dr. T. A. (Tom) Petersen
Millennium Project—Professors Emeriti Project   10p., s.s.

Dr. W. A. (Bill) Preshing
The Meanderings of an Emeritus   2p., s.s.

Dr. J. A. (Jim) Robertson
43 Years at the University of Alberta   4p., s.s.

Dr. J. W. (John) Scott
As the Chairmen Saw it Vol.1: Book I"—contributed by   19p., s.s.
    Dr. G. D. Molnar

C. D. (David) Sharplin
The University Library from a Publice Service Viewpoint: 6p., s.s.
    1962-1997

Dr. J. A. (Jim) Shaw
Association of Professors Emeriti "Millennium Project"   6p., s.s.

Dr. M. E. (Mary) Spencer
Vignette 1953-1961   8p., d.s.

Dr. G. H. (Geoffrey) Sperber
Memoirs of Geoffrey H. Sperber   3p., s.s.

Dr. B. R. J. (Brian) Sproule
Pulmonary Medicine in Alberta   8p., s.s.

Dr. L. G. (Lloyd) Stephens-Newsham
A Career at the University of Alberta   3p., s.s.

Dr. S. M. (Shirley) Stinson
U of A Nursing: Then and Now   5p., s.s.

Dr. W. C. (Bill) Taylor
1. Selections from History of the Department of the   1. 5p., s.s.
   Pediatrics of U of A, 1919-1992
2. MOANA (Medical Officers. Army. Navy. Air Forces)
   50 Years After

Dr. J. A. (John) Toogood
University-Farmer Cooperation in Fertilizer Research   4p., s.s.

Dr. E. W. (Ed) Toop
The Great Amaryllis Caper   1p., s.s.

Dr. B. (Balder) von Hohenbalken
Vignette #32: Peeling a Polyhedron and Other Adventures   7p., s.s.

Dr. G. R. (Gordon) Webster
Thirty Good Years at the University of Alberta   3p., s.s.

Dr. H. T. G. (Tom) Williams
History of the Department of Surgery   32p., d.s

Dr. D. R. (Donald) Wilson
"As the Chairmen Saw It" Vol.1: Book II as submitted by   21p., s.s.
 Dr. G. D. Molnar

Dr. W. S. (Fred) Ziegler
Why?   26p., d.s

Index of Contributors